Peter Shilton started out with Leicester City at 15, moved on to Stoke City, then won two European Cups, a league Championship medal and a PFA Player of the Year Award with Nottingham Forest. He also played for Southampton and Derby County before managing Plymouth Argyle. He completed his career record of 1,005 League appearances at Bolton Wanderers and Leyton Orient. His 125 caps for England are unlikely to be bettered.

PETER SHILTON

THE AUTOBIOGRAPHY

ORION

An Orion paperback

First published in Great Britain in 2004
by Orion
This paperback edition published in 2005
by Orion Books Ltd,
Orion House, 5 Upper St Martin's Lane,
London WC2H 9EA

1 3 5 7 9 10 8 6 4 2

A CIP catalogue record for this book is
available from the British Library.

ISBN 0 75286 572 2

Printed and bound in Great Britain by
Clays Ltd, St Ives plc

www.orionbooks.co.uk

CONTENTS

ACKNOWLEDGEMENTS

I would like to thank the following who, by way of expertise, friendship or access to statistics, have helped in the writing of my autobiography: Julian Alexander and all at Lucas Alexander Whitley; Ken and Jean Bolam; Brian Clough; Terry Conroy; Phill Dann; Leicester City; Don Mackay (at Middlesbrough AFC); Manchester United plc, in particular Mike Maxfield; Arthur Montford; Nottingham Forest; Ian Preece at Orion; Simon Lowe; Sir Bobby Robson; Steve and Deb Waterall.

I would like to say a big thank-you to my good friend Les Scott, who worked with me on my autobiography. Les has collaborated with Sir Stanley Matthews, George Best, Gareth Chilcott, Gordon Banks, Jimmy Greaves and Freddie Trueman on their respective books. He has written extensively for press, TV, radio and theatre, and wrote the screenplay for *The Rose of Tralee*. His knowledge of football is considerable, so when I decided to write my autobiography I immediately turned to Les for a helping hand. Thanks, Les. What I thought would be work turned out to be fun.

For Jane, Lauren, Ruby, Toni and Charley

PETER SHILTON, JULY 2004

MY AUTOBIOGRAPHY IS DEDICATED TO
SUE, MIKE AND SAM; MY MUM AND DAD;
GEORGE DEWIS – A SUPER GUY;
CHRIS GAMBLE; MIKE MORRISON;
AND LIONEL PICKERING

1

EARLY DAYS

'Go on, try and beat him, bet you can't,' said the Leicester City trainer, George Dewis. Frank McLintock hammered the ball low to my left but I got down in double-quick time to palm the ball away to safety.

Davie Gibson, the Scotland midfield player, was next up. Gibson could really connect with a ball. He was about sixteen yards away when he let fly, and the palm of my hand stung as I pushed his fiery effort wide of my goal. Mike Stringfellow stepped up. Although only fourteen yards away, he sliced across the ball, making it swerve wickedly. It didn't catch me out. I flung myself to the right and gathered the ball safely into my chest.

'Here, let me have a go,' said City's centre-forward Ken Keyworth. He drove his shot to my left. The ball was rising when I made contact with it, but I managed to hold on to it safely with both hands. Graham Cross was next to shoot and again I made the save. Then it was the turn of City's skipper, Colin Appleton. Frank McLintock tried again, followed by Davie Gibson and Mike Stringfellow. Stringfellow's effort was quickly followed by a snap shot from George Dewis himself. To George's obvious satisfaction, I saved every shot he and the Leicester first-team players fired at me that afternoon in City's gymnasium.

'What'd I tell you? Told you, didn't I?' said George, beaming, 'He's gonna be some goalkeeper this lad.'

The shooting session over, I swelled with pride and satisfaction at my efforts. Not one of the City players involved in this impromptu shoot-in had managed to beat me. Granted we were using a three-quarter-sized goal but that couldn't have mattered less to me. These were top-quality First Division players and I had denied them.

'Gaffer signed him up?' asked Frank McLintock.

'Ain't old enough,' said George Dewis to everyone's bemusement. 'Tell him how old you are, Peter, son.'

'Thirteen, Mr McLintock.'

Centre-forwards tend to take the glory; midfield players are glamorous; wingers are adventurous; there's respect for the ruggedness of centre-backs. Few youngsters aspire to be goalkeepers but, from early childhood, that's what I had set my heart on. Goalkeepers are part of a team and yet they enjoy a certain independence within it – they do their 'thing'. That was what tipped it for me. As a boy I was a keen team player who also had a great desire for independence. Being a goalkeeper fulfilled that need.

A full-back may be able to play in midfield, and a centre-forward as a centre-half, but goalkeeping is a specialist position. My childhood heroes were all goalkeepers, including the 'Black Octopus', Lev Yashin of Russia, Gordon Banks and Chelsea's Peter Bonetti. Like gun-toting marshals on a street in a cowboy film, they stood alone. Any mistake on their part would be crucial. They had to get it right. That appealed to the perfectionist in me.

Perfection would become a byword to me. I strove to achieve it throughout my career in football. Of course, I knew that, in reality, perfection was unachievable but that's what motivated me. I knew I would never be the perfect goalkeeper but by aiming to be, I reasoned that I would achieve a standard above that of others. 'You get out of football what you put into it,' my dad once told me. 'Always give it your best.' I studied goalkeeping and worked at my game from childhood to the day I retired as a player. In all that time I never stopped learning. After 1,400 senior games and thirty-two years as a professional footballer, I believe I have a story to tell.

I was born in Leicester in 1949, the middle one of three children. My parents, Les and May, were very supportive of my older brother Tony, younger brother Graham and me, and I grew up in a happy, loving family. I was actually born above an off-licence, which Dad ran before taking up the greengrocery business. During my formative years, Dad set up shop in various parts of the city. We usually lived above the shop and with Dad changing premises so often it meant we never stayed in one place for long. By the time I was fifteen years of age I reckon our family had moved home seven times, on two occasions occupying the same premises for a second time. This constant moving never made me feel insecure or rootless – I thought it was fun. Each home offered the promise of a new beginning and a new adventure. I am sure that was because I knew I was much loved by my parents. I simply accepted that the constant moving was all due to the nature of Dad's work in much the same way as children of people in the forces accept they will never stay in one place for long.

Looking back, perhaps the transient nature of Dad's work had something to do with my quest for perfection as a goalkeeper. Each new business of Dad's was a little more successful than the last and I grew up with the idea that success didn't come easily or quickly. You had to work constantly to be a success at anything.

A number of the shops Dad owned, all one at a time, were situated on council estates, some of which can best be described as being a bit rough. Wherever we lived we always appeared to be well respected in the neighbourhood, probably because Dad had his own business. Although we were not wealthy by any means, I gained the impression that many people thought of us as being 'fairly well-off'. My brothers and I were always well dressed and well fed and on some of the estates that singled us out.

I was quite a large baby at 9lb 4oz (4.5kg) and, aided and abetted by a healthy diet and a hearty appetite, I was soon towering above boys of the same age. Oddly, at around nine or ten years of age I stopped growing and began to fill out, which was a matter of some concern to me. I started training at Leicester City at the age of eleven and there were some at the club who felt I might not grow tall enough to make the grade as a professional goalkeeper. Fortunately, as mysteriously as I had stopped growing for a couple of years, I suddenly started again.

Perhaps the frequent moving of home has something to do with the fact that I remember little of my early childhood other than I was a happy young boy. My earliest recollections are from five years of age when we lived in Middlesex Road. Most people remember their first school teacher, but not me. I remember the school, though – Granby Road – and my abiding memory of it is school milk. You had to drink it but I didn't like it. Luckily, I made friends with a lad who loved school milk. When he had finished his and the teacher wasn't looking we'd swap bottles – problem solved. Our house was next to the gates of Leicester City's training ground. Many were the Sundays I would sneak in through the hedge for a kick-about on one of the pitches, only to be quickly discovered and chased off the premises by the groundsman.

Later, when I was seven, we lived above the shop on the Braunstone Estate, which is about five miles from Leicester city centre, and I attended Court Crescent Primary School. One teacher there was particularly keen on football and one day, during a PE lesson, he took us around the back of the school to a grassed area. He told us to put our coats down as makeshift goalposts and asked if anyone would like to play in goal. I found myself volunteering. That's my first recollection of playing football.

The school had a team and on Saturday mornings we played on one of the pitches in Braunstone Park. This was exciting because we boys had to carry the posts and crossbars from the school to the park, which was just across the road, and then help our teacher erect the goals. At the time, I was an outfield player, although I was equally happy to play in goal, and playing on the park pitch always gave me a thrill – with real goalposts I could believe we were playing on a 'proper' pitch.

I can remember being overjoyed the following Christmas to discover a brand new leather football and goalkeeper's jersey among the presents in the bulging pillowcase at the foot of my bed. We had a small garden at the rear of the shop and after breakfast I ran out bedecked in my new kit to spend a gloriously happy half-hour kicking my new ball around on the frosted grass. Mostly, I kicked the ball against the fence and dived to save the return. My enjoyment was shortlived, however, because when I dived to smother the ball as it returned from the fence I cut my hand on a sharp stone protruding from the hard ground.

My memories of childhood may be rather muddled, with few specifics, but I can recall some of the generalities of life at that time. Many young people were obsessed with Elvis Presley, and I remember the Dansette record players that every household seemed to have. I don't know how many Dansettes were sold in Britain in the late fifties but I reckon it must have run to millions. These small box record players came in two colours – red and blue. The Dansette had a lid that, when raised, was supported by two metal arms, and you had to raise the lid in order to play records. The grille on the front was made of cream-coloured plastic. The centre spindle enabled you to load six singles (forty-fives, as they were sometimes known), which would drop on to the turntable one after the other. That was the Dansette's unique selling point. Invariably, two records would drop together and the last record to play would, of course, be sitting on top of five other singles – not the best surface for sound reproduction. In addition, by then the needle had picked up a mini-carpet of fluff from the previous records, so the last one of the six often had a distinctly wonky sound to it. The other characteristic of the Dansette was that after an hour or so of use the top got extremely hot, too hot to touch at times. How they never burst into flames was a constant source of wonder to me, even as a child.

Grainy black and white television was another source of entertainment, and the prospect of being able to watch another TV channel as an alternative to the BBC was very exciting. The programmes we liked included 'Children's Hour', Eamonn Andrews presenting 'PlayBox', Christopher Trace and Leila Williams presenting 'Blue Peter' and Johnny Morris as the 'Hot Chestnut Man', who stood behind his stall every week and told us a story.

Saturday teatime viewing began with Clayton Moore as 'The Lone Ranger'. I thought his sidekick, Tonto, was a genuine Indian because his name was Jay Silverheels. After the news, we'd watch 'Six-Five Special', one of the few programmes to feature the latest in pop music. 'Six-Five Special' began with film of an express steam train hurtling towards camera. The long shrill of its whistle would be followed by the programme's theme tune, a rock-cum-skiffle number that began with the lyric 'The Six-Five Special's coming down the line / The Six-Five Special's right on time' – Virgin West Coast eat your heart out.

Later on a Saturday evening, the family would watch what the BBC billed as the series that 'portrays the gritty realism of police work' – 'Dixon of Dock Green'. Even then, far from 'gritty realism', it seemed to me to convey an idealistic view of policemen and their work. The opening of the programme was always the same – P.C. Dixon (Jack Warner) standing on the steps of the police station under the police lamp greeting everyone with 'Evening all', a phrase that was used in just about every comedy sketch that featured a policeman. In time, Dixon's words appeared clichéd, comic even, and a most inappropriate precursor to what passed for 'gritty realism' on TV in the late fifties.

I was still going to Court Crescent School and in 1959 I was chosen to play in goal in a representative match between West Leicester and North Leicester Boys. I can't remember anything about the game but I must have impressed someone because I received a glowing write-up in the Leicester *Green Un*. The head-line read 'Shilton Is A Fine Keeper' and the article said: 'The game revealed that at last we have a goalkeeper who shows every prospect of reaching the high standard of Heathcote, one of the stars of Leicester's Cup-winning side of 1945–46.' Somewhat over the top, I feel, as I still had another year at primary school! The piece continued: 'He is Shilton of Crescent who is fairly tall ... he positions himself well and follows every move in his half of the field [Presumably, at this early stage, my attention was elsewhere when my team were on the attack!] If he continues to improve he may have two years as Leicester senior keeper.'

In making reference to Leicester's 'senior' keeper the writer was somewhat incongruously referring to the Leicester Schools Under-11 team. I must have read that write-up a dozen times and I decided to keep the cutting because I thought it would be interesting to look back on it in later life. So I bought a scrapbook and pasted the cutting on to the first page, hoping, I suppose, to add more cuttings as time went by. I kept scrapbooks for the rest of my life in football, initially compiling them myself. Later my wife, Sue, took over the task. Not many footballers keep mementoes of their career in the game, let alone newspaper cuttings, match pro-grammes, tour itineraries, letters from managers and fellow players, telegrams, post-match dinner menus and Christmas cards from the

FA. I did and I'm glad I did. They provide a real jolt to the memory.

Just before my tenth birthday, I graduated from West Leicester to play for the City's Under-11 team. Others who played in these representative teams and went on to play professional football include David Needham (Nottingham Forest and Queens Park Rangers), Bobby Svarc (Derby County and later a very good player in part-time professional football with Boston United) and Jeff Blockley (Coventry City, Arsenal and England). I also played alongside Romeo Challenger, who would later find fame with the band Showaddywaddy.

Even then, I was somewhat of a perfectionist. On the Friday evening prior to the match I would clean my football boots and wash the laces so that they were sparkling white. My strip, which Mum had previously washed and dried, would be ironed on the Friday night. I felt I had to look the part if I was ever to have any chance of being the part.

I was quite good at school, always up there near the top of the class, but my real love was football. I used to love collecting the autographs of players from visiting teams as well as Leicester City. After a game at Filbert Street I would stand outside the players' entrance with my autograph book open and pen at the ready. So keen was I, I would also go down to the station, buy a platform ticket and hang about in the hope of catching a team – any team – returning from an away game via Leicester.

On one particular Saturday night, freezing fog descended on the city. It was a classic pea-souper and very cold. The fog was so bad that visibility was down to a few yards. Nothing deterred me, though, such was my enthusiasm for footballers and autographs, and I stuck it out at the station in the hope that at least one arriving train might have a team onboard. Eventually, my patience paid off. A train arrived carrying the Bolton Wanderers team. Through the mirk and gloom I recognised Nat Lofthouse, Doug Holden and goalkeeper, Eddie Hopkinson, so I knocked on the carriage window and held up my autograph book and pen. One of the Bolton players opened the small sliding window, took my book and pen and he and all his team-mates scribbled their signatures. That done, one of the Bolton players engaged me in conversation. I can't recall who it was but, at the time, the fact that all the Bolton players had signed my book and one took the time to have a little chat with me filled me with awe and delight. I made my way home through the freezing fog as if on silver wings, I was so happy and excited.

Supporters today have very little contact, if any, with top Premiership players. I find that sad. When a Premiership team arrives at a ground, supporters and would-be autograph hunters are kept at bay behind metal crush barriers while players are shepherded on and off the team coach. It is a case of never the twain shall meet. When I was a boy – and a player – the majority of footballers lived in the city in which they plied their trade, often in the same area as many of the club's supporters. There was contact between the two groups. Now there is little if any contact and when people are not in contact and communicating, it leads to mis-understanding and even distrust.

These days, not only do many top players not live in the city in which they play their football, they don't even live in the sur-rounding area. It's not the fault of the players that there is minimal contact with supporters. It's just the way things are nowadays. Many players are millionaires and I understand their concerns about security in this day and age. Not everything in football has changed for the better.

There was no bigger thrill for me as a boy than spending a few moments chatting to a player as he signed my autograph book. As far as I was concerned, I had been transported to another, exciting world, where my heroes lived. It meant so very much to me, which is why, when I became a professional player, I never refused a request for an autograph if I could help it.

Another real thrill for me was writing to clubs, requesting an autograph sheet and, if possible, a match-day programme. Most clubs responded. Some, such as Burnley, Charlton Athletic, Ipswich Town, Spurs and West Ham, were generous, sending not only a printed autograph sheet but half a dozen or so match programmes as well. Often, I had a reply from the secretary on club headed notepaper, thanking me for my interest in his club.

The printed autograph sheets were highly prized. It was like Christmas morning when the mail dropped through the letterbox and I discovered my bulging self-addressed envelope. A programme could be fitted into an ordinary-sized envelope then, unlike the magazine-type programmes of today.

The very fact that I had received a personal communication from a football club thrilled me. I would never tear the envelope open but place it on the dining table and finish whatever I was doing before the post arrived, savouring the moment, wondering what delights the envelope contained. I wanted to prolong the anticipation for as long as I could. Eventually, I would open it carefully, so as not to rip the envelope and spoil it. Should I receive a match-day programme from, say, Spurs, and it was for a game against Leicester City, I liked to believe the club secretary had selected that programme especially for me, having noted that I lived in Leicester. As far as I was concerned, there were no selfish or uncaring people in football. In my young mind, everyone connected with football was wonderful and god-like.

There were exceptions, of course. I soon found out which clubs never replied to requests from young boys for autograph sheets or programmes. Chelsea, Arsenal and Partick Thistle never replied although I wrote to each on more than one occasion. Curiously, their lack of response did not disappoint or dishearten me. I simply wondered what they did with the stamp I had sent them.

I couldn't get enough of football. The highlight of Christmas for me was receiving those mainstays of most boys' Christmas pillowcases, *The Topical Times Football Annual* and *Charles Buchan's Football Annual*, with their colour photographs of players. *Charles Buchan's Football Monthly* was the top-selling football magazine of its day – a status that was not hard to achieve, given the only other football magazine I knew was *Soccer Star*, which did not contain colour photographs.

In those days, photographs of players were always posed, comically so, although it didn't seem like that at the time. There seemed to be four standard poses. One was the upper body shot, with the player's arms folded across his chest. Then there was the full-profile shot, again with arms folded across the chest but with one foot on the ball. The swinging leg shot was a full-length view of the player that implied he had just kicked a ball. His kicking leg was somewhere up by his ribcage, and rather than looking towards where the ball had gone, he would be smiling at the camera. The throw-in was a head and shoulders shot of the player, arms behind his head, hands clasping a ball.

There was not the saturation coverage of the game we have today – no live games on TV other than the FA Cup Final, no 'Match of the Day' highlights. Even national newspapers restricted coverage of football to two pages at most, so *Charlie Buchan's Football Monthly* carried reports of major matches. Each edition came out in the middle of the preceding month. For example, I would receive the November edition at the end of the second week of October, and it would carry match reports of any major games that had taken place in July and August. With communications being what they are today, it seems ludicrous that a magazine should carry match reports that were anything up to two and a half months old. Yet because the coverage of football was minimal in comparison to that of today, these match reports had some immediacy about them.

The other basic function of *Charlie Buchan's* was to enable readers to put faces to names of players. As footballers were rarely seen on television, the only ways you could see what a player looked like was if he played at your home-town ground or was featured in the magazines or annuals, or in the sets of picture cards that came free with Chic or Anglo bubble gum. The latter were collected avidly by schoolboys, including me. There would be about fifty cards in a set, each featuring a different player. Every schoolboy would have two sets of cards, bound by thick elastic bands. One was his main set, the other his 'swaps'. All the boys who collected the cards would congregate in the school playground to compare swaps, in the hope of trading a card. You would be prepared to give up one you had several of for one you didn't possess.

The collection and trading of these bubble-gum cards gave rise to all manner of street myths. Invariably, there would be one particular card that remained elusive in your area. Tom Finney of Preston, for example, would be conspicuous by his absence whereas Johnny Dixon of Aston Villa, say, would be so common that just about every lad would have five or six examples of it in his swaps. Stories would circulate around the playground of how someone's cousin in Burnley – it was always some faraway place – had told him that, in his town, Tom Finney cards were two a penny and the one card you could never come across was – you've got it – Johnny Dixon of Aston Villa. Such was the joy and frustration of collecting bubble-gum cards of footballers in the fifties and early sixties, our angst perpetuated through playground myth.

I was fanatical about all things to do with football. One winter, after a heavy fall of snow, I remember going down to Filbert Street with some friends and volunteering to help the groundstaff clear the pitch. A photographer from the local paper arrived and took a photograph of us, which appeared in the *Leicester Mercury*. It was hard graft but the very fact I was out on the pitch that my heroes graced was ample reward. I still have that photograph in my first scrapbook – seven of us, duffle-coated, wearing wellington boots, woollen bobble hats and gloves, shovelling snow and smiling for the camera, all pals together. As it turned out, we laboured in vain. Once the pitch had been cleared of snow, the groundsman covered it with top soil. The moisture on the top soil simply turned to ice and the game was postponed, but the disappointment of not being able to use the free ticket I had been given in return for my labour was tempered by having set foot on the Filbert Street pitch itself.

Those three to four inches of top soil were to have a long-term detrimental effect. Following rain, the ground quickly turned into a Christmas pudding of a pitch, and it was still a pudding when I began to establish myself in the first team, a few years later.

My friend Chris Gamble and I were among the founder members of Blaby Boys Club, which became well known in the city for its many football teams. Blaby Boys Club was to become so successful it was considered a nursery club for Leicester City. Chris and I were bosom mates and he shared my enthusiasm for football. Not content to play for our school team and train and play with Blaby Boys Club, we devised our own training sessions, which took place in the back gardens of our respective homes or on the nearest strip of grass. I was fanatical about practising and I guess the friendship I formed with Chris had much to do with the fact that he was fanatical about it too.

Chris would hit shots at me from all angles and, even at this embryonic stage of my life as a goalkeeper, I was intrigued by the different positions I had to take up in order to produce a save. After heavy snow, Chris and I would be out practising. The feel of the ball was totally different and I realised that I had to adapt my footwork, as well as my handling and the way I gathered the ball into my body. I learned to take the sting out of a shot and cushion the ball with my hands. These days I see goalkeepers throwing their hands at the ball to take the pace out of a shot. In the snow, I learned to caress the ball.

The more I learned about goalkeeping, the more I realised how little I knew about it, but I wanted to know everything there was to know, so I practised at every given opportunity. People used to think Chris and I were mad because we would be out there, irrespective of the weather, but it was that variation that fascinated me because I realised that, as a goalkeeper, you had to adjust your basic technique in accordance with the conditions. I remember Chris and I practising in Braunstone Park on a piece of ground that was waterlogged. I had specifically chosen that spot so I could discover how the ball reacted and felt in such conditions.

While I was at Court Crescent School, when the afternoons were light, I would head for the park straight after school to train and practise for an hour or so before heading home for tea. After tea, I would quickly do my homework and then I would be out on the street with a ball. A wall near Dad's shop was illuminated at night by a street lamp and I would spend anything up to two hours on my own, whacking the ball against this wall and catching it to improve my handling. I would angle shots that necessitated me covering ground quickly. This, I found, helped my footwork. I also threw the ball up against the wall to practise catching it at its highest point. I devised my own exercises, which I would perform under the light of the lamp. At this point, I was still occasionally playing as a forward because I wanted to keep my options open.

When I played for the school team on a Saturday morning, my dad would make a detour from his delivery round. He would turn up at whichever school I was playing, wearing his white overall, and although he could stop for only ten minutes or so, for him to be there and watch me play always filled me with great pride.

A number of us from Blaby Boys Club used to travel to Glen Parva army camp in Wigston to train in a gym there. On one occasion, Colin Appleton and Albert Cheesbrough of Leicester City came to supervise our session. Meeting and being trained by two top First Division players was a tremendous thrill for us. Again, this shows how much contact there was between top professional players and supporters in those days. I wonder how many of today's top Premiership players give up evenings on a regular basis to help local boys' clubs. Some do, I know, but I should imagine they are the exceptions.

Blaby Boys was a very go-ahead club. As the sixties got under way, the vast majority of people still holidayed in Britain. Package holidays were in their infancy and I didn't know many people who had travelled abroad, other than those who had been in the services. Blaby Boys were pioneers regarding overseas travel. The first time I ever went abroad was with them, to Hamburg in Germany. I was eleven.

The club had arranged for us to play two games against local sides. I had been looking forward to the trip for weeks and in the days preceding our departure I could barely contain my excitement. On the journey by train and ferry, I felt as if I was travelling with a top English team on their way to play a European match.

I was enthralled by Hamburg. It was so different from Leicester. Everything about it was different – the look of the city, its smell, the way of life. In a way it frightened me, but with that delicious shiver of apprehension down the spine. So when we arrived at the ground at which we were to play the first of our two matches, I was never so disappointed in my life.

We had been told that the game was to take place at a ground with a perimeter fence around the pitch and a small grandstand, and I had imagined a real football ground as opposed to a school or park pitch. My heart sank when I saw that the pitch, rather than being of turf, was made of compressed shale. It looked like the hardcore tennis courts in the public parks in Leicester and, like those tennis courts, the surface contained myriad small loose particles that had been dislodged by constant use. To have travelled all that way to be confronted by what was not a proper pitch was a bitter disappointment. I had no tracksuit bottoms with me and no padding, so although I played in goal, I didn't enjoy the experience simply because the shale pitch did not allow me to play what I considered to be my normal game. The satisfaction of learning how a ball behaved on a shale pitch was negligible because I never wanted to play on such a pitch again in my life!

However, I did manage to buy some new and, to my young mind, innovative goalkeeper's gloves in Hamburg, from one of the sports shops in the city centre. The only goalkeeper's gloves that were available in Britain at the time were made of cotton. The ones in the Hamburg sports shop were made of leather and had dimples on the fingers and palms to give a better grip of the ball. I couldn't speak or read German but from the publicity material on display I gauged that these gloves were worn by some of Germany's top goalkeepers. I didn't have much spending money but I invested in a pair and couldn't wait to return home to test them. I thought they would help me enormously but another great disappointment was in store.

In England in the winter, football is usually played on a wet surface, even when there has been no rain for some time. I quickly discovered that the leather gloves were useless in such conditions. When the ball came at me off a wet surface I found it difficult to control and hold. The wetter the gloves became, the more the ball reacted like a bar of soap. After one game I confined my 'breakthrough' gloves to the bottom of my kitbag and there they stayed until I eventually filed them under 'D' for dustbin.

The trip to Hamburg was a real education for me in every sense of the word. It was a tremendous experience despite the football not living up to expectations. Travelling abroad on a football tour for the first time made me feel like a real professional player.

My first involvement with Leicester City came when I was around eleven years of age. By that time, I had moved up to senior school, King Richard III Secondary. I was still playing as a forward occasionally, and I scored goals, too. In consecutive games for King Richard III we beat Lancaster and Mundella Schools 8–1 and 9–3 respectively, with me helping myself to a hat-trick on both occasions. Those consecutive hat-tricks resulted in a little write-up in the local newspaper, but for all my success as a centre-forward in schools football, I still longed to keep goal.

I read in the *Leicester Mercury* that the club were to hold a 'Football Proficiency Test' at the Saffron Lane Sports Ground. Basically, all the Leicester schoolboy players were invited to attend this test, which was administered by the Leicester City trainer, George Dewis, and Bert Johnson, who was the City coach and right-hand man to manager Matt Gillies. Some of the first-team players were to be in attendance to assist Dewis and Johnson.

The test involved a series of skill exercises and I must have done well because George Dewis approached me at the end of the afternoon and invited me to come along to the ground to do a 'little training' straight after school. George held training sessions at Filbert Street on Tuesday and Thursday evenings for the City semi-professional and amateur players.

So that's how I began life at Leicester City. Every Tuesday and Thursday afternoon in the winter I would catch a bus to Filbert Street for training with George Dewis. When the evenings got lighter, I would cycle there and back, which was about an eight-mile round trip. I didn't mind cycling home after a training session.

On the contrary, I loved it because I saw it as an extension of my training and fitness programme.

George would give me one-to-one training sessions, which took place either on the Filbert Street car park or in the club's little gymnasium. Initially, because I was not yet twelve years old, George packed me off home before the semi-professionals and amateurs arrived at around 6 p.m. However, within two years, he considered my progress to be such that I was staying behind to train with them and taking part in the practice game that ended their training sessions.

George spent a lot of time working on the basic techniques of goalkeeping with me, such as how and when to catch the ball at the highest point and how to get your body behind the ball at every given opportunity. Occasionally, Matt Gillies would come out to watch George putting me through my paces. I hardly dared think that the City manager himself believed I had something about me as a goalkeeper, but I reasoned that he was a busy man and would only take the time to come to watch me if he felt I had real potential.

I can't overstate the influence George Dewis had on me, not only as a goalkeeper but as a person. He took me under his wing, spent countless hours with me and what he taught me about goalkeeping, football and life in general was to prove invaluable.

George had been a player himself. He began his career at non-league Nuneaton before signing for Leicester City in 1933 for the princely sum of £220. He was a good centre-forward, scoring 113 goals in 210 appearances for City. As with all players of his generation, George's prime playing years were lost to the Second World War, which he spent serving in the army. His best years were effectively behind him when peacetime football resumed, although he was City's leading goalscorer in 1946–47 with nineteen goals. He had three more seasons as a player before being appointed coach of the third team in 1950. He nurtured and developed many a City player over the years and remained at the club until 1983. George gave exactly fifty years of sterling service to Leicester City, the sort of loyalty you don't come across in football today. I was very grateful to George for the time he spent with me, helping my development as a goalkeeper, but what I didn't realise at the time was that, more than being simply my trainer, he was my mentor.

Towards the end of the season, when the Filbert Street pitch had dried out, George would supervise practice sessions in one of the goalmouths. With the pitch firm, our practice sessions would do it no harm. Even so, the groundsman would often appear and remonstrate with George but George had the authority to overrule the groundsman so our sessions continued.

George had a Mini-van and lived with his wife Edie in Stoke Golding. Sometimes, when I didn't have my bike, he would drop me off near my home and it always made me proud to be given a lift by the Leicester trainer. Under George's influence, my goal-keeping improved by leaps and bounds and I was soon to be selected for the Leicester Schools representative teams.

This was a magical time for me. I became a familiar figure around Filbert Street, getting to know all the players and the backroom and office staff. One Thursday afternoon I went to Filbert Street straight from school and arrived some fifteen minutes after City's reserve team match against Spurs had finished. As I was walking down the corridor, I saw the Spurs manager, Bill Nicholson, coming towards me. Nicholson had guided Spurs to the League and Cup double in 1960–61 and to the FA Cup the following season. He was a legend in the game even then.

I said 'Hello' and to my great delight and surprise he stopped to talk to me. He asked what I was doing at the ground and when I explained that I went there regularly for training sessions, he asked me what these involved. I remember him saying, 'That's unusual. Clubs don't usually allow lads of your age to attend training.' This was news to me. It dawned on me then that what I was doing at Leicester was indeed unusual, and that the club might think I had something about me as a goalkeeper for them to invite me to the ground on such a regular basis. Bill Nicholson wished me the best of luck and told me to keep working at my game and always be keen to learn.

The conversation lasted for some five minutes and I think it says much about him as a person that he took the time to show an interest in a thirteen-year-old schoolboy from another club. Bill Nicholson was arguably the top manager in England at that time. I've never forgotten it. I felt proud and humble at the same time.

Looking back now, there was a great contrast in my life at that time. I was regularly attending Filbert Street for training and knew all the players and staff but at home I pursued the normal interests of a boy of thirteen. I loved the TV series 'Robin Hood', which starred Richard Greene. In the days before 'Grange Hill' and 'Byker Grove' broke the mould for young people's television by extolling the 'gritty realism' that 'Dixon of Dock Green' strived for but never achieved, 'Robin Hood' was typical of the programmes that my generation sat down to watch while having their tea. 'Sir Lancelot' was another, and 'The Buccaneers', 'William Tell' and 'Sir Francis Drake' – adventure programmes that featured legendary characters from history. The stories, always exciting though simple and in many respects naïve, were products of the time. Life for my generation was simple and naïve. We made our own entertainment. We had no PlayStations, no DVDs, no computers, no picture-text mobiles, no internet chat rooms. We had our imaginations and we had friends.

I did well at school and enjoyed success in schoolboy representative football. In my later years at King Richard III school I concentrated on goalkeeping and was a member of a very successful Leicester Boys team. I played for them a year earlier than any other lad. Due to the physical development of boys at this age, it was unusual to find a fourteen-year-old playing in an Under-16 representative side, but I didn't think anything of it at the time.

In my first season, Leicester Boys reached the third round of the English Schools Trophy and I learned a valuable lesson. In the week leading up to the third-round fixture I was confined to bed with influenza. Come the day of the game, I believed I had recovered sufficiently to declare myself fit to play. I was far from being 100 per cent but I was desperate to play and thought I would get through the match without a problem. Our opponents, Chester-le-Street, had a very good team that included Colin Todd, who would later play for Sunderland, Derby and England, and Colin Suggett (Sunderland, West Bromwich Albion and Norwich City). Chester-le-Street defeated us 3–2 and I had a nightmare game in goal. I should never have played. That experience taught me that while you may be able to get through a game carrying a slight injury, you can't do it when you are not 100 per cent well. I remembered that lesson throughout my entire professional career.

The following season we went just about all the way in the tournament. In a two-legged semi-final of the English Schools Trophy we defeated a Liverpool Boys team that included Archie Styles and Alan Whittle, who would both go on to enjoy careers at Everton. That pitched us against Swansea Boys in the final. The first leg, played at the Vetch Field, ended in a 1–1 draw in front of a crowd of just under 10,000. The second leg at Filbert Street drew a crowd of 18,000 and also ended in a draw, which meant the two teams shared the trophy.

My performances for Leicester Boys earned me a call-up to a trial for England Schoolboys. Somewhat perversely, I found myself playing in a regional trial match for the South West of England against the South East at Andover. Most of my team-mates were from the South West, although our team did include Alun Evans from Mid-Worcester, who was destined to become British football's first £100,000 teenager when he was transferred from Wolves to Liverpool. One of our reserves that day was Willie Carr, who was to enjoy a long and fruitful professional career, in the main with Coventry City.

I didn't do well in this match but was selected for another trial between the North and South. There was little rhyme or reason about which team triallists played for. Geographical location appeared to be immaterial – I was selected for both the South West and the North although I came from Leicester.

In football, as in life, you need a bit of luck. I was originally selected as the reserve goalkeeper for the North, but the first-choice keeper, Steve Death (later to play for West Ham and Reading) was taken ill and so I played. The game took place at Maidstone United's ground on a very snowy day. The playing conditions were diabolical. The snow made life very difficult for goalkeeping but I played well, principally, I think, because of the training I used to do with Chris Gamble. I had learned how to cope with the ball when snow was on the ground, adjusting my handling and the way I executed a save to accommodate a slippery ball. I knew that, when struck, the ball may lose momentum suddenly or quicken when coming off a snowy surface.

As a result, I earned a call-up for England Schoolboys against the Republic of Ireland at Northampton Town's County Ground but the highlight of my appearances at this level was when I was chosen to play against Scotland Schoolboys at Wembley. A crowd of 85,000 saw England triumph 3–0. More often than not, just one or two players from either side in an international schoolboy match eventually went on to carve careers in the game. Players were often chosen for their physical prowess as much as their ability as young footballers. Boys are still developing at fifteen years of age and many who represented England Schoolboys found themselves overtaken within a year or so by lads with ability who could be termed, for want of a better phrase, late developers.

Of the England team that beat Scotland that day, to the best of my knowledge five players went on to enjoy careers as professionals. In addition to Archie Styles, Alun Evans and me, Bryan Chambers had a number of successful seasons at Sunderland and Paul Went played for Leyton Orient, Charlton Athletic and West Ham United. One of our goalscorers, Paul Shoemark, signed for Spurs, but failed to make a real impact in professional football.

I felt I had really achieved something when appearing for England Schoolboys at Wembley. As far as I was concerned, it was the pinnacle of my career, such as it was. Two years previously I had been to Wembley to see England Schoolboys play and had set my heart on trying to get there. I was overjoyed when I received the news of my selection and in the days leading up to the match itself, I was totally preoccupied with the occasion.

The England Schoolboys party stayed at a hotel next to the FA's headquarters in Lancaster Gate, where the full England team often stayed, which added to my sense of excitement. On the night before the game I wasn't nervous but I was anxious because I had developed a cold. I went to bed with a thick top over my pyjamas in the hope of sweating it out. The following morning I felt much better but in need of some fresh air, so my room-mate and I went out for a walk. We were wearing our blazers, ties and slacks and during the course of our walk in Hyde Park we came across the Olympic long jumper Lynn Davies. I recognised him straightaway and was taken aback when he stopped to talk to us. Lynn asked who we were and why we were in London. I explained about the game against Scotland Schoolboys and he wished us both the very best of luck. I had seen Lynn Davies on television and had always thought of him as being a decent guy. It was terrific that he stopped to talk to us. Lynn came across as a generous-spirited person and to meet him was a bonus on what was to be a memorable day.

My performances in goal for both Leicester and England School-boys brought me to the attention of a number of clubs. Arsenal and Manchester United were particularly keen to have my signature, but so too were Leicester City. There was also the issue of my education. I was fifteen and my head teacher at King Richard III wanted me to stay on for another year at school and take ten 'O' levels. The clubs that wanted to sign me as an apprentice professional required me to do so there and then.

I enjoyed school but my heart was set on becoming a footballer. I reasoned that if things didn't work out for me and I was released by a club in eighteen months' time, I would still be young enough to attend a local college of further education and take 'O' levels and possibly 'A' levels. I was, however, even at this tender age, supremely confident that I could make the grade as a goalkeeper in the professional game.

My dad went to see the headmaster and supported my quest to become an apprentice footballer. He agreed that I should leave school to pursue my dream, which is what I did.

Then my dilemma was which club to sign for. Arsenal and Manchester United were much bigger and more glamorous clubs than Leicester City but Leicester was my home town. I had been involved with the club since the age of eleven. The club had been very supportive of me and I felt a great affiliation to them. There was also the matter of George Dewis who had taken me under his wing and devoted countless hours to my embryonic development as a goalkeeper. I couldn't turn my back on him and City and sign for another club, irrespective of how big and successful they were. My parents had left the decision to me, but deep down I think Dad was pleased I finally decided upon Leicester City.

It was not unusual for a club to offer a financial inducement to the parents of a promising schoolboy they wanted to sign. My dad had heard about this from other parents when he accompanied me on trips with England Schoolboys. Dad didn't want me to miss out on any money that may be going, so he asked to see Matt Gillies.

Apparently, when Dad related the amounts certain parents had received from other clubs for signing their sons, Matt Gillies sat with an expression on his face that was as blank as the chequebook in his desk drawer was to remain. Matt listened to what Dad had to say, then said, 'Mr Shilton, do you want to ruin Peter before he has started?'

Matt went on to tell Dad that, although there would be no payment at this stage, should I develop along the lines he hoped and be offered a professional contract at seventeen, the club would make it up to me and 'look after me financially'.

So it was that in June 1965 I put pen to paper and became an apprentice professional with Leicester City for £8 per week. Although my progress through the ranks was swift, I wasn't excused any of the duties an apprentice was expected to carry out in addition to training and playing. These duties included cleaning the boots of the professional players, sweeping out and washing down the dressing room and treatment room and putting out the kit for first-team matches.

On Mondays and Tuesdays the apprentices had to sweep the terraces after the previous Saturday's game. Obviously, there was a lot more litter following a first-team match than a reserve game, but sweeping the terraces after a First Division match had its advantages. These were the days when pop bottles had a deposit on them, so we'd collect up the empties and take them back to the shop – 3d (1.5p) for each one returned. The other bonus was finding coins. The rule was 'finders keepers'. I was amazed at just how many coins were dropped during the course of a match. Most were small change but occasionally I would come across a half-crown (12.5p), which was a real find.

One of my jobs in the summer was to help the groundsman and his staff to paint the stadium. This involved painting the stands, the perimeter wall, the corridors, even the toilets. I didn't mind a bit. It was all part and parcel of the glamorous life of a young footballer!

2

WILY YOUNG FOX

The first-team goalkeeper at Leicester City was Gordon Banks, the England number one, and there were already two other goalkeepers on the books – George Heyes, the reserve-team keeper, and Dave Timson. Dave had also played for Blaby Boys Club and Leicester Schoolboys and, in 1964, had become Leicester's youngest debutant, a record I was on the point of breaking although I would never have believed it at the time.

I had a little taste of what it was like to be in the first team as early as the summer of 1965. A pre-season warm-up tour of Southern Ireland was followed by a game against newly promoted Northampton Town at Filbert Street. I was delighted when Matt Gillies named me as a reserve for this game although he made it clear I was there just to gain a little experience of what it was like to be involved with the first team and wouldn't be taking any part in the game. Gordon Banks was selected, with George Heyes on the bench. Even when Gordon Banks was injured during the first half and replaced by George Heyes, I was quite relaxed in the dug-out in my civvies. During the second half, however, George Heyes took a knock. He jumped to collect a cross and collided with a Northampton forward. While he was receiving attention, word was passed back to Matt Gillies that George may be suffering from concussion. As a reserve, my job was to ferry water for the trainer but when Matt Gillies was told about George Heyes' plight, he turned to me and said, 'Peter, you'd better get stripped.' My heart was beating like a drum as I hurriedly donned my kit. Once I was changed and ready, Matt told me to sit down and be on 'stand-by'.

In the event, George Heyes got to his feet and carried on playing but it was by no means certain that he would be able to complete the game, and it was a very nervous fifteen-year-old who sat on the bench for the remaining twenty minutes. I remember thinking, 'Crikey, I've just left school and I could be making my debut here.' George Heyes did finish the game and I didn't know whether to be disappointed or relieved. I reckon if I had been thrown in at the deep end, I would have been on the winning the side, though – Leicester defeated Northampton 6–1.

A landmark in English football was in place for the 1965–66 season – a substitute was allowed to replace an injured player although substitutions were still not allowed for tactical reasons. The first substitute to appear in English domestic football was Keith Peacock who, on the opening day of the season, replaced an injured team-mate during Charlton Athletic's match with Bolton Wanderers. Leicester City fielded a substitute on the opening day of the season, too, when Jimmy Goodfellow replaced the injured Graham Cross in City's 3–1 home defeat by Liverpool.

Gordon Banks missed City's first nine matches of the season due to the injury he had picked up against Northampton. George Heyes stepped up from the reserves but City made a shaky start, winning just two of those first nine matches and conceding twenty-six goals.

Meanwhile, I was making a competent start in goal for the City youth team and I was promoted to the reserves for a number of games. Again I did well, so much so that I began to think of the possibility of becoming Matt Gillies' second-choice goalkeeper.

With Gordon Banks back on first-team duty, Leicester shook off their bad start and began to produce decent results. Banks was not only first-choice goalkeeper for Leicester and England, he was establishing himself as one of the best goalkeepers in the world. It was his success at international level that gave me my big chance in the Leicester first team, in this my first season as an apprentice.

In the mid sixties, England played the majority of their matches on a Wednesday night but some games, especially those in the now defunct Home International Championship, took place on a Saturday afternoon when a full programme of Football League fixtures was also being played. With a club's top players away on international duty, those Saturday league matches gave reserve-team players the chance to gain some valuable first-team experience. Today, unlike cricket and rugby, the Premiership all but shuts down for a fortnight to allow players to prepare for an international match and one of the downsides of that is young players no longer have the opportunity to step in and cover for them. Having a full fixture list on the same day as a major international game serves to make leagues more competitive. In the Premiership, Arsenal, Manchester United and Chelsea dominate and, in some respects, it is good that English football has three very strong teams. On the other hand, it would make the Premiership more open if those clubs had to fulfil league fixtures when international matches are taking place.

When the England squad was announced for the game against Scotland in May 1966, Banks' name was there, and I was sure Matt Gillies would play me in Leicester's home game against Everton on the same afternoon. I was only sixteen but I was certain that I could do a job in the City first team.

A little while earlier, 2 May to be precise, I had played for Leicester in Alec Dowdells' testimonial against a Scottish XI. Their team, including Bobby Ferguson (Kilmarnock), Alex Hamilton and Willie Penman (both Dundee) and Pat Stanton (Hibs), was as strong as the team the Scottish League had fielded against the English League in the annual representative fixture earlier in the

season. Despite being a testimonial the game was keenly contested – Anglo-Scottish pride was at stake – and I found myself
pressed into action from the word go. The game ended 1–1 and
the following day I was the subject of newspaper headlines. 'Great
Display By Peter Shilton', said one. Another paper said, 'Sixteen-
year-old Peter Shilton bringing off a string of immaculate saves
must have been a heartening sight for the Leicester City management last night.' Even at such a tender age I knew not to let
such press coverage go to my head although it was a proud young
lad who glued those cuttings into his scrapbook.

My performance against the Scottish XI made me feel confident
that Matt Gillies would choose me to play against Everton on the
night Gordon Banks was on duty with England. When he pinned
up the team and I saw my name on the list, needless to say, I was
filled with a mixture of delight and excitement.

First-team debut or not, I soon discovered there was no question
of being excused my normal apprentice duties and that morning I
swept out the dressing rooms before laying out the kit. It was a
strange feeling hanging the goalkeeper's jersey on a peg and laying
out the shorts and socks on the bench below, knowing that I was
going to be the one wearing them later that day. After attending to
the kit I laid out towels and made sure there were enough bars of
soap for the bath and showers before going home for a light lunch.

I was a little nervous prior to the game itself, but relishing the
opportunity of playing for the first time in the First Division and
hopeful that, as a local lad known to City fans, the supporters
would give me every encouragement. Once the game got under
way, I was too busy concentrating to be nervous and I settled down
to enjoy the occasion.

Everton were on their way to winning the FA Cup and this was
the third from last game of the season. So I suppose there is an
argument for saying that some of the Everton players might have

had the Cup final on their minds and were not as committed as they might normally have been for fear of picking up an injury and missing Wembley. They were professionals, though, and they gave it what they could on the day but we were too strong for them. Goals from Jackie Sinclair, Derek Dougan and Paul Matthews gave Leicester a 3–0 victory.

As far as I was concerned, it had been a dream debut – a clear-cut Leicester victory in which I, as the youngest debutant in the club's history, had managed to keep a clean sheet. My performance didn't merit headlines in the press but the consensus of opinion was that I'd had a good game, and most writers were impressed by the potential I had shown.

Of course, I knew that when Banks returned from international duty he would go straight back into the first team and I would return to the reserves, which is exactly what happened. I wasn't disappointed. On the contrary, I had been given my chance in the first team in my first season as an apprentice and I had kept a clean sheet against one of the top sides in the First Division. Having had a taste of first-team football I wanted more but I knew that if I was to stand any chance of making a career out of football, I had one hell of a lot of work to do out on the training ground.

In addition to working on my technique and practising, I used to watch Gordon work at his game. George Dewis spent a lot of time with me but there were no specialist goalkeeping coaches in English football. Banks was an innovator. His training with the first team over, he would pay a few apprentices to stay behind on the training ground with him and pepper shots at him from various angles. I watched him work on his positioning, his angles and his footwork and observed the speed with which he took up different positions in accordance with the angle of the shot. Gordon worked tirelessly at his game and I was determined to do the same and some, adding my own ideas to those I was picking up from him and other goalkeepers I had seen in action. My enthusiasm knew no bounds and I had great energy. I was totally dedicated and wanted to learn all I could about goalkeeping.

One thing I learned at this time, which was to prove invaluable to me throughout my career, was that you should always go for everything. Even in practice sessions and when I knew a shot was going to pass the post safely, by a foot or so, I still attempted to make the save. Doing that teaches you good habits, keeps you mentally alert and ingrains the notion that you must never rest on your laurels or leave anything to chance. The process is what psychologists call 'over-learning'. It becomes instinctive that you should leave nothing to chance. There were occasions during my career when I went for a ball that appeared to be going wide, only for it to deviate in the air or hit the turf and be goalward bound, and I made the save.

The training facilities at Leicester were, by and large, good, but for a goalkeeper they had little to offer other than goalposts. George would give me shooting practice and I'd have to dive from one side of the goal to the other non-stop for half an hour. That was not only great shot-stopping practice, it also built strength, stamina and footwork.

George never attempted to fill my head with too much information at once. He concentrated on basic technique, introducing one or maybe two variations per session. For example, we would spend a session working on the different positions I would have to take up to counter shots from various angles, the golden rule being to get into position as early as possible. George would also drop the ball short so that I could practise diving at the feet of oncoming forwards. Some current Premiership goalkeepers can dive only one way when coming out at the feet of onrushing forwards – their preferred side – but George ensured that I practised diving to both my left and right. All of this really helped my reading of the game but to take things further, and reinforce George's coaching, I had to use my initiative and imagination. One of my self-created training routines was to get team-mates to shoot at me from wooden poles positioned at various angles in and around the penalty area. These poles helped me to acquire a good appreciation of the positioning and techniques required to execute a save from any distance or angle.

Again, through constant practice, this technique became over-learned so that, eventually, wherever an opposing player might be during a game, I would quickly be able to take up the optimum position from which to make the save just before he took the shot. Of course, the world's best players would react instantly and, seeing the scoring opportunity blocked, or at least limited, they would decide not to lose possession and opt for passing the ball to a team-mate in the hope of creating a better chance. Either way, I had denied them a shot at goal. When you are talking about a shot from sixteen yards or ten yards, it's a matter of a split-second's difference. This very fine point of goalkeeping is one that the majority of goalkeepers never go into.

All the practice and what amounted to my journey of self-discovery regarding goalkeeping filled me with so much con-fidence that at times I felt unbeatable. In time, I worked out every position I had to take up in order to save from every conceivable angle. I was painstakingly meticulous in my training and in my pursuit of perfection.

Many footballers practise the things they are good at but often never work at the weaker aspects of their game although some top players are able to compensate for that by becoming specialists in certain areas. I made huge efforts to improve what I perceived to be my weak points. For example, during the embryonic stage of my career I spent six months, off and on, exploring and perfecting the technique of punching the ball. I found I would get it right one day but flap at the ball the next day. It occurred to me that there must be a reason why I was not connecting properly all the time and perhaps it was more a question of technique than practice. When I thought about it, I realised that when attempting to punch a high ball clear, I was often too far away from the ball and punching with an outstretched arm. Whenever a major fight was screened on television, I watched the boxers carefully and noted the way they delivered a punch. Without exception, they moved close to their opponents and delivered punches with a snap of the arm. I went out and bought a punchbag. The pummelling not only strengthened my arms, wrists and hands but improved my footwork immensely and I soon found the closer my feet were to the bag, the better and more effective the punch.

Eventually, I discovered there were six basic ways to punch a high ball clear, each one appropriate to a given situation, such as the height and angle at which the ball entered the penalty box and how much pressure was being exerted by opposing forwards. The two-fisted punch achieved height and length when under pressure. Punching the ball forwards, sideways and even backwards were all options to alleviate pressure. Each technique was dependent on the type of cross and whether it was being delivered straight or at an angle from the byline. If the cross was coming from wide or from the byline, I discovered it was best to get one fist to the ball, and I practised punching to both the left and right. A two-fisted punch was the most effective when the ball was delivered straight at me from deep. The object of all this work was for me to have no big weakness in my game.

While I was dedicated to football, I did have other interests outside the game. I met and fell in love with a beautiful girl called Sue and spent more and more time with her. We would go to the cinema, occasionally have a meal in a restaurant or pop into a pub for a drink. I have never been a big drinker but in those early days of courting Sue I would enjoy a couple of beers if we visited a pub after a match.

My other interest was music. The Beatles and the Stones were in their pomp in the mid-sixties and I was a massive fan of both bands. Sue had the advantage over me because she had actually seen the Beatles when they played a concert in Leicester some years earlier. Many couples have a song that they feel is special to them. Ours was 'Baby Now That I've Found You' by the Foundations. All these years later, it's still 'our song'.

Although I loved music and still do, I have never been one for attending live concerts. This might have something to do with the fact that the one and only gig I attended as a boy was a great disappointment. I was about thirteen and spent my pocket money on a ticket for a Freddie and the Dreamers concert. That may induce a wry smile in some. Freddie and the Dreamers were a middle-of-the-road pop band, hardly cutting edge in terms of popular music. Their lead singer, Freddie Garrity, wore large spectacles and his gimmick was to jump and dance around the stage in a comic way, like some medieval court jester – or, at least, that's how I imagined such court jesters would have danced. Freddie and the Dreamers had enjoyed a number of hits with songs such as 'If You Gotta Make A Fool Of Somebody', 'I'm Telling You Now' and 'You Were Made For Me'. I was just a young lad and Freddie and the Dreamers' catchy, happy-go-lucky songs and stage act appealed to me.

I had been looking forward to seeing Freddie Garrity live for days, but before the concert began, someone came on stage and said they had 'bad news and good news to announce'. The 'bad news' was that Freddie Garrity was unable to appear that night. The 'good news' (insert your own joke here) was that the concert was to go ahead with just the Dreamers. I was bitterly disappointed and I wasn't the only one. The audience never warmed to the

Dreamers playing their hits minus their effervescent front man. The songs were just not the same and I was left with the feeling that if anyone 'had made a fool of somebody', it had been the concert promoter and the Dreamers making a fool out of me. I felt cheated. That was the first and, to date, last concert I attended.

I collected records, as they were then, and for a time considered learning to play the guitar. I bought one second-hand and signed up for lessons but, unfortunately, the stocky fingers I was developing through goalkeeping were not conducive to playing the guitar. I gave up after a few lessons and decided to concentrate on football instead, which must have come as a great relief to my mum and dad, who had patiently endured my attempts to master 'Bobby Shaftoe' on the guitar for hours on end.

The 1966–67 season was largely dominated by the aftermath of England's victory in the World Cup final. The success of Alf Ramsey's team had a knock-on effect on English football. Attendances were up and there was a general feel-good factor throughout the game as a result of England being world champions.

A particularly parochial aspect of that post-World Cup pride was that Gordon Banks had been England's goalkeeper throughout the tournament. Gordon's success provided a boost to the image and status of the club and his performances in the World Cup had established him as England's number one after his battle for the jersey with Chelsea's Peter Bonetti. There was possibly an element of reflected glory when Matt Gillies was appointed as a local magistrate.

I spent most of the 1966–67 season playing in the reserves, having signed as a professional for the club, and attempting to establish myself as Gordon's deputy. My second outing in the first team came in November 1966 in a 2–1 victory over West Bromwich Albion.

Matt Gillies was not averse to playing youngsters in the first team whenever established players were on international duty, or at the end of the season when little was at stake, and I enjoyed a run of three games in the first team during the following April. Although we drew one and lost two of the games in question, I knew I had played well.

My performance against West Bromwich Albion earned a favourable headline in the *Daily Express* – 'Hero Shilton Defies Albion'. Press headlines never affected how I thought of myself as a player. I wasn't a hero but the fact that I had played well in those first-team games further boosted my confidence and led me to believe I wasn't a million miles away from having a career in the First Division, possibly at another club.

Deep down I felt there was not much chance of a long-term future for me at Leicester City. I estimated Gordon had quite a few more years at the top and I didn't want to play reserve-team football for that length of time, so I decided to have a word with Matt Gillies. I had total respect for him. I thought I would be capable of playing regular first-team football in the not-too-distant future. A number of First Division clubs had expressed an interest in me, despite my age, and I realised that I might have to move on.

Matt listened to what I had to say and told me that he recognised my ability as a goalkeeper and felt I had a great future ahead of me. He asked me to be 'patient for a little while longer'. I understood the manager's dilemma and resigned myself to concentrating on reserve-team football for the time being.

The financial situation at Leicester meant the club were not averse to selling, even star players. The first inkling I had of this occurred in March 1966 when Matt sold Derek Dougan to Wolves for £50,000. 'The Doog' was a terrific centre-forward and a cult hero with Leicester supporters. His departure did not go down well with them. Given the club were always strapped for money, I still thought they might consider selling me or Leicester's other prize asset – Gordon Banks – at some time, even if they weren't particularly keen to do so at the moment.

Leicester's money worries did not stem from paying high wages. They were among the lowest payers in the First Division, if not the lowest. Wolves were in the Second Division at the time of Derek Dougan's transfer, but he earned more with them than he did at Filbert Street. Leicester did not have the financial resources of many of the other First Division clubs and I suppose the offer from Wolves was just too good to turn down.

The club were always pleading poverty and, having sold one of the team's prize assets to generate income, the board decided to repeat the exercise by selling another – Gordon Banks. In March 1967, unbeknown to me, Matt Gillies had a chat with Gordon on the training ground. The gist of the conversation was that the club were ready to sell Gordon should they receive an acceptable offer. There had been rumours in the press about the possibility of either Gordon or me moving on but, up to this point, nothing concrete had materialised.

I later learned that the club reached the decision over Gordon, in the main, because they wanted to cash in on him while he was at the top of his game. Also, Matt saw me as a long-term investment.

Over the next few weeks, speculation about where Banks was headed was rife. At one point, he seemed ready to sign for West Ham United, then it was Liverpool. Neither move came off and, in April 1967, Gordon joined Stoke City.

Stoke City were not as big and glamorous as Liverpool, or even West Ham, whose playing staff included Bobby Moore, Geoff Hurst and Martin Peters, but the move was a good call at the time. Stoke were an established First Division club and one that was on the up. They had a lot of potential and their manager, Tony

Waddington, was in the process of creating a very good team. As in the case of Derek Dougan, Banks was much better off financially at Stoke than he had been at Leicester. I suppose the move worked out well for everyone. Leicester received a then world record fee for a goalkeeper of £60,000. Banks joined a club that was in the ascendancy and for better money. Stoke had a world-class goalkeeper and Leicester had a ready-made replacement for him in me. I have to say that I did wonder whether it would have been better for me to have a fresh start rather than Gordon. The pressure on a seventeen-year-old taking over from England's, and at that time possibly the world's, best goalkeeper was tremendous.

I was as surprised as anyone that Gordon left Leicester. He was under contract and didn't have to go. Even during all the talk of a possible move, I didn't think Gordon would leave. To my mind, he could have told the club that he didn't want to go and that would have been the end of the matter. He wouldn't have been dropped.

When I succeeded Gordon, the Leicester fans were very supportive. I was a local lad. They knew me from my schoolboy career and from City's youth and reserve teams and the occasional first-team match. They got behind me and gave me a really good chance to show what I could do, which I appreciate to this day.

During the 1966–67 season, I had the honour of being selected for the England Youth team. As with England Schoolboys, in those days players had to undergo trials for the Youth team and the one I attended, at RAF Cosford, featured several players destined to make names for themselves in the game – Dave Latchford (Birmingham City and Celtic goalkeeper), John Craggs (Newcastle United), Frank Lampard (West Ham United), Mick Mills (Ipswich Town), Tony Want (Spurs), Trevor Brooking (West Ham), Colin Todd (Sunderland), Vic Halom (Charlton, Luton and Sunderland), Paul Went (Leyton Orient, Charlton and West Ham), Chris Garland (Bristol City and Chelsea), Colin Suggett (Sunderland, West Brom and Norwich), Joe Royle (Everton), Mick Channon (Southampton), Steve Kember (Crystal Palace), Brian Kidd (Manchester United) and Alun Evans who, as mentioned earlier, became Britain's first £100,000 teenaged signing. George McVitie (Carlisle and Oldham) and Steve Death (Reading and Lincoln) had good careers in the lower divisions. In fact, the number of players in that trial who made the grade in First Division football is remarkable – seventeen, including myself. That statistic is indicative of the quality of home-grown talent that was around in the sixties.

I played for England Youth in the qualifying stages of the International Youth Tournament, including two matches against Scotland. England beat Scotland 1–0 on aggregate and on both occasions I found myself the subject of flattering headlines in the national press. I was dubbed 'Superkid', 'Boy Wonder' and one newspaper even went so far as to say 'This Leicester Boy Is Great', but I had my feet firmly planted on the ground. I knew I was good enough to be playing First Division football but I also knew I had much to learn about goalkeeping and a long, long way to go before I would reach the standard I had set myself.

When Gordon Banks left Leicester City, many newspapers featured photographs of us shaking hands and bidding one another 'goodbye'. Over the years I have heard stories that Gordon and I never got on but nothing could be further from the truth. We were, and still are, good friends. In my scrapbooks there are a number of letters from Gordon, received at various stages of my career, offering congratulations and expressing pleasure at my achievements. We both now appear as after-dinner speakers and, on occasions, have teamed up for 'goalkeeping special' dinners. Apart from anything else, Gordon Banks is a gentleman in every sense of the word, and it is just not in him to be resentful of the progress of others.

Progress is what my career did in 1967–68. With Gordon having departed for Stoke, I played in all but seven of Leicester's league games. My deputy was the experienced Brian Williamson. He had been brought in on loan from Nottingham Forest after I was injured at Old Trafford in our third match of the season. That injury frustrated me more than anything had done before. I was just beginning to settle and was looking forward to a long run in the first team. I sprained my left ankle after about half an hour of the game and, as there were no substitute goalkeepers, I carried on playing, only to sprain my right ankle. I was in a lot of pain and discomfort but managed to carry on until about ten minutes from the end when it all became too much. Matt Gillies brought on Alan Tewley as substitute and Bobby Roberts took over from me in goal. I was taken aback when the Old Trafford crowd gave me an ovation as I left the pitch but that was not the only surprise.

While I lay on the treatment table in the dressing room, there was a knock on the door and in walked United manager Matt Busby. I was amazed, especially as the game was still in progress. Matt Busby had tried to sign me at one point but this was the first time I had ever encountered him in person. He asked how I was and I was very taken with the concern he showed for my injury. Before he left, he said, 'Don't be in any hurry to get back out there on the pitch, son. You have an injury and you could make it worse by getting back out and playing. Rest up and take it easy, you're in good hands.' Matt Busby's sympathetic words touched me, although later I did joke that the real purpose of his visit was to ensure I didn't return to the pitch. The game was finely balanced at 1–1 and perhaps Matt believed that with me sidelined and an outfield player in goal, his team stood a better chance of winning the game!

I played in just one of our next seven matches but returned fully fit in October in time to play in the 2–1 home defeat of Liverpool. Thereafter, I remained Leicester's number-one choice goalkeeper, but I was far from thinking I had made it. I knew the really hard work was only just beginning.

I think the best word to describe my attitude then – and perhaps even now – is 'single-minded'. From the age of eight I had been single-minded in my quest to be a top goalkeeper. Throughout my childhood and teens I had spent countless hours making drawings and diagrams of the angle and trajectory of a ball when kicked from various positions in and around the penalty area. Even as a small boy I had a grasp of angles, lines and positioning. The subject fascinated me and this fascination was to become almost an obsession when I became a professional goalkeeper.

Matt Gillies told the story of how one afternoon he walked out to the training ground to watch me putting myself through one of my self-imposed training schedules. Matt said he watched me for five minutes or so before engaging me in conversation about goalkeeping. The way Matt told it, that conversation was stilted and after a few minutes he realised his presence was an unwelcome distraction from my work, so he left and let me get on with my training. I would have been around eighteen at the time. Most eighteen-year-old professionals welcome the interest of the manager when training. It's a great fillip. I wasn't being rude or unwelcoming. It was just that my mind was fully applied to the training I was doing. Had Alf Ramsey himself stopped for a chat, it would still have been a hindrance.

One of the constants in my life was my obsession with goal-keeping. When practising, or making those diagrams, I immersed myself in a world where I felt comfortable and secure. As the years passed and I began to develop new goalkeeping techniques that were unknown to other keepers, I felt increasingly comfortable and secure in this world of mine because I was in control, dictating events. I felt I possessed certain knowledge that others didn't have. That sense of security was the result of my single-mindedness although I never thought of it in that way at the time. Something inside just told me 'I want to be a top goalkeeper' and I have never entered into anything half-heartedly. For me, it is always a case of all or nothing. I am finding that now with golf!

Throughout my life I have always set myself goals. One of the first was to play for the school football team. I knew that in order to do that I would have to work hard at my game, which is what I did. Once in the school team, I set myself the goal of making it into the Leicester Primary Schools team. That would involve more hard work, to which I applied myself totally, and so it went on all the way through to playing for England. After that, I set myself more goals, establishing myself as the England number one, trying to achieve perfection in a certain goalkeeping technique, and so on.

Football is a team game and I was very much a team player but my obsession with my role in the team meant that I spent a lot of time training and practising on my own, or with the help of anyone I could coerce into staying behind after normal training to assist me.

Goalkeepers enjoy a special fraternity. It is a highly specialised position within the team, a position apart if you like. There is a bond between goalkeepers that I don't think exists for other positions, a sort of union of goalkeepers. The empathy endures partly because we don't come into direct opposition with one another during a game, and partly because we know and understand the special pressures that go with the job. A forward can make several mistakes and nothing comes of them. A goalkeeper makes one and the consequence of that can be great. It is a case of 'There but for the grace of God go I.'

*

Hindsight is a wonderful thing. It is all too apparent now that in the late sixties when I was establishing myself in the first team, Leicester City were letting the grass grow under their feet – literally when the pitch was relaid in 1967, the turf being cut from our Belvoir Drive training ground. In 1967–68, all Matt Gillies' attempts to bring in new signings to improve the team came to nothing. Perhaps it was a case of players such as Mike Doyle (Manchester City) and Fred Pickering (Everton) not wanting to take a drop in wages. For a good stretch of the time, there was inadequate cover for me. A number of goalkeepers were taken on loan – Jack McClelland from Fulham was one – but, in the main, junior goalkeepers were pressed into service with the reserves, with local amateur players turning out for the 'A' team.

Matt did make one or two signings. Frank Large joined us from Northampton and Len Glover came from Charlton Athletic, but a mid-table finish was the best we could manage in my first full season.

One match I readily recall was our away game at Southampton in October. We recorded a fine away win beating Southampton 5–1 but the reason this game sticks in the memory is because I scored our fifth goal! It happened in the last minute of the game when I punted the ball deep into Southampton's half of the field. We were 4–1 to the good and I simply wanted to keep the play in Southampton's half of the pitch until the final whistle. To my utter amazement the ball sailed into the Southampton penalty area, bounced high enough to avoid the home keeper's attempt to collect it and carried on into the net. That was the only goal I ever scored as a professional but I didn't realise I had scored until much later. When I punted the ball upfield, City winger Mike Stringfellow chased after it and, as it bounced towards the goal, I thought Mike got a touch before it crossed the line.

We had no time to hang about after the final whistle. The game ended at around 4.40 p.m. and it was one mad rush to catch the five o'clock train back to Leicester. During the journey, my team-mates started to chipper me up about my goal. The lads were great mickey takers and I thought they were having me on, hoping I would rise to the bait. I was having none of it and dismissed their comments about 'a rare and unusual goal' out of hand. It was only later, when I saw the game on 'Match of the Day', that I realised they hadn't been winding me up and Mike Stringfellow hadn't touched the ball. One goal in 1,400 games – eat your heart out Alan Shearer!

In 1968–69, Allan Clarke arrived from Fulham. Having been subjected to much criticism from fans who believed the board were 'unambitious', the directors broke the British transfer record in signing him. The deal, valued at £150,000, involved City paying £110,000 and Frank Large moving to Craven Cottage as the make-weight.

Allan Clarke was a super player but our performances as a team were, by and large, very disappointing. Come the end of November we had won just three of our twenty-one league games and the board held an emergency meeting to discuss the situation. Matt Gillies was given the dreaded 'vote of confidence'. Assistant manager Bert Johnson and assistant coach George Dewis, my mentor, were relieved of their duties. George was appointed trainer of the 'A' team.

On 29 November, Matt Gillies tendered his resignation and the directors decided to make it public prior to our away match against Everton. Ironically, that week Matt Gillies had become the first Leicester manager to stay in the post for ten years. Off the pitch, the club was in turmoil and, within a few hours, we were in turmoil on the pitch as well. Everton beat us 7–1.

In December, the club appointed Frank O'Farrell as manager. Frank had done a good job at Torquay United and this was a big step up for him. In my opinion, he did well at Filbert Street but the rot had set in and, as a team, we were unable to turn things around sufficiently to avoid relegation to the Second Division. The former West Ham winger Malcolm Musgrove was appointed first-team coach, and secretary Eddie Plumley joined Coventry City. Given the other changes that had taken place, it meant that within a couple of months the entire backroom staff at the club had changed.

The season proved to be somewhat of a dichotomy. For all our performances in the League left much to be desired, we had a very good run in the FA Cup that took us all the way to the final at Wembley. On the way, we accounted for Barnsley, Millwall, Liverpool and Mansfield Town. Allan Clarke scored the only goal of our semi-final against West Bromwich Albion at a packed Hillsborough to send us into the final against Manchester City.

It is one of the curious things about football that, despite players coming and going over the years, there always seems to one club that is a bogey side for another. In the case of Liverpool, it has been Leicester City. Even in the days of the 'Mighty Reds' in the seventies and eighties, more often than not Leicester would get a result against Liverpool at Filbert Street, irrespective of previous form. I can remember Leicester upsetting the odds by beating Liverpool in the 1963 FA Cup semi-final. In 1969 we repeated that feat although on this occasion in the fifth round.

The first match at Filbert Street attracted a capacity crowd of 42,002 but ended goalless. I don't think anyone outside Leicester gave us any chance of winning the replay at Anfield but we did. A solitary headed goal from Andy Lochhead, who had been signed that season from Burnley, sealed Liverpool's fate. I was very busy that night. The pressure Liverpool exerted was phenomenal. Somehow we withstood the barrage and I had the satisfaction of pulling off a series of saves to keep the home side scoreless, at one point saving a penalty from Tommy Smith in front of the Kop.

My dad had travelled to Anfield to watch the game and found himself seated in the main stand surrounded by Liverpool supporters. When I saved the penalty, he jumped up and threw his hat in the air. It hit a rather large Liverpool supporter seated in the row in front, who swung around and glowered at Dad.

'I'm sorry,' Dad said, 'I got carried away. That's my son who's just saved the penalty.'

The big Liverpool fan studied Dad for a moment, handed him back his hat and said, 'It's OK. If my son had just saved that penalty, I'd be proud of him, too.'

Our goal apart, it had been more or less one-way traffic but we held out to claim a memorable victory. It says much for the sporting nature of the Anfield crowd that, although they must have been gutted by the result, they gave me a standing ovation as I left the field. It's a moment I have never forgotten. Elated as I was by our victory and my own performance, I felt humbled by that great sporting gesture. Those supporters were used to seeing their team win at Anfield but they were gracious in defeat.

Our semi-final against West Bromwich Albion was similar to the Liverpool game in that West Brom dominated but couldn't put the ball in the net. Allan Clarke always seemed to reserve his best performances for the Cup and this semi-final was no exception. He worked tirelessly up front, often as a lone striker, and managed to score the only goal of the game with just three minutes of the match remaining. West Brom threw every man forward bar their goalkeeper. I particularly remember an incident in those closing stages when a West Brom player sent a looping ball into my penalty area. The ball seemed to hang in the air for ages and I was aware that Jeff Astle and Tony Brown were barnstorming into the box in the hope of getting on the end of this 'Garryowen'. I told myself, 'You gotta stand firm.' I knew I was going to be clattered but I jumped up and collected the ball. As I did so, both Astle and Brown hit me. It was as if I had been hit by a fridge freezer swung by a crane. I went flying but hung on to the ball as if my life depended on it. For me, it was one of my most memorable saves. It wasn't a great one because it was merely a matter of collecting the ball but, given the circumstances, I felt it was brave.

Naturally, I was thrilled at the prospect of playing in an FA Cup final at Wembley. I was nineteen and this was only my second full season at the club. However, I was not euphoric because we had just eleven league games left in which to preserve our First Division status.

The final took place on 26 April and my memory of it is of a decent game of football. Manchester City were a good footballing side and I felt we more than matched them for long periods, but we failed to take our chances and a single goal from Neil Young sealed our fate.

I was very disappointed but consoled myself with the thought that I had plenty of time ahead of me to return to Wembley and play in the winning side. Oddly, for all the success I was to enjoy in my long career, this never happened – 1969 was my only appearance in an FA Cup final.

I didn't enjoy the post-match banquet. I felt as flat as a pancake and didn't feel much like talking, not even to Sue. It was the same on the train journey home. Leicester had appeared in two previous FA Cup finals in the sixties and had lost on both occasions. To end the decade losing a third was a bitter experience and nothing could raise my spirits. Sue told me later that it was in the aftermath of that game that she realised just how much I had wanted Leicester to win.

Following our appearance at Wembley, we had five more league matches to play. We faced Manchester United in the last one needing a victory to avoid relegation. There was nothing at stake for United but this was to be Matt Busby's last match as manager and I suppose the United players wanted him to sign off with a victory. We took the lead in the first minute through David Nish, but a characteristic piece of dribbling magic from George Best resulted in United drawing level and they drew ahead courtesy of Denis Law. A goal from Rodney Fern fuelled our hopes but although we battled hard, Willie Morgan scored United's winner and Leicester City were relegated.

I could not remember Leicester City in any division other than the First. To be a part of a Leicester team that was relegated hung heavily upon me but I faced up to the prospect of Second Division football, determined to do all I could to help the team get back up into the top flight at the first time of asking. I was also determined to make myself the top goalkeeper in the country and to undertake all the hard work that would entail. I was to be encouraged in my quest by someone who saw some potential and came calling for me. That person was Alf Ramsey, the England manager.

3

TO CAP IT ALL

So a season that had promised much had ended in relegation. We all felt the pressure as the season reached its end. It was unlike anything I had experienced before. The pressure of trying to win the FA Cup is one thing but this was all together different. In those last few league games, every mistake seemed to be vital and to have dire consequences because time was running out and the opportunity to put matters right was forever diminishing. The players knew this better than anyone else and it brought an edge to our play. Only those who have been involved in a battle against relegation know this sort of pressure. The weight of expectation in an important Cup match didn't bother me – in fact, I thrived on it – but the pressure of a relegation dogfight was something I found strange. It was as if foreboding hung over every game.

On a personal note, however, I felt my game was continuing to improve with every match I played. Some members of the press seemed to feel the same, among them Alan Holby of the *Daily Express*. He put himself on the line by selecting four young players he believed would go on to achieve 'great things in the game' – Brian Kidd (Manchester United), Alun Evans (Wolves), Eric McMordie (Middlesbrough) and yours truly. Alun Evans, as has been said, eventually joined Liverpool and although he played a number of games for them in the First Division, he never fulfilled his early potential. Eric McMordie, a cerebral midfield player, enjoyed a fine career with Middlesbrough and became an established international with Northern Ireland, but he never scaled the lofty heights achieved by Brian Kidd, who deputised for Denis Law in the 1968 European Cup final. When Holby wrote his piece, Brian was already establishing himself as a fine young player at Old Trafford.

As for myself, I felt flattered that Alan Holby predicted I was 'destined to one day succeed Gordon Banks as England goalkeeper'. That was one of my aims, but I knew I still had a long way to go before I reached a standard whereby that could ever happen, and I was anxious about playing in the Second Division. If I was to continue to develop, I needed to be playing top-flight football – in the First Division. At this stage, I was dedicated to doing that with Leicester City.

It was around about this time that I first went into business for myself. Tebbitt and Brown was a well-known sports shop in Leicester. I knew the owners, who had spotted what they believed to be a relatively untapped market for innovative, endorsed sportswear. After a series of meetings, I set up my own company and entered into a partnership with Tebbitt and Brown whereby I would design and promote sportswear and they would arrange its manufacture.

The first project undertaken by Peter Shilton Limited was to market a goalkeeping jersey I had designed myself and some goalkeeping gloves. I had always wanted to wear a goalkeeper's top that was different from the conventional style and more suited to my needs. At the time, every goalkeeper's jersey was green, had a circular collar and resembled a sweatshirt. They were made of cotton and were rather nondescript. The one I designed had a two-way collar and a zip down the front, which enabled it to be worn as a sort of V-neck in warm weather and as a roll-neck in the winter. The goalkeeping gloves featured black string and, I felt, offered a better purchase when handling the ball.

I had plans to introduce a tracksuit of my own design and follow up with a complete range of sports clothing. Even at nineteen, and hopeful of a long career in the game, I thought I should prepare for when my days as a footballer were over.

The Football League were not visionary with regard to the goalkeeper's jersey. I had worn one for several league outings already but following a game at Bournemouth the referee intimated he felt the jersey with its zip and buttons was a potential danger to other players and the Football League upheld that view. There had been no official complaint about the jersey but, nevertheless, the League wrote to Leicester City pointing out that there were certain rules governing football kit that my jersey contravened.

I didn't agree with the Football League but I had to adhere to their ruling, which effectively put an end to that particular business venture. The initial sales of the other lines of sportswear were good but it came to a point when Tebbitt and Brown had to decide whether they were going to channel all their resources into manufacture or concentrate on their core business, their retail shops. In the end, they decided manufacturing was too much of a gamble and they concentrated their efforts on the shops.

Before the contentious goalkeeper's jersey was abandoned, it involved me in a curious incident before one match at Filbert Street. I was lining up ready for the kick-off when the referee delayed the start. He ran to my goalmouth and told me to remove the jersey I was wearing. I couldn't understand why he had chosen that moment to ask me to change my top. He had, after all, visited our changing room to check every player's studs. I had been wearing the top then and he had said nothing. The fact that he delayed the kick-off while I changed my top made me feel I was being made an example of. It was all rather embarrassing. The chairman, Len Shipman, who was also president of the Football League, was never keen on the top and I did wonder if he had had a word with the referee. It seemed strange to me that the referee had seen me wearing it in the dressing room but had not thought fit to make an issue of it then.

Football reflects society and football kit is apt to mirror fashion. When the Beatles appeared on the scene wearing suits with Nehru collars, it wasn't long before football shirts mirrored that fashion. Before 1963, players had worn V-necked shirts with short sleeves. The Beatles fashion for suits with round-necked collars filtered down from mainstream fashion to football and come 1965 just about every team had adopted round-necked shirts, and that included the goalkeeper's top. Within a few years the style of football shirts was to change yet again. As the seventies got under way, the fashion was for young men to wear shirts with long collars, and soon football tops sported that style, too.

I like to think I had been innovative in designing a goalkeeper's jersey with a collar when all strips boasted a circular neck. The notion that the zip and buttons represented a potential danger to other players – unlike aluminium studs, of course! – seemed odd. In cold weather, many goalkeepers took to wearing a tracksuit top with a zip underneath their normal goalkeeper's jersey but to the best of my knowledge nothing was ever said about that.

In 1969, West Bromwich Albion, then a top side in the First Division, enquired about my availability for transfer. It was reported that they were prepared to pay £100,000 for my signature, which would have smashed the previous record fee for a goalkeeper, the £65,000 that West Ham had paid Kilmarnock for Bobby Ferguson. I was, however, committed to Leicester City and proved it by signing a new contract. Despite being concerned that playing Second Division football might be detrimental to my chances of being called up for England, I felt Leicester had the potential to gain promotion at the first time of asking. As things turned out, we didn't bounce straight back up to the First Division. We came very close but it took two seasons to get there.

During the close season, Allan Clarke left Filbert Street for Leeds United for £165,000. It was a very big fee at the time but the club appeared in no mood to spend any part of it on new players to strengthen the team for our push for promotion. The only new signing was full-back Billy Houghton, who joined for a nominal fee from Ipswich Town.

The 1969–70 domestic season started in early August and was scheduled to conclude in mid-April to allow the England team time to acclimatise for the defence of the World Cup in Mexico the following summer. We got off to a good start in the Second Division, winning our opening game at home to Birmingham City 3–1 in front of a healthy crowd of over 35,000. I saved a penalty.

In fact, we did well in the first half of the season, losing just four of our twenty-one matches, which kept us in touch with the promotion pace-setters Huddersfield Town, Blackpool and Middlesbrough. During the season, Andy Lochhead was transferred to Aston Villa while Frank O'Farrell brought in winger John Farrington from Wolves for £30,000, the same fee the club had received for Lochhead. Come Easter, Huddersfield looked set to clinch one of the two automatic promotion places with Leicester challenging Blackpool for second place. Despite remaining unbeaten in our final eight league games, Blackpool pipped us for the runners-up spot by two points, which was a bitter disappointment.

We enjoyed a certain distraction from our efforts to win promotion with good runs in both the FA and the League Cup. Our progress in the League Cup ended in the quarter-finals. We drew 0–0 with West Bromwich Albion at Filbert Street in front of a record League Cup crowd of 35,121. In the replay at the

Hawthorns, a goal from Graham Cross proved insufficient when West Brom triumphed courtesy of two goals from Jeff Astle.

In the fifth round of the FA Cup, we once again found ourselves up against mighty Liverpool but this time there was to be no fairytale ending. Having secured a worthy 0–0 draw at Anfield, we had high hopes of progressing at the expense of our more illustrious opponents. A crowd of over 42,000 packed Filbert Street for the replay but two goals from my old England Schoolboys team-mate Alun Evans put paid to our hopes of repeating our success of the previous season.

In earlier rounds we had beaten Sunderland and Southampton and now we had run Liverpool very close, all First Division clubs. To me that suggested we could compete at the highest level and Frank O'Farrell was creating a side that could not only win promotion but stay in the First Division.

I was by now a well-established member of the England Under-23 team and was pushing to make the full squad. I'd first been chosen for the Under-23s in April 1969 for a game against Portugal at Coventry. Alf Ramsey was not only the manager of the full England team, he was also manager and coach of the Under-23s. These days the England coach enjoys the assistance of anything up to four coaches for an international match. Also on the bench are physios, trainers and, for a friendly, another entire team of substitutes. It's worth noting that when England won the World Cup in 1966, Alf Ramsey's backroom staff consisted of trainers Les Cocker from Leeds and Harold Shepherdson from Middlesbrough. During the actual tournament, Alf also had Wilf McGuinness from Manchester United to help him with the coaching. That was the extent of Alf's backroom staff. In addition to his responsibilities with the full England team and the Under-23s, Alf was often involved with the coaching of the England Youth side. I don't know how much Alf was paid by the FA, but whatever his salary was, he earned it!

The team Alf selected for my debut at Under-23 level included Glyn Pardoe, Mike Doyle and Tommy Booth (all Manchester City), Joe Royle and John Hurst (both Everton), Bryan 'Pop' Robson (Newcastle), Peter Osgood (Chelsea) and Ralph Coates (Burnley). I got the nod for the goalkeeper's jersey ahead of Peter Springett of Sheffield Wednesday, whose brother, Ron, had preceded Gordon Banks in goal for the full England team.

England won comfortably on the night and I made a decent debut at this level although, to be honest, Portugal were not the best of sides and I found myself with nothing to do for long periods. It can be a real test for a goalkeeper when his team are exerting a lot of pressure in the opposition's half of the field. For one thing, he must keep full concentration at all times and, however long the play unfolds at the other end of the pitch, he must remain part of the game. One sweeping pass can turn attack into defence in a matter of seconds. The keeper may suddenly have to spring into action and make a save, so he must keep himself mentally alert with his reactions primed. To be called upon suddenly to pull off a save after a period of inactivity can catch out a goalkeeper if he isn't careful. His reactions may be just a fraction of a second slower than usual, but that could be crucial. That is why, whenever I endured periods of inactivity, I always concentrated fully on the game while keeping on the move to ensure my agility would be optimum should I suddenly be called into action.

In May 1969 I joined the Under-23s for a short tour of the Continent where we played Holland, Belgium and Portugal. Alf was busy with the full England team so Ron Suart, the Chelsea manager, was in charge, assisted by Les Cocker. Again, the competition for the goalkeeper's jersey was Sheffield Wednesday's Peter Springett, who took over for our game against Belgium.

Peter Knowles of Wolverhampton Wanderers, a player with tremendous potential, was part of the squad. A good-looking young guy who had become something of a pin-up for teenaged girls, Peter's career was just taking off in a big way at Wolves when he stunned everyone by announcing his retirement from the game at the age of twenty-three. The reason was that he had become a devout Jehovah's Witness and, rather than continuing his career as a top-flight footballer, he wanted to devote his life to spreading the gospel door-to-door in the Wolverhampton area. His decision came as a surprise to most but Peter was totally devoted to his beliefs. He lives near Molineux now and works as a window cleaner, and to this day he knocks on doors in the Wolverhampton area, looking for converts to his religion.

After the second game of the tour, in Belgium, the players were given permission to have their customary night out. More often than not when playing for the Under-23s, I roomed with Brian Kidd. Brian and I became good pals and we tended to stick together on tour but for some reason, I can't remember why, we didn't go out together that night. The players broke off into small groups and I went off with Peter Springett, Joe Royle, Roy McFarland and my Leicester team-mate David Nish. We had a quiet enough time, talking football over a few too many beers. When I returned to our room Brian wasn't back, so I simply got into bed and went to sleep. The following morning when I woke up, Brian was in bed asleep with his back turned to me. Not wanting to disturb him, I had a shower and dressed as quietly as I could and went down to breakfast.

When I saw Brian later that morning, I was amazed to see his nose was red and swollen. Apparently, a local had taken exception to Brian for some reason, and socked him on the nose. In comparison, my heavy head was a small price to pay for an evening's entertainment.

'I think we'd better stay together on nights out,' I told Brian, 'so we can look out for one another.'

The incident involving Brian's skirmish never made the press, nor did the FA launch an inquiry into it. In fact, I should imagine those FA officials present on the tour never mentioned the incident on returning to England. The matter of the brawl blew over as quickly as it had started. I shudder to think what would happen should such an incident occur these days on an England Under-21 tour.

Shortly after arriving home, I was surprised and delighted to be called up to join the full England squad on a short tour of South and Central America, which was being undertaken as part of the preparations for the defence of the World Cup the following summer. My call-up came as the result of sad circumstances. Gordon Banks had returned to England, having received the news of the passing of his father. The other goalkeeper on the tour was Gordon West of Everton.

It was one mad rush to pack a bag and get down to Heathrow and I nearly didn't make it out to Mexico. When I presented myself at the airport, I was told a visa was required and no one had made provision for one. Fortunately, the matter was resolved by FA officials and, after an anxious wait, I was on my way.

As part of the tour, England were to play a Mexican XI in Guadalajara and I was absolutely thrilled when Alf Ramsey informed me I would be playing in this game. The press stated that 'three new caps' were to play against the Mexicans but that wasn't strictly accurate because the game was given unofficial status and no caps were awarded. The other two debutants were Allan Clarke, still my Leicester team-mate at the time, and Colin Harvey of Everton. The game took place in the Jalisco Stadium and the fact that it was unofficial mattered not one jot to me. I was so proud to wear an England shirt and be part of a tour that was so important to English football. Alf Ramsey played a number of fringe players from the squad against a team that formed the nucleus of the full Mexican national team.

For the record, the line-up for my first full, albeit unofficial, international match was: Peter Shilton (Leicester), Tommy Wright (Everton), Bob McNab (Arsenal), Colin Harvey (Everton), Jack Charlton (Leeds), Bobby Moore (West Ham), Alan Ball (Everton), Colin Bell (Manchester City), Jeff Astle (West Brom), Allan Clarke (Leicester) and Martin Peters (West Ham).

The match, a highly competitive game in which I saw plenty of action, ended in a draw. I felt I had played well and Jack Charlton made a point of saying, 'Well done, you kept us in it, son,' which gave me a boost. The match reports in the newspapers were favourable. Desmond Hackett wrote in the *Daily Express*, 'The temperature may have been eighty-five degrees but debutant keeper Peter Shilton remained cool and composed, his highly competent performance belied his tender years.'

For the official international against Mexico in Mexico City, Alf opted for Gordon West. The match ended in a goalless draw and Gordon gave an impressive display but then astonished Alf – and everyone else in the squad – by asking not to be considered for any more internationals because he was homesick. As it happened, his request didn't do me any favours because Gordon Banks returned to the squad and was immediately recalled for the remaining games of the tour against Uruguay and Brazil.

When the 1969–70 international season got under way with a game against Holland in November, Alf selected Peter Bonetti as his goalkeeper. Peter played in England's next game, against Portugal, and thereafter it was business as usual with Gordon Banks as the number-one choice and me on duty with the Under-23s.

I was called into the squad for the game against Portugal, one of four goalkeepers in an initial squad of thirty. The others were

Gordon Banks, Peter Bonetti and Alex Stepney (Manchester United). I knew I wouldn't be selected but the fact that Alf had included me in the squad was a tremendous source of encouragement and went some way towards making me believe my chances of gaining recognition at full international level were not being harmed by playing my football in the Second Division.

In the summer of 1970, I was again included in the initial squad of thirty players, this time preparing for the World Cup in Mexico. Though hopeful of making the final twenty-two, realistically I expected to be put on stand-by, but just being part of the initial England squad for Mexico was a great experience for me.

I was very interested in how methodical Alf was in his preparations for the World Cup although on occasions his ideas did border on the bizarre. Alf was very concerned about players spending too much time out in the sun in case we got sunburned or, even worse, suffered from sunstroke. To avoid this, Harold Shepherdson had to time our sunbathing with a stopwatch. We were allowed a total of twenty minutes. First of all we would lie on our backs for five minutes. Harold would then blow his whistle to signal we were to turn over. After five minutes of lying on our stomachs, Harold would blow his whistle again and we would all turn over, and so it went on.

In addition to the training and acclimatisation programme, we were required to attend various diplomatic functions. At one such party, a band was playing and, as representatives of England, the players had to dance with the wives and daughters of those in attendance. Every female in the room had danced at least once except a rather plain young lady, who was looking very solemn. It became obvious that she was upset because no England player had asked her to dance and the captain decided something had to be done. Bobby Moore, being his usual gracious self, stepped up and away they went across the dance floor, where they stayed for quite some time. The other young women present, many of whom were akin to supermodels, looked on in envy.

When they finally left the dance floor, the young lady seemed to think that Bobby had a crush on her and he handled her overtures with grace, dignity and sensitivity. In keeping with the occasion, he was the consummate diplomat.

When Alf named his final twenty-two for the World Cup, Bob McNab, Peter Thompson, Ralph Coates, Brian Kidd, David Sadler and I were the unlucky ones. The experienced Alex Stepney was chosen as number-three goalkeeper behind Gordon Banks and Peter Bonetti.

I was, of course, disappointed not to have made the final squad but I consoled myself with the fact that I was just twenty years of age and time was on my side. No sooner had I arrived home than Sue came round to see me. We were now engaged but we had precious little time alone together. Minutes after Sue knocked at my parents' house, a gaggle of press photographers arrived. If they expected a shot of me looking forlorn and upset, they didn't get it. The photographs that appeared in the newspapers the next day were of me smiling, sitting in the garden next to Sue with my dog Buster at my feet.

Like the rest of the nation, I sat and suffered in front of the television, watching England exit at the quarter-final stage against West Germany. Having led by two goals to nil, England contrived to lose the game. It was unheard of for an Alf Ramsey England team to concede a two-goal advantage. More unbelievable is the fact that it was twelve years before England qualified for the finals of another World Cup.

Peter Bonetti was in goal against West Germany and the illness that kept Gordon Banks out is now part of English football's legend and folklore. He succumbed to a debilitating stomach upset and to this day no one, including Gordon himself, knows for sure if he contracted the illness through bad luck or whether his food or a drink had been tampered with.

My scrapbooks contain a number of interviews I gave to the press in the wake of England's exit. All the journalists wanted to know how I thought I might have done against West Germany if Alf had not sent me home. As I said at the time, 'It's irrelevant because even if I had been in the squad, I don't think he would have chosen me ahead of Peter Bonetti.'

Leicester's opening game of the 1970–71 season offered no indication of the success to come – we lost 1–0 at home to Cardiff City. However, we quickly put that reverse behind us, winning our next game 3–1 at Queens Park Rangers and losing just one of our next seventeen league matches, which put us in pole position.

Sue and I were married in the September, two weeks after my twenty-first birthday, in the Mayflower Methodist Church in Leicester. My best man was my pal Chris Gamble with whom I had spent all that time practising as a young lad. Frank O'Farrell and his wife were among the guests, as were team-mates David Nish, Graham Cross and Rodney Fern. It was the most wonderful day but I have to admit I felt more nervous than I did playing in the 1969 FA Cup final or on my debut for England. I remember thinking how beautiful Sue looked. Life was great. Leicester City were on course for promotion, I was on the fringes of the full England team and I had married the love of my life. I didn't think life could get any better for me, but it did.

Sue worked as a secretary with a firm of Leicester solicitors and I had met her a little under four years previously in the Penny Farthing, which was a dance hall-cum-nightclub. As we were married in September, we had a two-day honeymoon because I had to be back to play for Leicester against Middlesbrough on the Wednesday night. To cap what for me had been a wonderful week,

Leicester beat Middlesbrough 3–2 – though let it be said, the fact that I conceded two goals had nothing at all to do with having just returned from honeymoon!

Leicester hit a bad patch during December and January, with four defeats and one win in seven matches, but after that we never looked back. We didn't lose another league game for the remainder of the season and clinched the Second Division championship three points ahead of runners-up Sheffield United. We conceded thirty goals throughout the campaign and I broke a club record by keeping twenty-three clean sheets.

Frank O'Farrell had proved himself an astute manager. One masterstroke was the October signing of Willie Carlin from Derby County. Willie had a tremendous influence in midfield. Two City stalwarts, Peter Rodrigues and Davie Gibson, left during the season. Rodrigues' replacement at right-back was Steve Whitworth, a local boy who eventually played for England.

One interesting aside to the 1970–71 season was the introduction in February of decimalisation. In keeping with most clubs, prior to 'D' day Leicester issued 'Think Decimal' leaflets to all supporters as they passed through the turnstiles, itemising the cost of entry in the new decimal currency and including a handy conversion guide. It's interesting to see the cost of admission in 1971. The price for children was 15p on the ground terracing and 20p in the paddock enclosure. The cheapest admission price for an adult was 30p on the terraces and this rose according to which section of the ground you were going to stand in – 35p for the paddock enclosure, 50p for the double-decker stand. The top price of admission was 80p for a seat in the main stand.

The average wage in 1971 was, according to the Government's Office of Statistics, around £21 per week. So, in relative terms, the cost of attending a football match was much cheaper in 1971 than it is today. Football was still very much a working-class game and the bedrock support of all clubs consisted of working people. This was before the degeneration of our traditional industries, such as mining, shipbuilding and steel, and before the breakdown of the nuclear family, when people sought work in their local area and few, other than graduates, sought employment in other areas of Britain. Football was still community based and acted as a social glue.

Attendances were healthy. In 1970–71, over 28 million people attended Football League matches. Come 1985–86, that figure had fallen by 12 million to just over 16 million. The Taylor Report, which led to greatly improved facilities for supporters, the creation of the Premier League and the TV deals that were struck in the nineties, particularly those with Sky Sports, revolutionised English football and popularised it again. Throughout the nineties, football gradually returned to being a family game and attendances grew accordingly, season by season, so that in 2002–03 the total number of people attending Premier League and Football League matches was the same as it had been in 1970–71 – 28 million. That is the highest figure since 1971.

On the international scene, following England's painful defeat by West Germany in Mexico, Alf Ramsey was looking forward, hopeful of creating another England team capable of winning the World Cup in 1974, and for that he turned to a number of younger players. He made four changes when East Germany came to Wembley in November 1970. Emlyn Hughes (Liverpool) replaced Keith Newton (Everton) at right-back, David Sadler (Manchester United) came in for Brian Labone (Everton) at centre-half and Allan Clarke (now at Leeds) replaced Bobby Charlton, whose illustrious career with England had come to an end following his substitution against West Germany in Mexico. Gordon Banks was still very much the number-one choice goalkeeper but I was very pleased to be given the chance to show what I could do.

In winning their previous four internationals, East Germany had scored sixteen goals, but on the night it was a case of the Germans promising much more than they produced. Goals from Allan Clarke, Martin Peters and Francis Lee gave England a comfortable 3–1 victory. Despite conceding a goal, I was pleased with my performance and relieved to get through the game without making a telling mistake. Sir Alf seemed satisfied and after the game he made a point of telling me I had done well, which set my mind at ease.

In the lead-up to the game, the press were up in arms because they thought Sir Alf had dropped Gordon Banks. He came in for a lot of criticism and that wasn't ideal for me either. Alf hadn't dropped Gordon. He just wanted Ray Clemence and me to 'have a go', as he put it at the time. He didn't include Gordon in the squad because he didn't want him to sit on the bench. The negative press placed added pressure on me. I felt I was really under the microscope and any mistake I made would be highlighted in the newspapers. Fortunately, I was able to stay focused. The one goal I did concede took a hefty deflection and the consensus of opinion was that I had made an excellent debut.

I was immensely proud to have represented my country but I didn't kid myself that I would remain in the team. I'm a realist and I knew that for the next international match, against Malta, Sir Alf would recall his preferred choice of goalkeeper, Gordon Banks.

However, the East Germany game wasn't my sole international appearance in 1970–71. In April, Sir Alf picked me for the Home International match against Wales at Wembley. For this game, Sir Alf continued his policy of giving a chance to players he felt might be good enough to make the squad for the qualifying stages of the 1974 World Cup. Against Wales, Sir Alf played Chris Lawler,

Tommy Smith, Emlyn Hughes and Larry Lloyd (all Liverpool), Ralph Coates (Spurs) and Tony Brown (West Brom). Geoff Hurst came in for Martin Chivers, making eight changes to the England team that had beaten Northern Ireland four days previously. It was most unusual for Sir Alf to make so many changes from one game to the next, even if he was keen to blood young players. We had a heavy schedule of four matches in ten days, so I guess he wanted to rest key members of the team in order to keep them fresh for the final match of the sequence, the 'big one' against Scotland.

At this time, players still considered it a great honour to be called up to the England squad. For most, it was the pinnacle of their careers. Making the England squad was like being elected to some very exclusive club. In addition to the pride you felt, there was considerable kudos attached to it. This changed in the seventies when Don Revie became England manager and, for his first match in charge, called up a hundred players for what he termed an 'England get-together'. I think calling upon so many players went some way towards tarnishing the pride felt at being chosen. In some respects, it diminished the status of being an England squad player. Prior to Don Revie's 'get-together', an England call-up meant you were among the best twenty-two English players in the country. When a hundred-plus players were summoned, almost overnight it appeared that you did not have to be of international class to be part of the England set-up, merely a decent player.

The team Sir Alf sent out against Wales was, I suppose, experimental. Larry Lloyd, Tommy Smith and Tony Brown all made their international debuts and, with so many changes to the team, our performance lacked cohesion and fluidity. Francis Lee did get the ball in the net but it was disallowed for offside. Wales battled every inch of the way and no one could deny them their joy when the final whistle blew with the game scoreless. It was a disappointing England performance, but the press did find some plus points. I was singled out for some praise, producing, as the *Daily Mail* put it, 'a highly competent and safe performance that ensured England denied what at times was a rampant Welsh attack'.

It was back to the tried and trusted for England's next game against Scotland at Wembley and the stalwarts, such as Gordon Banks, Bobby Moore and Alan Ball, were not found wanting. England triumphed 3–1 to win the Home International Championship.

Leicester City's preparations for life in the First Division received a jolt when, in June 1971, Frank O'Farrell accepted an offer to become manager of Manchester United and took coach Malcolm Musgrove with him. Frank had done a good job at Leicester. He was more of a hands-on manager than Matt Gillies had been, occasionally donning a tracksuit and joining us out on the training pitch, but it was Malcolm Musgrove who did the majority of the work in training sessions. I liked Frank as a manager and as a person. In my opinion, he struck the right balance with discipline, man management and preparations for matches. He was a gentleman and I should imagine his grace and dignity were two aspects of his character that attracted Manchester United. Matt Busby possessed such traits. Wilf McGuinness, whom Frank was replacing, was a good manager but perhaps the United board thought he lacked those old-school, gentlemanly and sage-like qualities that both Matt and Frank possessed.

Also, at the time, United were having one or two problems with George Best, who was creating headlines that were, for want of a better phrase, not in the Manchester United tradition. Perhaps the United board also thought that Frank could bring George back into line and restore the image of the club.

It was around this time that Brian Clough, manager of Derby County, made Leicester City an offer for my services but nothing came of it. Having moved to Manchester United, Frank O'Farrell returned to Leicester in an attempt to sign David Nish. Nothing came of that either but, eventually, Clough signed David Nish – such is the transfer merry-go-round.

Clough's offer for me resulted in a typical piece of business gamesmanship on the part of the City chairman Len Shipman. Seemingly, Leicester were not keen on me leaving the club but, as always, were pressed for money. Apparently, on receiving the official bid, which I was led to believe was in the region of £200,000, Len Shipman went to the club's bankers and, on the strength of it, managed to increase the club's overdraft. The new overdraft facility meant Leicester did not need Derby's money and the board turned down Clough's offer. That solved Leicester's financial plight in the short term and when David Nish was sold to Derby, the money the club received for him meant they had no need to sell me. So, for all the interest in my services, a Leicester City player I remained.

Frank O'Farrell's replacement was the former Birmingham City and Arsenal winger Jimmy Bloomfield, who had done such a good job of managing Leyton Orient. Jimmy Bloomfield must have felt the team that had won promotion wasn't good enough to keep Leicester in the First Division because the 1971–72 season was only a few weeks old when he embarked upon the first of what would be wholesale changes. Jon Sammels was signed from Arsenal for £100,000 and was included in the team for the Charity Shield match against Liverpool, who had been the defeated Cup finalists.

Now you may find it odd that the Charity Shield was contested between the Second Division champions and the runners-up in the FA Cup. At the time, the Charity Shield had declined in status and was no longer a contest between the champions and Cup winners. The Charity Shield was staged at the home ground of one of the participating clubs and had been contested since 1908. However, in the early seventies, clubs who had won the championship or Cup preferred to play what they perceived to be more prestigious pre-season friendlies against top foreign opposition. These games generated more income and the clubs donated a good slice of the receipts to various charities. The Charity Shield was revived in 1974 when the FA and Football League switched the game to Wembley and invited the League champions and Cup winners to contest the trophy. With the clubs being allowed a percentage of receipts and some 20 per cent going to charity, plus the carrot of another big day out at Wembley, the Charity Shield became an attractive proposition to top clubs and remains so to this day.

The Charity Shield has since given birth to an annual 'contest' in a sports column that appears in the Stoke-on-Trent evening newspaper *The Sentinel*. Every August, readers write in hoping to be the first to have spotted the cliché that is always used to describe the Charity Shield – 'the traditional curtain raiser to the new season'.

Yet again, a Leicester team got the better of Liverpool. A rare goal from full-back Steve Whitworth added the Charity Shield to the club's trophy cabinet. Although not the auspicious occasion it is now, none the less, beating mighty Liverpool and winning another trophy served to boost confidence.

I was relishing the prospect of playing top-flight football again and I was quietly confident that Leicester would more than hold their own in the First Division. We couldn't have asked for a better start. Playing away to Huddersfield Town, Ally Brown scored the first goal of the new season after just forty-five seconds. The game ended 2–2 which, considering we were First Division new boys playing away from home, was a satisfactory start.

Things went even better in our second match, an East Midlands derby against Nottingham Forest that attracted a crowd of nigh on 33,000 to Filbert Street. A goal from Ally Brown and an own goal from Forest's Liam O'Kane gave us our first victory of the campaign. After that, the reality of life in the First Division set in. We lost our next four matches and won just one in a sequence of ten league games. That's when Jimmy Bloomfield really set about ringing the changes. Keith Weller was signed from Chelsea for £100,000 and Alan Birchenall from Crystal Palace for £45,000 with Bobby Kellard going in the opposite direction as the makeweight in the deal. David Nish, who had not yet moved to Derby, and I were the subjects of interest from a number of clubs. According to press reports, Everton and Arsenal enquired about me and Arsenal went so far as to offer Leicester £150,000 plus Bob Wilson for my services.

It was an unsettling time, especially as, deep down, I never wanted to leave the club. Leicester was my home town and I genuinely felt we could consolidate in the First Division. In the event, I was proved correct. We shrugged off our poor autumn results and settled down to play some attractive attacking football, finishing a creditable twelfth. In a very tight end to the championship, Derby County finished a single point ahead of Leeds, Liverpool and Manchester City. In fact, Derby, having completed their fixtures, went on holiday to Majorca while both Leeds and Liverpool still had one game remaining. Leeds lost their last match at Wolves and Liverpool drew at Arsenal. The Derby players were sunning themselves on the beach when the news came through that they were League champions. I bet that was some beach party!

Leyton Orient put one over on their former manager in the fourth round of the FA Cup, winning 2–0. I was absent through injury and my deputy, young Carl Jayes, didn't have the best of games. He was considered to have been at fault for Orient's second goal. Jimmy Bloomfield felt the need to have what he perceived as 'more capable cover' for me and asked me to look at a young goalkeeper whom I'd heard was beginning to turn in good performances for Walsall.

So I travelled to Bristol Rovers' Eastville Stadium to watch them play Walsall, my attention focused almost entirely on their young goalkeeper, Mark Wallington. Mark had made just eleven appearances for Walsall and, at twenty years of age, he was raw but I liked what I saw and was of the mind that if he worked at it, he could become a very good goalkeeper indeed.

On returning to Filbert Street, Jimmy Bloomfield asked for my opinion of the player. My reply was short and concise – 'Don't hestitate. Sign him.' Jimmy took my advice and signed Mark for £30,000. He was arguably the best buy Jimmy ever made while manager of Leicester.

Mark wasn't the most athletic of players at that time but he was dedicated to learning his trade and worked hard at his game. It was good for me to have another goalkeeper to work with who shared my enthusiasm on the training field and, in time, we became good pals. Mark continued to improve as a goalkeeper and was a capable deputy on those occasions when I missed a first-team game. Although we were, in essence, rivals for the first-team jersey, it never seemed that way to me. When I eventually left the club, Mark stepped up to take my place in the first team. I like to think I played a significant role in grooming my replacement, not only in terms of having been instrumental in him coming to the club, but also through all the work we put in out on the training ground. Mark went on to give Leicester sterling service. Having initially been in my shadow, he eventually played 460 first-team games, which included a club record of 331 consecutive appearances.

The spirit in the Leicester camp was excellent, with good camaraderie between the players both on the field and off it. We liked to socialise with supporters, and every fortnight or so the players would visit a pub or working men's club and play the locals at darts and dominoes. We charged the pub or club in question £100 for our presence and the money was invested in a fund that was used to buy equipment for local hospitals.

I used to enjoy those social get-togethers. It was good to go out with team-mates, meet the supporters, have a bit fun and a laugh while at the same time raising money for worthy causes. The £100 the club or pub paid to our charity fund was quickly recouped because the presence of the Leicester players ensured the place was packed. We used to visit on a weeknight when it would usually have been quiet. Invariably, we would be well beaten by the local darts and dominoes teams but the result was of no consequence. These visits were great for public relations and good for team spirit, and we all felt good about doing something to help the local hospitals.

The 1972–73 season was similar to the previous campaign in that Leicester City again consolidated in the First Division, finishing just below halfway in the table. Personally, however, it was a highly significant year because I began to establish myself in the England team. It was distressing that the opportunity came about as the result of a bad car accident involving Gordon Banks in which he lost an eye.

I was shocked and saddened when I heard news of the accident, which, to all intents and purposes, put an end to his career although he did play successfully in the USA for a while. I had followed Gordon's career at Leicester since he joined the club from Chesterfield in 1959 and I had seen at close quarters how he had worked at his game and developed new goalkeeping techniques. When he first came to the club, Gordon had not been particularly adept at taking crosses but he had worked tirelessly to perfect that art. When he made the England team, the London press were forever trumpeting Peter Bonetti, often to the detriment of Gordon. He had the character to ignore those press reports and, over the years, he devoted himself to becoming a better goalkeeper, eventually becoming the best in the world and helping England win the World Cup.

England played eleven international matches during the 1972–73 season and Sir Alf chose me for nine of them, opting for Liverpool's Ray Clemence for the other two. Ray and I could never have known it at the time, of course, but he and I would be vying for the England goalkeeper's jersey for another ten years.

The highlight of the international season was England's 5–0 victory over Scotland at Hampden Park in a match played to celebrate the centenary of the Scottish Football Association. England were three up after a quarter of an hour and we skated to victory on a treacherous snow-carpeted pitch. It was a nightmare start for the new Scotland manager, Willie Ormond, but a dream game for England skipper Bobby Moore. The game marked Bobby's one hundredth appearance for England.

If the game against Scotland was the high point, there is no doubting the lowest point of that international season. In June, England travelled to Katowice for a vital World Cup qualifying match against Poland. One team would qualify from our group and England were locked in a head-to-head battle with Poland.

On the night before the game, Alf stipulated that the players were to receive no telephone calls because he wanted us to get a good night's sleep. A restful night's sleep is what we didn't have. Throughout the night, the hotel staff continually put calls through to every player's room from people I can only describe as ladies of the night. I don't know if the local mafia were behind this ploy. All I know is that the calls kept coming. No sooner would I settle down to sleep than the phone would ring and some young woman would be asking if I wanted to 'come to a party'. Our protests to the hotel reception fell on deaf ears. It was annoying, irritating and not the best preparation for a crucial World Cup qualifying match.

The Poles had a very strong team but we were confident and hopeful of achieving a result. I replaced Ray Clemence in goal for this game, played out before a hostile crowd of 100,000 crammed into a forbidding granite stadium. The gamesmanship extended to the pre-match kick-about, which was something of a misnomer because there were no practice balls. I didn't go out on to the pitch for a warm-up. There seemed no point if I couldn't get a 'feel' for the ball. I was left thinking that the Poles had done everything in their power to disrupt our preparations for this match and I wasn't alone in this view. Alf was livid.

The game was nine minutes old when Poland won a free kick wide on the left and played the ball in towards my near post. Gadocha stuck out a leg and so, too, did Bobby Moore. The ball ricocheted off Bobby's leg, spun into the ground and flew up in the air, which caught me out. The ball hit my shoulder and spun into the net at my near post.

The second half had barely got under way when Bobby shouted for Roy McFarland to play the ball to him. Roy made the pass and it seemed that Bobby had plenty of time to play the ball forward. In a flash, Poland's Lubanski was on to him. Bobby reacted with his usual impeccable instinct, looked up to see where he was going to play the ball and pulled it across Lubanksi with his right foot with the intention of going wide into space. I'd seen Bobby successfully conduct that manoeuvre on countless previous occasions and my goalkeeping instinct told me there was no danger – but this time, Bobby didn't move quickly enough. Lubanksi got a touch on the ball and flicked it behind Bobby. The momentum of Lubanski's run carried him past Bobby and the ball fell perfectly in his path. Bobby gave chase but to no avail. I came quickly off my line to narrow the angle but Lubanksi slipped the ball past me and just in off the post.

It was a bad goal to concede at a terrible time in the game. Our momentum and belief that we wouldn't be beaten were knocked for six. Conversely, as the clock ticked on and we became increasingly desperate in our efforts to claw back a goal, Poland grew in confidence and stature. In the latter stages, Alan Ball was sent off, to rub salt into what were now gaping wounds.

Bobby Moore played two more games for England. When Poland came to Wembley for the return match in October, his career at international level was over. In truth, he had played well against Poland until that uncharacteristic mistake, but certain elements of the press thought he was now too slow to play international football and that Sir Alf had picked him out of sentiment. I doubt whether Sir Alf had ever played anyone in the England team out of sentiment – he was far too professional.

That defeat put one hell of a dent in England's hopes of qualifying for 1974 World Cup finals in West Germany. We still had Poland to play at Wembley, however, and everyone was confident that we would win on the night – and what a night it turned out to be! The consequences of that game proved to be a watershed for English football at both international and domestic level.

The 1973–74 season was also to be a watershed for me. When Leicester City kicked off the season against Ipswich Town under gold-leaf sunshine at Portman Road, the furthest thing from my mind was that this would be my last season at the club I had been with since I was eleven years of age.

4

MOVING ON

In September 1973, a month before the crucial return match against Poland, when the England squad assembled for a friendly against Austria, Sir Alf took Bobby Moore aside after a training session at the British Aircraft Corporation Sporting Ground in Stevenage.

'I've got a disappointment for you,' he told him. Norman Hunter had being doing well of late, and Sir Alf told Bobby that he was going to play Norman in the game. Sir Alf's aim was to field a settled England team and the significance was not lost on Bobby.

'Does this mean I'm no further use to you?' he asked.

'No, no,' replied Sir Alf. 'If we beat Poland and therefore qualify, I will need you. You will be there with us in Germany.'

Bobby wasn't there in Germany because England weren't there. Bobby Moore's international career was at an end.

England overran an Austrian defence that had no answer to the combined power of the four Cs – Mick Channon, Martin Chivers, Allan Clarke and Tony Currie were all among the goals in a resounding 7–0 victory. Colin Bell and Martin Peters dictated the pace and pattern of the match from midfield. It was a perfect confidence booster for the big showdown against the Poles.

Confidence was further heightened when, during his post-match interview, the Austrian manager, Leopold Stastny, said, 'England can still teach the world how to play. On the evidence of tonight's performance, England will be in Germany and strong contenders for the World Cup.'

To qualify for the finals in Germany we had to beat Poland at Wembley on 17 October. On the night, Bobby Moore donned an England shirt for the last time but it sported the number twelve rather than his favoured number six. He took his place on the substitutes' bench, where he sat and suffered along with the rest of the nation who watched the game live on television.

Poland needed a draw to qualify but I believe they half expected to lose. No sooner had the referee blown his whistle to start the game than England went on the attack. Throughout the first half we laid siege to the Polish goal with shot after shot after shot but the breakthrough just wouldn't come. So relentless was England's attack that I was a virtual spectator throughout those first forty-five minutes. The Poland goalkeeper, Jan Tomaszewski, on the other hand, was a very busy guy, making a string of saves to deny England.

We came off the field at half-time having enjoyed most of the play but so far without a goal in sight. During the interval Brian Clough remarked on television that Tomaszewski was a 'clown'. It was a description prompted by a first-half performance in which the Polish goalkeeper had blocked all those England efforts with every conceivable part of his body. In keeping England at bay, Tomaszewski had invariably failed to hold on to the ball. His goalkeeping, though effective, had been haphazard, wildly eccentric and, at times, downright lucky.

In referring to Tomaszewski as a 'clown', Clough was not only implying that the Polish keeper's technique left much to be desired, he was intimating that if we kept the pressure up on his goal, his luck would run out, as everyone believed it would. Clough was tempting fate all right.

We took to the field for the second half and picked up the same script, laying siege to Tomaszewski's goal again but still finding no way through. Tomaszewski made some good saves and when they weren't good, he saved the ball anyway, once blocking it with his chest and on another occasion with his backside. We had dominated the game. Tomaszewski had been like a cat on a hot tin roof, sometimes rushing so far out of position that our crosses dropped behind him. I'd never witnessed such a game. Shots were hitting the woodwork and firing off bodies on their goal line. We couldn't have put in more effort than we did. Yet still the game remained goalless. Then disaster struck.

The Poles cleared the ball down our right-hand side and Norman Hunter went to meet it. Norman got his foot on the ball and tried to pull it back inside the oncoming Gadocha. Gadocha got a touch on the ball and it spun behind Norman and fell perfectly in the path of the Pole. Roy McFarland was left with two Polish players to mark. Gadocha played the ball forward to Anton Domarski and alarm bells started clanging in my brain. I came out of my goal to narrow the angle but at the very moment that Domarski let fly, I was momentarily unsighted by Emlyn Hughes, who had raced back to offer cover. It was vital that I saw Domarski's striking foot make contact with the ball so that I could gauge its speed and trajectory and act accordingly. In that split second, my sight of him was blocked unwittingly by Emlyn Hughes. The Wembley pitch was very greasy, the ball skidded under my body and I knew from the position I had taken that it was goal bound.

Wembley fell as silent as a minister's study – so silent that I heard the whoops of joy from the Polish players. For a moment it was almost as though all the strength had left my body. I felt weak. My stomach churned. Unbelievably, we were chasing the game. One goal would not now be enough. We needed two.

Six minutes later, in the sixty-fourth minute of the game, we were given a lifeline when Allan Clarke equalised from the penalty spot. Thereafter, it was *déjà vu*. We bombarded the Poles, but yet again Tomaszewski denied us. In the final minute the ball was played across the face of the Polish goal. Substitute Kevin Hector came sliding in at the far post but, with the goal gaping, Kevin failed by a fag paper's width to get the toe of his boot to the ball. Seconds later the referee blew his whistle for the end of the game and the end of England's World Cup hopes.

The England dressing room was like a morgue. Everyone was totally drained and devastated. All that effort, all that application had counted for nothing. I have never known such a feeling of emptiness. The statistics showed that England had thirty-nine goal attempts to two by Poland. It was unbelievable that the game had ended 1–1. On the pitch where, some seven years earlier, England had won the World Cup, our hopes of emulating that achievement in 1974 had ended. I felt our performance and spirit deserved a better fate, but football can be a cruel mistress.

Poland deserve some credit, though. A disastrous defeat in their opening match in the group against Wales had galvanised them and they turned things around. Against England at Wembley they had fought a tremendous rearguard action before the most partisan crowd to attend an England game since the 1966 World Cup final.

The next day, while travelling home to Leicester, I analysed my reaction to Domarksi's shot. He struck the ball well. It wasn't an easy shot to deal with because the Wembley Cumberland turf was springy and lush, which, on a wet night such as this, made the ball very greasy. When the ball hit the turf it came off it lightning fast. Having been unsighted when Domarski struck the ball, and given the conditions, what I should have done was make a blocking save, or parry the shot away for a corner. But I tried to get hold of the ball by scooping it into my body and retaining possession. It was the speed of the ball coming off the turf, together with the fact that I had been momentarily unsighted when Domarski actually struck it, that beat me. That went into the memory bank for future reference. I was gutted by our exit from the World Cup but there was some consolation in knowing that I had learned from my mistake, though very little.

The press vilified Sir Alf Ramsey, saying his overtly cautious approach in previous games, particularly in the draw against Wales, had been the reason behind our failure to qualify for the World Cup finals. The media accused him of being negative and of being out of touch with current developments in football tactics. Six months after the Poland game, the Football Association relieved him of his duties as England manager. Sir Alf was devastated.

Even if the FA were desperate to get rid of this faithful servant of English football, I feel they might at least have allowed him the opportunity to resign. To sack the man who had led England to World Cup success was, to my mind, shabby. The FA's decision came out of the blue and shocked Sir Alf enormously. He never really got over it but it was the mark of the man that, for all that hurt, his grace and dignity remained flawlessly intact.

The former Ipswich Town centre-forward Ted Phillips, who had played under Alf when Ipswich won the Second Division title in 1960–61 and the First Division championship in 1961–62, boarded a train at Liverpool Street that afternoon. Ted had retired from the game and was heading back to his home in Ipswich after a business meeting in London. As he searched for a seat on the train, he came across his old boss. Sir Alf was delighted to see Ted again and went off to the buffet car, returning with two miniature bottles of whisky. Sir Alf asked Ted what he was up to, Ted told Sir Alf about his business interests, and over a couple of drinks the pair had a laugh, recalling their days together with that successful Ipswich team. When the train reached Ipswich, they bade one another goodbye with Sir Alf saying it had been great to see his old centre-forward again.

When Ted got home, he picked up the local evening newspaper

and was shocked to read the headline: 'Alf Ramsey Sacked As England Manager'. Sir Alf hadn't mentioned a word of the meeting he'd just had with the FA.

Perhaps it was something to do with Sir Alf's pride or perhaps he felt shame at the fact he had been sacked. Sir Alf was seen by many as stoic, taciturn and cold. That was how he came across in the media but I knew him well and he was, in fact, a man of generous spirit, and one who empathised and understood the emotions and feelings of the players under his charge. We were loyal to him because he was totally loyal to us and he never put us in a situation where we felt uncomfortable or embarrassed. I'm certain that the reason he never mentioned a word to Ted Phillips on that train was because he didn't want to embarrass him.

The fall-out from the Poland game was partly instrumental in Brian Clough leaving his post as manager of Derby County. The Derby County board had been very uncomfortable about Brian's high profile in the media and in particular his outspoken views. So much so, they feared it might result in Derby being charged by the Football League. Clough's description of Tomaszewski as a 'clown' was controversial, and since the Polish goalkeeper had only conceded one goal from a penalty, Clough's comment proved embarrassing both to him and the club.

Matters came to a head when, in his ghosted newspaper column, Brian was said to have accused the Derby players in the England team of 'cheating' by not giving 100 per cent to County because of their preoccupation with the Poland game. For the Derby board, that was the last straw. They took both Brian and Peter Taylor to task but Clough and Taylor were having none of it. They refused to be gagged and handed in their resignations. Brian and Peter took their talents to Brighton but Brian was there for less than a season before moving on to manage Leeds United where his idiosyncratic ways found no favour. He fell foul of dressing-room power and his reign at Elland Road ended after only forty-four days. He was appointed as manager of Nottingham Forest in 1975 and the rest is history of the most glorious kind.

Joe Mercer took over from Sir Alf Ramsey in a caretaker capacity until the new England manager was appointed. That man was Don Revie, his departure from Leeds prompting the arrival of Brian Clough at Elland Road.

Thus the consequences of our inability to beat Poland went far beyond England not qualifying for the 1974 World Cup finals. Two mistakes, one from Norman Hunter and one from me, plus a large slice of Polish luck, set off a chain of events that brought about the end of an era in English football. Bobby Moore and Sir Alf Ramsey departed from the England scene. Brian Clough's comments led to the end of his time as manager of Derby County. Leeds United lost the services of the most successful manager in their history and the whole sequence eventually led to Nottingham Forest, a hitherto modest provincial club, conquering Europe.

I got on well with Jimmy Bloomfield at Leicester City. He was a nice guy and a decent manager although some of his policies were somewhat quixotic. In 1972–73 he put Leicester into an all-white strip, which upset the traditionalists among the fans, of which there were many. I think the idea behind this was to ape the successful Leeds United side who, in the early sixties, had changed from their traditional blue and gold strip to all white, mirroring the great Real Madrid. Jimmy preferred the all-white strip as, curiously, he believed the players looked bigger in it.

The following season, however, the board decided the team should revert to the traditional strip of blue shirts and white shorts. There seemed to be a lot of time and attention given to cosmetic matters when really what the fans wanted was success on the pitch. I was with the fans!

Leicester were marginally more successful in 1973–74 than in the previous season, finishing ninth as opposed to sixteenth. We also enjoyed a good run in the FA Cup. Having accounted for Spurs, Fulham, Luton Town and QPR, we were yet again pitched against Liverpool, this time in the semi-finals. Liverpool were red-hot favourites to win but, as had been so often the case, Leicester proved to be a thorn in their side. The semi-final took place at Old Trafford and, for all their pressure, Liverpool couldn't break us down. I felt particularly pleased with my performance in this game although I did enjoy a slice of luck when, minutes from the end, I was beaten by a header from Kevin Keegan. The ball struck the inside of a post and, as luck would have it, rebounded into my waiting arms.

The semi-final replay took place at Villa Park and for this game I was wearing an innovative white goalkeeper's jersey. Liverpool took the lead through Kevin Keegan and I remember the goal for a comment made by Jimmy Hill on television. Liverpool played a long ball over the top of the City defence and Kevin was on to it in a flash. He was looking over his shoulder following the trajectory of the ball and when it came to him he took a chance and volleyed it into the top corner. I wasn't expecting that. Luck was with Kevin and the ball flew into the net. After the game, in his analysis of the goal, Jimmy Hill said, 'Kevin Keegan saw Peter Shilton off his line out of the corner of his eye because of the white goalkeeper's jersey Shilton was wearing.'

I had to laugh. It was nonsense. In following the trajectory of the ball, Kevin kept his eyes on that ball all the time. He had to in order to swing his foot and volley the ball first time. If his eyes had been averted for a split second he wouldn't have been able to execute the volley.

The goal was a blow but we were back in the game almost immediately through Len Glover, after which we began to take charge. For a time I really did think we could make Wembley again but we failed to capitalise on all our possession. Having soaked up our pressure, Liverpool stepped up a gear. A quick shot on the turn from Kevin Keegan put them ahead and as we went in search of the equaliser, Liverpool suddenly broke from defence and it was 3–1. Game over.

Jimmy Bloomfield had brought some decent players to the club – apart from Alan Birchenall and Jon Sammels, he had signed the mercurial Frank Worthington – and Leicester were far from being a bad First Division side but I was of the mind that this was as good as it was ever going to be. Throughout the 73–74 season I became increasingly convinced that, as a club, Leicester would never go the whole mile and bring in the one or two top-quality players who could bring major success to the club. I felt the quality of the team as it stood was such that we were destined to be fair to middling in the League and, although we might enjoy the occasional good run in one of the Cups, we were never going to win a trophy. I had been attached to the club for nigh on ten years. I loved the club – and still do – but in 1974 I felt I was ready for another challenge.

I was forever looking at ways to improve my game and around this time I sought the advice of Len Hepple. Len was the father-in-law of Bryan 'Pop' Robson, a prolific goalscorer for Newcastle United, Sunderland and West Ham United. Len Hepple was a brilliant ballroom dancer who had innovative ideas concerning balance, foot movement and running. I'd heard he had helped 'Pop' Robson, particularly regarding turning and balance, and thought he might be able to pass on some pertinent advice that would help me as a goalkeeper.

One of many things I learned from Len was to turn from the hips when upright. This motion was not only suited to my body, it also enabled me to save a valuable second when turning. That may not seem much but, for a goalkeeper, getting into position quickly is of paramount importance and saving a second can mean the difference between making a save and conceding a goal. Len also taught me to have my weight slightly forward, shoulders also forward and knees slightly bent when addressing a shot. I discovered that, to a goalkeeper, the correct body position could make the difference between being a winner or a loser. If you think back or see a photograph and note my posture and body position when opponents were on the attack, you will be aware of the influence Len Hepple had on me.

Another thing I picked up from Len was speed off the mark. He taught me to throw my head forward first when taking off on a sprint. I found this helped my initial propulsion and subsequent momentum. To this day I see goalkeepers dancing up and down on their toes, especially when a free kick or corner is about to be taken. Len told me not to do this because you lose a vital second when taking off. He taught me to keep my feet light and close to the ground, moving them as if skating on ice. Many goalkeepers keep their feet too far apart, which puts them at a disadvantage when saving shots from close range. Len Hepple taught me to keep my feet closer together and collapse my legs down when saving shots from close range.

Many people have said I had a very distinctive style as a goalkeeper. I suppose I did and much of that was down to Len Hepple. He taught me about body movement and starting position, which is crucial to good goalkeeping and to defending as a whole. I sometimes think that if a player like Tony Adams, who had a very upright stance and posture, had benefited from Len's teaching, he could have been an even better centre-back.

By now, I had acquired an agent, or rather two. Jon Holmes and Jeff Pointon ran a company called Pointon and York and I had asked them to represent me. I was a young guy and the subject of increasing attention from sports companies who wanted me to promote their sportswear or endorse ancillary products, and I received many requests for personal appearances. I needed professional people to deal with all this both in terms of advice regarding what I should do and the actual business side of the projects.

One of the deals Jon and Jeff struck on my behalf was for me to promote Admiral sportswear, including an all-white strip – hence the white jersey that Jimmy Hill singled out. Jimmy Bloomfield never said as much but I should imagine he loved this kit. It was far removed from the goalkeeper's conventional green jersey plus shorts and socks in club colours. Peter Bonetti had taken to wearing an all-green strip, as had one or two other goalkeepers. The all-white strip I wore was very distinctive and received blanket coverage in the sporting press. It was never a commercial success, probably because it showed up all the mud and dirt, but the publicity it generated for Admiral was phenomenal. In the early seventies, Admiral were keen to make a name for themselves in the sportswear market and the all-white kit certainly brought their brand to the attention of the nation. The deal was beneficial for me, too. It was financially lucrative and I enjoyed a lot of fun publicity.

During the course of the season, a number of clubs had expressed an interest in signing me, including Arsenal and Manchester United. The fact that clubs of such stature were interested fuelled the notion in my head that now was the time to seek pastures new. When the club offered me a new contract I said, 'No thanks.'

I played my last game for Leicester City at Filbert Street on 29 April 1974 – a 3–0 victory over Norwich City. It was one hell of a wrench to leave but I knew if my career was to be re-energised, I had to move on. It was 'Catch-22'. I was leaving because I felt the club were not prepared to spend on players. Yet with the transfer fee I would generate, the club would have a good chunk of the necessary money. There was some degree of comfort in the fact that I had been instrumental in signing and developing Mark

Wallington as my replacement. I wasn't leaving the club in the lurch.

Negotiations were still going on as the 1974–75 season got under way. Although I was still at the club, Mark Wallington took his place in the first team. In essence, Leicester were willing to sell me to the highest bidder. Offers were received from Arsenal, Manchester United, Derby County and Stoke City, at the time all top clubs. Surprisingly, considering their financial clout, both Arsenal and Manchester United dropped out of the bidding, neither willing to match the offers made by Derby and Stoke, which were in excess of £300,000. Jon Holmes and Jeff Pointon told me the decision about which one to join was solely down to me. It was a tough choice.

Both Derby and Stoke were among the pace-setters in the First Division and both stood a good chance of winning the title. Sometimes in life people make a big decision on the strength of something small, even cosmetic. You and your partner may have decided to buy house on the strength of the garden or the design of the units in the kitchen. I made a similar decision when opting for Stoke City rather than Derby County. In truth, there wasn't much to choose between the two clubs. The one thing that swung it for me was the pitch. Derby's Baseball Ground pitch was, if anything, worse than the one I had known at Filbert Street before it was relaid. In comparison, Stoke City's pitch at the Victoria Ground was a beauty.

I informed Jon and Jeff of my preferred choice of club and they in turn informed the Leicester City board. Stoke City were a club on the up. They had won the League Cup in 1972 and had been really unlucky to lose to Arsenal in the 1971 and 1972 FA Cup semi-finals. The Stoke team boasted players of real quality in Alan Hudson, Geoff Hurst, Jimmy Greenhoff, Jimmy Robertson, Terry Conroy, Mike Pejic, Dennis Smith, John Mahoney and Geoff

Salmons, and there was another attraction. One of the members of the Stoke City coaching staff was Gordon Banks.

I was looking forward to seeing Gordon again and had an inkling that he may have had something to do with my move, perhaps recommending me to the Stoke manager Tony Waddington. The thought of linking up with Gordon at Stoke was very appealing to me, especially as I had now set my sights on becoming the best goalkeeper of my generation. To have any chance of doing that I would have to continue to work hard and develop my game.

Jon, Jeff and I met Tony Waddington and some members of the Stoke City board in a hotel just off the A45 near Northampton. I warmed to the directors straightaway and was impressed by the great enthusiasm they displayed for me joining their club. The transfer fee had been set at £325,000 and all that needed to be sorted out were my personal terms. At the end of the meeting, the Stoke directors said they looked forward to hearing my decision soon before asking Jon, Jeff and I if we would like something to eat while we discussed the possible move among ourselves. We said we would appreciate that very much and one of the directors, Alec Humphreys, went to arrange some food for the three of us. We were expecting a plate of sandwiches and a pot of tea. What arrived was akin to Balthazar's feast. There were several bottles of champagne and enough food to have fed around twenty people.

'Well, Peter,' said Jon, 'should you decide to sign for Stoke. I think we can safely assume you will be looked after up there.'

I did decide to sign for Stoke. I told Jon and Jeff that I had been impressed by Mr Humphreys and his colleagues and I didn't want to disappoint them.

I made my debut for Stoke City in November 1974 in a 2–2 draw at Wolverhampton Wanderers. The *Evening Sentinel* reported, 'Peter Shilton went some way to justifying his club record

TOP LEFT: Aged seven with my uncle Fred, who played in goal for Leicester City reserves in the 1930s. After trying to stop centre-forwards with a lethal finish, he took to applying a matt finish – when his playing days were over he became a painter and decorator.

TOP RIGHT & LEFT: With Dad, Mum and my brother Graham at Mablethorpe circa 1959. There was no fridge so the coolest place to keep bottles of milk was under the caravan.

LEFT: Aged 7 on holiday at Mablethorpe. Later in life I placed many a bet on horses like this one.

RIGHT: My first ever dance and my first ever suit. The dance took place at Trustville Holiday Camp in Lincolnshire in 1960. I was so shy I couldn't pluck up the courage to ask for a dance.

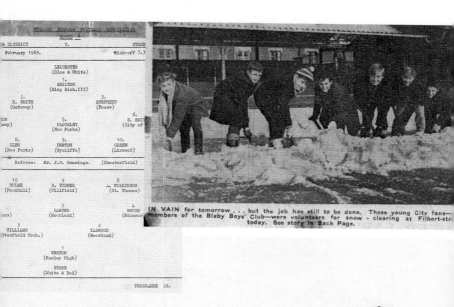

IN VAIN for tomorrow . . . but the job has still to be done. These young City fans—members of the Blaby Boys' Club—were volunteers for snow - clearing at Filbert-str today. See story in Back Page.

INSET TOP RIGHT: I'm wearing the bobble hat *(Leicester Mercury)*.

BELOW: In action for Leicester Schools against Chester-le-Street in the English Schools Trophy Final. Behind me is David Needham. I rose from my sick bed to play in this game and learned a valuable lesson about football.

TOP: The Leicester Boys team that shared the English Schools Trophy with Swansea in 1965. On my left is Jeff Blockley, who went on to play for Coventry, Arsenal and England. Far left, front row, is Romeo Challenger, who earned fame as a member of Showaddywaddy.

ABOVE: Signing as a pro for Leicester City aged 17. Behind me is City secretary Eddie Plumley, Dad, manager Matt Gillies and some sixties fabric wallpaper (*Leicester Mercury*).

Leicester City squad of 1965–66. Note the washing hanging out to dry in the background. As an apprentice I had to peg it out and gather it in when it was dry (*Leicester Mercury*).

LEFT: In the zip-up goalkeeper's top I designed, which caused so much controversy and led to the idea for the programme *What Not To Wear* (*Ken Coton*).

ABOVE: In action at Maine Road, April 1969 (*Popperfoto*).

Feeling fairly relaxed, passing the time at the hotel prior to the 1969 FA Cup Final against Manchester City (*Mirrorpix*); and saving at the feet of Francis Lee and Neil Young at Wembley. Also in the frame are, l to r, Graham Cross, Alan Clarke (putting a real effort in to come back and cover), Andy Lochhead and Mick Doyle (*Leicester Mercury*).

In action at Upton Park (*Mirrorpix*), and with my son, Michael; both shots in the 'infamous' all-white goalkeeper's strip, which was the result of a deal my agent, Jon Holmes, had struck with Admiral. It never caught on as all-white was somewhat impractical for goalkeepers on what were in those days Christmas-pudding pitches.

LEFT: An action shot from my later days at Filbert Street (*Popperfoto*).

BELOW: In action for Stoke, with Burnley's Peter Noble, 1975. My manager at Stoke, Tony Waddington, was one of the best I ever played for. He was the man who described football as 'the working man's ballet' (*Popperfoto*).

LEFT: Signing on at the City Ground with Peter Taylor and Brian Clough, this time minus the squash racket (*Nottingham Evening Post*).

BELOW: With Nottingham Forest following our League Cup victory over Southampton. It was a proud day for me. I had been to Wembley twice as a fan, played there in a Cup Final for Leicester, but never won a trophy before (*Empics*).

TOP: Possibly one of my greatest, certainly one of my most crucial saves. Tipping Mick Ferguson's header over the bar at Highfield Road helped bring the championship trophy back to the City Ground in the spring of 1978.

ABOVE: Forest team photo for the 1978–79 season: Back row, l to r: Ian Bowyer, Viv Anderson, Tony Woodcock, Kenny Burns. Centre, l to r: Jimmy Gordon, Frank Clark, Larry Lloyd, Chris Woods, me, Colin Barrett, Brian Clough. Front row, l to r: Peter Withe, David Needham, John McGovern, Martin O'Neill and John Robertson (*Nottingham Evening Post*).

In the thick of the action at Forest: against Ipswich (*right*, *Sporting Pictures*) and at Anfield (*below*, *Popperfoto*).

TOP: Lining up for one of our early European adventures, in Athens (*Nottingham Evening Post*).

LEFT: After beating Malmo in the final in Munich, 30 May 1979. I didn't have a great deal to do in this match but always had to maintain optimum concentration (*Mirrorpix*).

BELOW: Receiving my PFA Player of the Year Award for the 1979–80 season.

FROM TOP: Giving the green light to my defenders following our trip round the red-light district of Amsterdam, prior to our second European Cup semi-final, against Ajax, 1980 (*Nottingham Evening Post*); a relaxed Cloughie just prior to our second final in as many years (*Mirrorpix*); we've done it again . . . Forest 1–0 Hamburg, holding the trophy with Ian Bowyer (*Nottingham Evening Post*).

Life at The Dell: no trophies but a successful spell, and probably one of the happiest times of my career. I also won 49 of my caps while at Southampton (*Sporting Pictures*).

fee by producing a string of world-class saves to ensure City returned from Molineux with a valuable point.'

Initially, the move proved to be a very good one. Sue and I settled into life in North Staffordshire. At first we rented a house in the Endon area of Stoke-on-Trent before buying a home of our own on the Westlands, which is not actually in Stoke but in the borough of Newcastle-under-Lyme.

Stoke continued to post good results and, with three games of the season remaining, we were joint leaders of the First Division, albeit trailing Derby County and Liverpool on goal average. Ipswich Town were also in the frame at this late stage of the proceedings and any one of those four teams had a chance of winning the title.

Some bookies favoured Stoke as they felt we had the slightly easier run-in, our final three matches being against Sheffield United, Newcastle United and Burnley, but a 2–0 defeat against Sheffield United put a serious dent in our title hopes. This was followed by 0–0 draws against both Newcastle and Burnley, which resulted in Stoke finishing a very disappointing fifth. Injuries to centre-half Denis Smith and winger Jimmy Robertson hadn't helped our cause. In fact, the loss of two such key players proved crucial to our chances of winning the title.

Derby County won their second League championship in four years, again without having to kick a ball. On this occasion, Derby weren't sunning themselves on a Spanish beach because they still had one match to play. Stoke's poor run-in was mirrored by Liverpool, and when Ipswich Town failed to beat Manchester City at Maine Road, the title was Derby's. It had been a really competitive campaign with the lead changing hands a record twenty-one times.

The season had been one of change for English football. Don Revie had been installed as the England manager, Bill Shankly announced his retirement and another great manager, Bill Nicholson of Spurs, also retired. The previous season the Football League had experimented with three-up and three-down between the First, Second and Third Divisions and now they announced the new format was here to stay. My old England team-mate Bobby Moore reached the FA Cup final with his new club Fulham, only for them to be beaten by his old club, West Ham. The FA decided to dispense with the traditional rendition of 'Abide With Me' because in previous years the singing of this wonderful and moving hymn had been besmirched by terrace chanting. Happily, the singing of 'Abide With Me' has been brought back as part of the pre-match ritual of the Cup final and it says much for the behaviour of football supporters these days that the hymn is always afforded due respect.

Leicester City once again consolidated in the First Division, which was no mean achievement seeing as they failed to win a game from early November to the end of February. At one stage, in mid-January, Leicester found themselves in the bottom three but recovered sufficiently to finish in eighteenth place. I wish I could say the £325,000 the club received for me was used wisely but, in my opinion, a number of poor signings were made. Frustration was to become something of a permanent state of mind at the club. Come the end of the 1976–77 season, Jimmy Bloomfield resigned and the following season Leicester were relegated to the Second Division.

Under Matt Gillies the predominant accent in the Leicester dressing room had been Scottish. When Jimmy Bloomfield found his feet it was most definitely southern as he returned time and again to sign players from London clubs. Jimmy Bloomfield favoured an attacking game and his teams were entertaining but, in the eyes of the supporters, they were destined to be 'nearly' teams. Considering he had, at one time or another, such gifted but maverick players as Frank Worthington, Keith Weller, Alan Birchenall and Len Glover under his charge, Jimmy showed he certainly wasn't lacking in matters of man management.

Jimmy was a friendly guy. As Leicester manager he liked to involve himself with supporters and the local community and often accepted invitations to present awards at the end-of-season dinners of local leagues or amateur clubs. He was, however, apt to forget the names of people he did not know well. On one such occasion, Jimmy was asked to introduce Roy Hitchkiss, a former stalwart of the league in question. Being the bright chap he was, Jimmy waxed lyrical in his introductory remarks.

'I am particularly delighted to have been asked to introduce a man who has given great service to this league,' began Jimmy, 'a man who rejoices in a great surname, the last part of which is synonymous with love and pleasure. Gabrielle Rossetti called them messengers of love. Polynesian women believe that to have one placed on their lips is the first step to a heavenly experience, while in medieval English tapestries, young maidens are depicted longing for such a thing from knights returning from war.

'I am sure that many of you here tonight will have indulged yourselves with one at some time today and that is why, without further ado, I hand you now to, Mr Roy . . .' There was a pregnant pause as Jimmy racked his brains for the surname of the guest speaker. '. . . Mr Roy Hitchcock!'

Tony Waddington was a superb manager. It was Tony who described football as 'the working man's ballet', an apposite description if ever there was one. Tony was not the best tactician I ever came across. In fact, he didn't bother too much about tactics at all. Signing good players who were also good professionals had been Tony's policy ever since he had been appointed as Stoke manager in 1960. He had brought Stanley Matthews back to the club and acquired a number of quality players who were very experienced and had two or three years left in the game – Eddie Stuart, Eddie Clamp, Jimmy McIlroy, Jackie Mudie and Denis Violett, for example. The Stoke City side that clinched promotion by winning the Second Division title in 1962–63 had the oldest average age of any team to win a championship in the history of English football.

Over the years Tony had continued his policy of signing good-quality players and mixing them with the products of his excellent youth system. When I joined the club, Denis Smith, Jackie Marsh, Alan Bloor, Alan Dodd and Eric Skeels were coming through.

Stoke City had a very good squad of players and hopes were high that the 1975–76 season would be another successful chapter in the history of a club that was now competing with the best in the First Division. We never produced the scintillating form we had shown in much of the previous season but, come Christmas, we were in the top half and handily placed for a push to secure a place in the UEFA Cup. In December, we posted a fine 2–0 win at Highbury and although we lost our next game at West Ham, on Boxing Day we gained a highly creditable point in a 1–1 draw with Liverpool. In January, it all began to go pear-shaped.

The FA Cup was our last realistic opportunity of winning silverware. We had been drawn away to Spurs and on the Friday morning the team assembled at Stoke station to catch a train to Euston. During the previous night a raging storm had swept across the Midlands. I'd heard of the damage the storm had caused on the local radio news that morning but nothing had prepared me for the sight that greeted our eyes as the London-bound train passed the Victoria Ground. The ground looked as if a bomb had hit it. The roof of the Butler Street stand on the side of the ground backing on to the railway had been stripped away in the storms. Parts of the roof lay scattered about on the waste ground behind the stand and even on our training ground, some 300 yards away. As the train picked up speed, more debris from the stand was to be seen by the railway track. We didn't realise it at the time but the damage was to plunge the club into a long period of financial hardship that would necessitate selling players. My days at Stoke City were numbered.

Stoke's problem was that the cost of rebuilding the Butler Street stand was far in excess of what it had been insured for. The club had gone to the hilt in order to acquire players such as Alan Hudson, Geoff Salmons and me. Attendances were holding up so meeting wages and the general costs of running the club were not a problem. What would be a problem was if any unforeseen large financial outlay had to be made, which was exactly what happened when the Butler Street stand blew away and there was a large shortfall in the insurance compensation.

The immediate worry was where to play. Neighbours Port Vale offered the use of their ground and Stoke won their first 'home' match away from the Victoria Ground when we beat Jack Charlton's Middlesbrough on 17 January.

I think Alan Hudson and Mike Pejic sensed trouble ahead because both players handed in written transfer requests, just before we were about to meet Sunderland in the fifth round of the FA Cup. Having previously accounted for Spurs and Manchester City, everyone was confident that we would progress to the quarter-finals at the expense of Second Division Sunderland. I dare say the Stoke board saw it as essential that we enjoyed a good run in the Cup. Making it to the final would ease the club's financial plight slightly.

A crowd of over 41,000 turned up to see Sunderland produce a fine rearguard action that resulted in a goalless draw. The Sunderland keeper Jim Montgomery was their hero producing a string of fine saves. The replay at Roker Park was a cut-and-thrust cup tie. Mel Holden gave Sunderland the lead in the second half but in less than a minute we were on level terms when Denis Smith bundled the ball across the line after an Alan Bloor effort had rebounded into play off the post. Roared on by a home crowd of over 48,000, Sunderland took the game to us. We soaked up all the pressure until ten minutes from the end when Bryan 'Pop' Robson scored what was, in all honesty, a fortuitous goal. There seemed no danger when Robson fired off his shot. I had the effort covered but the ball glanced off the back of Denis Smith and I was wrong-footed. That deflection took the ball on a different course, away from me and into the net. Roker Park erupted. Sunderland were bound for the quarter-finals of the FA Cup whereas Stoke were bound to be in financial difficulty.

So it proved to be. Apparently, the Stoke board made it clear to Tony Waddington that the new roof for the Butler Street stand would have to be financed by the sale of players. Tony Waddington did his best to raise funds by selling some of the club's youngsters and those on the fringe of the first team rather than his main players. Sean Haslegrave went to Nottingham Forest for £35,000 and Ian Moores joined Spurs for £75,000. The money generated wasn't enough, though, and faced with a growing overdraft, impatient creditors and the Butler Street bill, Tony Waddington's hands were tied. He had no option but to sell prime assets.

Jimmy Greenhoff joined Manchester United for £120,000. Alan Hudson was sold to Arsenal for £200,000, which was £40,000 less than Stoke had paid for him three years earlier. Not only were the board selling key players, they were doing so at knock-down prices. Alan was still only twenty-five and had been called up for England. Next to leave was Mike Pejic, who joined Everton for a fee of £140,000 during the 1976–77 season.

The creative heart had been ripped out of the team. Youngsters were called up from the reserves and 'bargain buys' were drafted in. Results suffered accordingly. In 1975–76, Stoke City finished in twelfth place. As the club continued to decline, Tony Waddington became an easy target for disgruntled home fans and, unbelievably, considering all he had done for the club, chants of 'Waddington Out' were heard from the terraces. Tony was devastated and tendered his resignation. He was replaced by former Arsenal, Newcastle and England player George Eastham, who had been a member of Sir Alf's squad for the 1966 World Cup. George Eastham couldn't make a silk purse from a sow's ear and, come the end of the 1976–77 season, Stoke were relegated.

Perversely, those two seasons produced benefits for me as a goalkeeper. I was under a lot of pressure because Stoke were invariably forced to defend and I was able to display my ability to the full. The players who were supposed to be creating goals weren't doing the job and in such circumstances, goalkeepers often get the blame when their team doesn't post good results. I tried to capitalise on the situation. In giving of my best when under a lot of pressure, I felt my individual game was improving. Tony Waddington very kindly said that my presence in goal for Stoke was, 'in terms of goals not being conceded, worth thirty goals a season to the club'.

I did my utmost to live up to that plaudit. The relegation season was a real backs-to-the-wall job. The youngsters who were thrown in at the deep end were, quite simply, not up to the task. The team wasn't good enough for the First Division and our main weakness was our inability to score goals.

I had a great rapport with the Stoke supporters and felt loyalty to both the club and its directors. I never sought a move while we were fighting relegation. I received a call from Jimmy Greenhoff who told me that the United manager, Tommy Docherty, wanted to sign me. I guess Jimmy had been asked to ring to gauge my reaction to a possible move to Old Trafford. Nothing ever came of it because a week later Tommy Docherty's managerial career took a familiar turn – he was sacked.

Of the so-called big-name players, I was almost the last to leave, but this period of my life was very unsettling. In addition to playing for a club that was in rapid decline, I was not popular with the England manager, Don Revie, who preferred to play Liverpool's Ray Clemence in goal.

In fact, Revie never gave me a look-in from the word go. His first game in charge was in October 1974, a European Championship qualifier against Czechoslovakia. England took the field newly decked out in white shirts with red and blue shoulder stripes, provided by Admiral, the first time the national side had departed from wearing white-only shirts. I wasn't with them. I took my place on the bench with the substitutes.

England beat the Czechs 3–0 and Don Revie preferred Ray Clemence for the next two games against Portugal (0–0) and West Germany (2–0). He recalled me for the European Championship match against Cyprus at Wembley, a game memorable for the fact that Malcolm Macdonald scored all England's goals in a 5–0 victory. Malcolm became the first player to score five goals at Wembley and his feat equalled the record of Tottenham's Willie Hall who had scored five for England against Northern Ireland at Old Trafford in 1938. I didn't have too much to do in this game, but the fact that I had kept a clean sheet seemed to cut no ice with Revie. He recalled Ray Clemence for the return match with Cyprus in Limassol and I found myself out of the team for England's next eighteen matches.

Having last played in the 5–0 defeat of Cyprus, oddly I was recalled by Don Revie for a game against Northern Ireland in May 1977 following England's 5–0 defeat of Luxembourg. I had been out of the England team for two years and at one point I had become so frustrated at never being picked that I informed Don Revie that I didn't wish to be included in the squad any more. I hated saying it.

During that time, my unhappiness at being out of favour with Don Revie and at playing in a Stoke team in decline was such that I felt I needed to talk to someone in the game whose opinion I respected. I rang the Nottingham Forest manager, Brian Clough. I was not seeking a move. I was simply in need of some good advice and Brian turned out to be a good listener. He agreed to meet me for lunch in a Midlands hotel. We chatted in general terms about the state of the game and I told him my troubles. He simply advised me to continue doing what I was doing – to apply myself fully to my game and to Stoke City and to be patient where England was concerned.

The way he handled our conversation was incredible. He seemed to know exactly how I felt and exuded empathy. The way he conducted himself and our conversation made a big impression on me and I was left thinking it's the way people say things that often matters, rather than what they say. Afterwards, I felt a little better about things and I adopted the Micawber philosophy that, in time, 'something would turn up'.

During the two years I had spent in Ray Clemence's shadow, I had been playing well for Stoke. After one particularly poor run of results in early 1977, when Stoke lost to Everton in the FA Cup, then scrambled a 0–0 draw with Newcastle before losing 1–0 at home to Leicester, the *Evening Sentinel* said, 'Regarding recent performances, only Peter Shilton can hold his head high. Time and again he has been City's saviour, but the omens do not bode well. Even Shilton's heroics may not be sufficient to save Stoke from relegation this season.' But my good club form didn't endear me to Don Revie.

Following my appearance against Northern Ireland – a 2–1 victory for England – I played in a 1–0 defeat by Wales. It was Wales' first victory over England for forty-two years and their first ever at Wembley. Leighton James scored from the penalty spot after I was adjudged to have brought him down. The press were highly critical of England, and Don Revie in particular. Regarding keeping my place for the next game, against Scotland, I feared the worst. Revie chose Ray Clemence and England lost 2–1. It was the first time England had lost consecutive matches at Wembley and the press censured the manager.

No matter how hard I tried, I could not win over Don Revie. The chemistry between us was never right. At the time, I tried to think of possible reasons why Don never appeared to like me. Brian Clough was a big fan of mine and Don not liking Brian was one reason I came up with.

Another reason concerned a column I wrote for a local newspaper during my time at Leicester City. Don had a close association with Leicester, having once played for the club, and word reached him about one particular article I had penned. While praising the Leeds side he had created, I had gone on to criticise some of their tactics in a game against Southampton, which Leeds had won 7–1. While the Southampton players attempted to gain possession, the Leeds team played keep-ball, gleefully passing the ball to one another, even indulging in some mickey taking. Rather than seeing this as the ultimate demonstration of possession football, I saw it as being unprofessional and unethical. Don, seemingly, took exception to my views. Whether he harboured resentment about it I don't know, but he seemed to take great delight in seeing me put down.

An example occurred at a gathering of the England squad one Sunday. The previous day I had played for Stoke City against Newcastle United. Stoke were leading 1–0 when, with minutes remaining, Newcastle played a long ball over the top of the Stoke defence. I came out of my goal and ended up in a race with Newcastle's Alan Gowling for possession. We collided, Alan got to his feet first and had the simple task of rolling the ball into the net for the equaliser, for which I received some mild criticism in the press.

When the England squad assembled, the Stoke–Newcastle game was being screened on ITV and everyone settled down to watch it. At half-time our coach summoned us to a training session but Don insisted everyone should stay to see the second half. Of course, when my clash with Alan Gowling and the resultant goal was shown, I came in for some good-natured stick from my team-mates, which I took in good part. What shocked me was Don Revie's reaction. I turned to see him laughing gleefully. I was convinced then that Don had insisted everyone should watch the game for the sole purpose of seeing my howler. As for him clapping his hands and laughing, suffice it to say Alf Ramsey would never have done such a thing, nor subsequent England managers I served.

Following the defeat by the Scots, England embarked upon a summer tour of South America and drew their three matches against Brazil, Argentina and Uruguay. It was England's first ever undefeated tour of South America and, considering the quality of the opposition, no mean feat. Revie preferred Ray Clemence for all three games and, given the results, I believed my chances of playing for England again in the near future were remote. However, not long after the squad returned to England, Don dropped his bombshell, announcing he had resigned as England manager to take up the role of national coach of the United Arab Emirates. He had missed the game in Brazil, joining the England squad in Buenos Aires, but, at the time, I don't believe anyone thought that untoward. In fact, he had been in Dubai negotiating with UAE officials.

The South American tour apart, Don had been subjected to a lot of criticism in certain quarters of the press for a sequence of uninspired performances, and for the way he had managed

England. That 'get-together' involving a hundred players didn't go down well and some of his selection policies had been questioned.

In March 1976, Don picked two of my Stoke team-mates, Alan Hudson and Jimmy Greenhoff, for a game against Wales. Alan and Jimmy had been playing particularly well and their selection was widely approved. They were set to be Stoke's first two outfield players to be capped in the same England team since Stanley Matthews and Neil Franklin had faced Scotland in 1947. Unfortunately for Alan and Jimmy, Stoke rearranged a league match against Derby County for the same night. As clubs had first call on players, Alan and Jimmy played for Stoke at the Baseball Ground. Sadly, Alan broke his leg against Derby and neither he nor Jimmy Greenhoff was ever selected by Don Revie again. (A shame, after Alan's superb game for England against West Germany.) For the following international, Don raised eyebrows when Jimmy Greenhoff's place in the squad was handed to Colin Viljoen of Ipswich Town.

At one point, when criticism of Don had reached a crescendo, he named an England team that contained five central defenders, seemingly a result of his fear of losing. Having appointed Alan Ball as England captain, Don promptly turned his back on his new skipper. Alan Ball went public with his criticism of Don Revie and the tabloid press had a field day.

Talented and creative players such as Alan Hudson, Tony Currie and Charlie George, for all their fine performances for their respective clubs, never really found favour with Don, and neither did Malcolm Macdonald. Those players had something in common – they were all individualists with strong characters who didn't fit into the regimented way Don ran the England team. During a period when England failed to qualify for the finals of a major international tournament, it was odd that some of the country's most gifted individuals were constantly overlooked for the national team. Flair in the England team was unfashionable.

In the seventies, individualists often lost out to the team ethic. Those who played to the gallery found little favour with some coaches and managers. In some ways, players such as Alan Hudson, Stan Bowles, Rodney Marsh and Tony Currie were seen as being 'unprofessional' because they diverted from the preconceived game plan. Perhaps that was why they never found favour with Don Revie, who wanted his players to carry out his instructions to the letter.

Previously, players such as Bobby Charlton, Danny Blanch-flower, Johnny Haynes and Dave Mackay dictated the game out there on the pitch. What happened in the wake of the 1966 World Cup, and in particular in the seventies, was that the onus of dictating play shifted from talented individuals to coaches. Today we see managers, coaches, technical directors, call them what you will, directing and conducting play from the designated technical area by the touchline. The seeds of this were firmly planted in English football with the growing importance and influence of managers and coaches throughout the seventies.

There were no 'stars' in the England team when Sir Alf Ramsey was manager. Every player was treated the same. Under Don Revie it was different. Don warmed to Kevin Keegan. He liked Kevin's work ethos, which was in keeping with the sort of player Don preferred. Kevin was not a flair player but he made the most of what he had. He knew he wasn't the best player in England at the time, but he was always working on it. Don made Kevin the Eng-land captain and for his part, Kevin capitalised on his new-found status by promoting himself in the media and securing various commercial deals. I didn't think there was anything wrong in that and Kevin always had that side of his career firmly under control.

There were some bizarre incidents regarding players and commercial deals during Don Revie's reign as England manager although, of course, these had nothing directly to do with Don. Don selected Stan Bowles to play in a crucial World Cup qualifying match against Italy in Rome in November 1976. Stan had signed two deals with football boot manufacturers that involved him wearing a particular style of boot they made. Stan was in a dilemma. The Italy game was a big international match and he knew each boot manufacturer would want him to wear their particular brand of footwear. Stan got round the problem by wearing one manufacturer's boot on one foot and the other make on the other foot. I dare say the companies in question were aware of this, but to the best of my knowledge no one, apart from the rest of the team, noticed Stan was wearing odd boots against Italy.

If certain quarters of the press had not approved of the way Don Revie managed the England team, they hated the way he managed his departure. Apparently, Don had told the FA that he was willing to resign if his contract were paid up and he also received a tax-free bonus of £5,000. The FA didn't take him up on his offer. This had been going on behind the scenes but a few weeks later, Revie went public. He gave an interview to the *Daily Mail*, announcing that he was heading for the United Arab Emirates and a £60,000-a-year tax-free job as their national coach. He was vilified for his actions, some newspapers going so far as to refer to him as being 'a traitor to English football' and 'a money-grabbing mercenary'. 'Don the Deserter' was a new nickname that he couldn't shake off.

It all became very messy. The FA, in particular chairman Sir Harold Thompson, went gunning for Revie. Amid allegations that he had made illegal approaches to certain players when manager of Leeds – Alan Ball was one who was cited – the FA charged Don with 'bringing the game into disrepute' and suspended him indefinitely.

Don returned from the United Arab Emirates a year later to face an FA Commission who put a limit of ten years on the ban. Revie had taken most of the criticism on the chin but he was determined to lock horns with the FA. He sued for damages and asked that the ban be ruled illegal. Don won his case in court and the FA were instructed to lift the ban but his success was something of a Pyrrhic victory. The judge ruled that Sir Harold Thompson had behaved as an 'honourable man' in chairing the FA disciplinary committee but nevertheless it was considered that there had been a 'bias against the former England manager'. He went on to describe Don as 'deceitful, greedy and selfish'.

The lifting of the ban enabled Revie to receive an income from Leeds United as part of a long-term consultancy contract he had negotiated with the club, but he was never to have an active role in English football again. Throughout his career Don had been motivated by a great desire to win matches and trophies but also to make money. You could say he was the ultimate professional.

Personal differences apart, I recognised his contribution to the English game and played in his testimonial at Elland Road. I had no alternative but to accept the fact that he preferred Ray Clemence to me but I have to be honest and say I wasn't sad to see him leave. After he'd gone, I was hopeful that my performances for Stoke would come to the attention of the next England manager, whoever it may be, and that I would be given a chance to re-establish myself in the national side.

However, Stoke had been relegated and I didn't think playing Second Division football was going to help me. I didn't think Stoke would bounce back up in the next couple of seasons, as Leicester had done. I needed to be playing at the highest level. I had remained loyal to Stoke throughout their problems on and off the pitch and given them 100 per cent commitment at a time when the club's best players were leaving but if I was to develop my career further, I knew I had to leave. I was very unsettled and I asked for a transfer. The club were reluctant to sell me but given their dire financial situation had little option but to do so. I had no idea what the future had in store for me or which, if any, club would want to sign me. In the event, I did not have to wait long to find out.

Stoke City kicked off the 1977–78 season with an away game at Mansfield Town – hardly the setting for someone with aspirations of regaining the number-one goalkeeping position with the England team. It was an ignominious start to life in the Second Division as Mansfield ran out winners by two goals to one. I played in Stoke's next two games, a 0–0 draw with Southampton and a 2–1 victory over Burnley. That was to be my last game for Stoke.

To start with, I loved the atmosphere at the club. On my very first pre-season tour, the club's directors got all the players together in the lounge bar of our hotel and the drinks and conversation flowed. It was very convivial and relaxed.

One another occasion, Stoke City were on tour. The night before a match Tony Waddington had, as usual, confined all the players to the team hotel. Needless to say, this rule applied to the players only and not to Tony or the directors, who enjoyed a night out on the town. To while away the evening a group of us had got together in my room for a game of cards. Alan Hudson, Geoff Hurst, Terry Conroy, Jackie Marsh, Alan Bloor and I were just about to wrap up the card school when Tony came in. His tie was loose, the top buttons of his shirt were undone and it was obvious to us all that he had enjoyed a good drink. Tony asked us what was going on and we told him we were having a game of cards. Unsteady on his feet, Tony walked across the room to where the 'pot' of money lay on the bed. To our surprise, he scooped it up, saying, 'I'm confiscating all this.' He did it as a bit of joke but just as he was scooping the money off the bed, the chairman, Albert Henshall, came on the scene, wearing his pyjamas.

'Is there a problem here, Tony?' Henshall asked.

'No problem. Just breaking up a late-night card school, Mr Chairman,' replied Tony.

Albert Henshall seemed to be having difficulty in focusing and was swaying a bit.

'Card school, eh? That's the work of the. . .'

He didn't complete his sentence. He swayed back, then forwards, then collapsed on my bed. Tony gave a little laugh and lolled back in a chair. Some of us carried the chairman to his room, and put him into bed, while the remainder of the card school guided Tony to his room. We never did get the money back.

The social life at Stoke was good. The players often enjoyed a day out at the races, Wolverhampton or Uttoxeter. However, after a time, I felt the convivial social atmosphere degenerated into something that was too lax. At one point, when Waddington was manager, and in the heat of the moment immediately after a game, I gave an interview to a newspaper in which I mentioned that I thought Stoke were 'too relaxed and unprofessional' in their attitude to the match. Tony was upset at this and, looking back, I can understand why but at the time I felt it needed to be said. Things were becoming too free and easy. Unlike one or two of the other players, I was keen to stay at Stoke 'if the club is prepared to change its Corinthian style approach'. I had moved to Stoke because I felt they were a great club with a lot of potential but in order for potential to be realised you have to work at it and I didn't think some players were doing that.

Stoke's decline was not purely down to bad luck and the destruction of the Butler Street stand. The club and dressing room had taken on an increasingly *laissez faire* attitude. If Stoke were ever to be successful, I felt they needed a more professional approach all round. Too many things had been brushed under the carpet and it was time for plain, honest talking. For eighteen months, Stoke had regularly not performed to our potential on the pitch and things were lax off the field, too. I liked a drink as much as anyone, but one or two players had a real penchant for drinking sessions.

It had all gone horribly wrong for me at Stoke. I needed someone to give my career a fillip, to say, 'This boy can play…he's a great goalkeeper.' The person who came along was Brian Clough.

5

LIFE WITH BRIAN

The true managerial greats of our game are a select band. Arguably, their number includes Sir Alf Ramsey, Bob Paisley, Bill Shankly, Jock Stein, Bill Nicholson, Arsène Wenger, Sir Alex Ferguson and Brian Clough. Football is a game of opinions and the guy standing next to you in the pub would no doubt disagree, but I think few people would argue with the inclusion of Brian Clough on that list. He was the best manager England never had.

Brian Clough doesn't suffer fools gladly, if at all. He is impatient, dogmatic, arrogant and confrontational but also sympathetic to the needs of others. He insisted his players followed the rules he laid down, but then often encouraged us to break them. He was brash and belligerent but also understanding, crude yet impeccably well mannered, hard-faced yet compassionate, complicated yet a believer in simple homespun philosophies. Undoubtedly conceited, he also displayed considerable humility. Clough was an antagonist but a great friend to his players. He aroused contradictory reactions in everyone because he was, and is, a man of wild contradiction, an enigma in football management. I never thought that I would come across a manager with more self-belief than I had as a goalkeeper but I did the day I signed for Nottingham Forest.

The most common thing said of Brian Clough as a manager is that he was a bully. Significantly, you never hear that said by anyone who played for him. John McGovern followed Brain Clough from

Hartlepool United to Derby County to Leeds United to Nottingham Forest. John O'Hare was a player with Clough at Sunderland and played under him at both Derby and Nottingham Forest. Would either player have followed Clough when asked, knowing he bullied his players? Would I have signed for Nottingham Forest? The simple answer to those questions is no. More significantly, if Brian Clough had bullied the players at Forest, we would not have gone out and given him our all on the pitch, and without exception we always did give him 100 per cent effort and commitment.

Clough made things uncomplicated. He believed football to be a simple game and asked that his team played it accordingly. His style of management was straightforward – in some respects like Sir Alf Ramsey's. He was always in control. I felt that all I had to do was to get on with my job. That was not always the case with other managers I played for, some of whom sought the advice of players about how to handle certain situations, or how to counteract a particular opponent, which, more often then not, led to disagreements in the dressing room.

One of his greatest strengths as a manager was discovering players' hidden talents and encouraging those players to demonstrate them to the full. When Clough and long-time friend and assistant Peter Taylor signed Kenny Burns from Birmingham City, Kenny was a half-decent striker who occasionally played in midfield. Kenny was bemused about why Clough and Taylor needed him at Forest because the team seemed to be well off for strikers. When Clough informed Kenny that he wanted him as a centre-back, Kenny was even more bemused.

'I've never played as a centre-back in my life,' said Kenny incredulously.

'I know,' said Clough, 'but that's where you should be playing. You can play there and we're going to show you that you can.'

Although you never felt you knew where you stood with Clough, oddly you always did. He could be wildly eccentric and erratic, yet you were always comfortable with that because it was how you expected him to be. It was the manager whose emotions were always on one level but who then suddenly threw a tea-tray across the dressing room at half-time that made players worry. Like a centre-forward who always expects the unexpected in an opponent's penalty area, there was comfort and security in knowing your manager was given to the unconventional.

I discovered how unconventional he was when Jon Holmes, Jeff Pointon and I went to see him in his office at the City Ground in September 1977, after Forest had made an official approach to Stoke City for me. We hung about outside his office for ten minutes or so before someone informed us 'Mr Clough is ready to see you now.' Jon and Jeff went in first and I was slack-jawed to see them both go sprawling across the floor. From behind the open door, I heard Clough laughing impishly. He had been hiding to one side of the door and as Jon and Jeff entered, he angled a squash racquet across their path and tripped them both up. I have no idea if Clough did this to gain some sort of psychological advantage for the following negotiations or whether it was just a prank. It certainly threw Jon and Jeff for a time.

When we did sit down to discuss my personal terms, Clough seemed disinterested to the point of dissociating himself from what was being said. As Jon or Jeff outlined a point, Clough would stare at the ceiling while beating the squash racquet against his right leg. After nigh on three hours, Clough brought the meeting to a close, saying something on the lines of, 'Well, this has got us nowhere, has it? And I'd prefer to be somewhere rather than nowhere, so good day, gentlemen. Thank you for coming.' He stood up, turned to Peter Taylor and said, 'I'm going for a bloody meal.'

I was left utterly perplexed. Forest had agreed a fee of £250,000 with Stoke for my services but as we had not agreed personal terms, I wasn't sure if I was joining Forest or not. The sticking point was the salary rather than bonuses and extras. Clough had offered £15,000 a year and I was on £22,000 at Stoke.

Jon and Jeff tried to break the deadlock by speaking to Stoke. Jon asked if they would be willing to pay the £5,000 loyalty bonus that was due at the end of my contract with them on the understanding that the money would be offset by the substantial fee Stoke would be getting from Forest. The board declined Jon's request. Albert Henshall, the chairman, called it 'the most incredible financial demand I've ever experienced'. In fact, Jon hadn't made a demand; it was just a request. Stoke were in desperate need of the money they would get for me and I was desperate to leave the club. I thought Stoke might pay the loyalty bonus to push the deal through rather than have pressure from their bank and an unsettled player on their books.

A few days later I received a telephone call asking me to meet Clough at a local hotel on my own. I was desperate for the move to happen so I went. When I walked into the room Clough and Taylor were already present, and so was a bottle of champagne in an ice bucket. I took that to mean he expected a successful conclusion to our meeting.

It transpired that Clough was as keen to have me sign for Forest as I was to join them. He came up with a compromise figure of £20,000 a year and I immediately agreed. I think, within reason, he and Taylor would have paid anything to get me. For my part, my mind was so made up about joining Forest that the money didn't really matter too much, so I signed on the dotted line.

Following the tremendous success we enjoyed together at Forest, Clough said, 'I rescued Peter Shilton's career. Never mind about what he has done for us, how many matches he helped win for us, I saved his career! He has earned X-amount of pounds a week plus bonuses and all that. But I have given him things that money can't buy, even if he was a millionaire. I've given him medals to show his children and grandchildren.'

That is true but I feel there were occasions when I went a long way towards helping Brian achieve success at Forest. That season, 1977–78, we exceeded all expectations, including my own. On paper, Nottingham Forest didn't appear to have the best team in the First Division. Viv Anderson, Colin Barrett, Ian Bowyer, Martin O'Neill, John Roberston, Peter Withe, Tony Woodock, Larry Lloyd, John McGovern, Frank Clark and, the player no other club seemed to have wanted, Kenny Burns were all good players but not household names. Clough and Taylor, however, forged us into a team in every sense of the word and unearthed gifts those players never realised they had.

Nottingham Forest had just been promoted and the majority opinion was that we could consolidate in the First Division although some pundits believed that, given our squad, we would be relegated. Neither happened. Nottingham Forest won the First Division championship at the first time of asking and we did so with four games to spare. We also won the League Cup at Wembley – I missed out on that because I was cup-tied, my place going to Chris Woods. The Forest fans, who for years had endured disappointment and, prior to the arrival of Clough and Taylor, downright despondency, roared their approval as we created their memories.

We clinched the title with a 0–0 draw at Coventry City in which I produced what many believe to have been one of the best performances of my career. It was a game in which I made what I believe to have been one of my greatest saves. Coventry played the ball into my penalty box towards the byline at my far post, some ten yards from where I was positioned at the near post. Ian Wallace played the ball back across goal to Coventry's David Ferguson. I immediately changed direction, moving swiftly from my near post across the goal. Everything that followed seemed to happen in a split second. Ferguson let fly with a bullet header towards goal, I took off from the ground and knocked the ball over the bar. Ferguson brought his hands to his head in frustration. It proved a crucial save as the game ended goalless and the draw clinched the championship for Forest. In the dressing room after the game there were no hysterical celebrations. Our dressing room took on a stilled atmosphere of satisfaction and achievement. Of a job well done. I was thrilled and delighted but, along with my team-mates', my joy was restrained.

We lost just three league matches in the entire season. Our undefeated run, which spilled over into the following season, lasted a year and thirteen days. All told we remained unbeaten for 42 league games, a record in English football.

Having played three games for Stoke in the Second Division, I went on to play 37 league matches for Forest. John Middleton was in goal for the other five. Forest were unbeaten at home throughout the entire season and in those 21 home matches conceded just eight goals. Away from home we won ten, drew eight and lost three, conceding just 16 goals on our travels, the lowest of any team in the Football League.

We were not prolific goalscorers although our season's tally of 69 was laudable. We scored more goals than runners-up Liverpool but not as many as teams below us, such as Everton, who scored 76, and Manchester City and Coventry, both of whom scored 75. Manchester United were the only team to score more than us away from home – 35 as opposed to our 32.

The key to that Nottingham Forest team was organisation. Everyone played his part to the full and we built from the back. Our defence was the bedrock of our success and I like to think my presence in goal made a difference. Full-back Viv Anderson grew in stature as the season progressed. We nicknamed Viv 'extension' because of the way his leg seemed to extend to take possession of the ball when tackling. Viv's attributes as a full-back are well known but he could also play a quality ball and he got forward to support our attacks. I was delighted for Viv when, in November 1978, he was chosen along with Tony Woodcock and me to play for England against Czechoslovakia. As the first black player to represent England at senior level, Viv made all the headlines. To a man, every England player was delighted for Viv and applauded the significance attached to his international debut.

Larry Lloyd and Kenny Burns complemented one another perfectly. Both were good in the air, particularly Larry. Like Viv, both could play a bit. Kenny was a very good reader of a game and his distribution was excellent. Not the tallest of central defenders, he more than made up for his lack of inches with his superb timing. Many's the time I saw him win the ball in the air against a forward who was much taller than him.

Left-back Frank Clark was an astute acquisition from Newcastle United. Many people thought Frank's best days were behind him because he was in his thirties but, in reality, Frank's best days were spent at Forest, certainly in terms of success. Frank was one of those players who had been there and done it. His experience was invaluable to us. He may not have been as pacy as he had been at Newcastle, but his ability to read and assess the game thwarted many an opposing attack.

The work rate of Ian Bowyer and John McGovern in midfield was phenomenal. They were both good at winning the ball and, once it was at their feet, their distribution was always superb. McGovern was the anchor in a midfield in which Martin O'Neill was the prime creator. Martin had great football nous and acumen and a keen eye for goal. Archie Gemmill was rapier-like in attack and, like O'Neill, possessed an excellent football brain. Colin Barrett was a fine player. Tony Woodcock was very quick and worked the channels extremely well.

John Robertson was the enigma of the team. His creative talents sometimes seemed to be taken for granted. He was a creator of goals, a player whose speed of thought matched the skill and subtlety of his play. John didn't miss a single league, FA Cup, League Cup or European game in over two years. That bears testimony not only to the way he was able to look after himself when up against the most rugged of defenders, but also to the importance Clough and Taylor placed on him as part of the team.

John was not what you would call the consummate professional. He liked a beer and more than the occasional cigarette. I remember quite a few occasions at team meetings, where Clough or Taylor would ask him, 'Have you had that frying pan out again?' John would look slightly uneasy but the message got through: to keep an eye on his weight. Clough and Taylor need not have worried, though. John never let them down with his weight; in fact, his performances were great.

Clough did, however, pass comment on John's dress sense, which was anything but elegant. Footballers tend to be smartly dressed even when turning up for training but John would sometimes arrive wearing an old jumper, and nearly always wore a pair of scuffed Hush Puppies. Occasionally, he even wore his old Hush Puppies with a dark suit. Clough would look John in the eye, transfer his gaze to the shoes and back to John's face. John would shuffle uncomfortably. Neither would say a word but John was left in no doubt about what Clough thought of his appearance.

John's eccentricity was tolerated by Clough and Taylor, I suppose, because they felt that to try to change him would affect his performance in the team. John was happy being who he was and managers like happy players, especially when they also happen to be very good.

My commitment to Clough, Taylor, my team-mates and the Forest cause was such that I was mentally and physically exhausted at the end of every game. There is, as I discovered, a very thin line between being sufficiently involved in a match to help the players around you and being too involved. The mark of a good keeper is how well he positions himself and organises the players in front of him to deny the opposition shooting opportunities. I was playing behind a very good defence at Forest, yet I attached much importance to my role as a motivator, shouting instructions, offering words of encouragement, complimenting team-mates when they did even the simplest of things right.

As a goalkeeper, you must boss your penalty area. Occasionally, I would remonstrate with defenders, and occasionally they would have a go at me. I relied on my defenders as much as they relied on me. It was a two-way street. Larry Lloyd and Kenny Burns helped me because, in addition to their technical ability, they were both very positive individuals. It was easy for me to read what they were going to do in certain situations and, if necessary, do a mopping-up job. What a goalkeeper does not want is defenders who are indecisive, who stand off opponents and let them play. You have to make things happen in a game and Larry and Kenny were very good at seizing the initiative.

I always took on a lot of responsibility and I expected the defenders in front of me to do the same. When a goalkeeper is very positive, as I was, there is the danger of defenders relying on him too much. For example, if a high ball is pumped into the penalty area, they might think, 'I'll not go for this, it's the keeper's ball. He likes to boss his area,' when what they should be doing is taking the initiative themselves. I adhered to the principle of honesty, of defenders doing their jobs. Rarely, if ever, did that Forest defence let me down.

However, footballers are only human and even in the most crucial games there might be a ten-minute spell when Larry Lloyd's and Kenny Burns' concentration was not what it should have been and they weren't quite clicking as central defenders. I would be on to them and, even though they were liable to eyeball me as if to say 'shut up', I wouldn't until their concentration had returned to the optimum level. Larry and Kenny may have glowered at me but they never said anything because they knew I was doing my job.

Larry Lloyd used to say he enjoyed playing in front of me at Forest and Ray Clemence at Liverpool because having a good goalkeeper behind him instilled confidence. 'With a dodgy keeper, I'm almost afraid to commit myself for fear that, if I miss the tackle, the ball will end up in the net,' Larry once told me. 'That was never the case with you or Ray. I was always relaxed and confident when playing in front of either of you.'

Both Brian Clough and Peter Taylor were happy for me to command my penalty area and organise the defence. For instance, they were happy, if we were short on numbers when defending a dead-ball situation, for me sometimes to take a player off a post. What I didn't like as a goalkeeper was an opponent standing in or around my six-yard box. I preferred to have my defenders mark opponents outside the six-yard box because I considered a ball into that area as being my responsibility. I didn't see any point in coming for a cross and having to reach over two players – my defender and the opponent – in order to collect the ball. If an opposing player stood in or around my six-yard box, I ordered my team-mate to drop away and accepted the responsibility for winning the ball against the opponent.

In my early playing days the only player who really caused me problems, flicking the ball on at the near post, was 'the giraffe', Jack Charlton, but, overall, at Forest, I was happy to assume the responsibility for taking the player off the line, and the ploy worked well because every Forest player did his job.

In John Robertson, Forest possessed a speedy winger who was a superb crosser of the ball. When we broke from a corner we often caught opponents on the hop. John's speed and ability to deliver pinpoint crosses resulted in many a goal. My scrapbook contains numerous match reports of how, having soaked up pressure from an opposing team, we won possession of the ball from a corner and swiftly switched the play to the opposite end of the pitch before delivering a killer blow.

If winning the First Division championship in 1977–78 had come as a surprise to most people, what Nottingham Forest went on to achieve in the following season must have defied the belief of many.

Brian Clough set out to win every game, irrespective of its status. Even friendlies were keenly contested and Clough would field his strongest side. We were hopeful of retaining the title while contesting both the FA and League Cups, and having won the championship, we had also qualified for the European Cup. Not at any time did anyone at Forest think we were spreading ourselves too thinly. Clough and Taylor spurred us on to make a real go of winning everything. I can't say any particular competition was given priority over another. We embarked upon the 1978–79 season hell bent on winning every competition we entered.

That said, I think Clough's greatest desire was to retain the championship. In Cup competitions, a little bit of inspiration, or luck, can tilt the balance in your favour but that doesn't happen over forty-two league matches. The league programme is tough and demanding. In the course of a season you have to overcome every sort of difficulty, all manner of problems. To Clough, winning the League championship carried real status, proof that his team possessed genuine character and could display endurance and application over a long period of time. Sir Stanley Matthews once said, 'For a team to win any cup, it needs to have a little luck.' No team wins the championship with luck – it simply can't be sustained through an entire season.

Most clubs who had won the title and the League Cup in a single season would settle for maintaining standards at that level the following season but for Clough and Taylor, life without progress was just not acceptable. It was a hallmark of the Forest team that we were not only able to remain a power in English football but took our talents into Europe with great success. I think Clough and Taylor saw entry into Europe as another yardstick by which they and the Forest team could be judged. They were both very forthright and outspoken and some members of the media were very wary, if not downright afraid, of them. If Forest had failed miserably in Europe, I think one or two press people would have seen that as a way of getting back at Brian and Peter.

Forest could not have asked for a more attractive start to the 1978–79 season. We set out to defend our title against newly promoted Tottenham Hotspur. The fixture attracted a lot of national interest. People were keen to see if we could pick up where we had left off and continue the unbeaten run and glamorous Spurs had the added attraction of two Argentinian internationals in their team.

During the close season, Spurs' manager, Keith Burkinshaw, had completed a sensational double transfer swoop for Argentine World Cup stars Ossie Ardiles and Ricardo Villa. The pair joined Spurs for a joint fee of £750,000 and their arrival marked an important breakthrough for English football. They were the first overseas players to make a serious impression on the English game. At the time, a lot of people wondered if the pair could adapt to our fast and physical style of football. I thought they would because they were quality players, and quality players can play anywhere in the world.

In the event, Ardiles and Villa both adapted well and their success paved the way for English clubs to sign more overseas players, who, it was believed, would simply be absorbed into the culture of our game. In the case of Ardiles and Villa, I think this was largely true. In addition to their skill and technique, Ardiles and Villa had novelty value. People were curious to see how they coped with the hurly-burly of the First Division but when more and more overseas players arrived, the novelty value of seeing foreign players in English football disappeared. Something else also changed. The increasing number of overseas players and coaches who have come to this country in recent times have had a profound effect, to the extent that our game to a degree has been absorbed into overseas football culture.

The prime example of this is Arsène Wenger. When Wenger arrived at Highbury in 1996, he changed the training methods, the players' diet and general lifestyle and placed a total ban on alcohol. It was revolutionary and when Arsenal won the League and Cup double in 1997–98, his methods were vindicated and adopted at numerous other clubs.

In 1978 I could never have predicted the effect overseas players would have on English football although Ardiles and Villa made their presence felt on the opening day of the season. Such was the interest in the game, the gates of the City Ground were closed twenty minutes before kick-off. A capacity crowd of 41,223 saw Martin O'Neill put us ahead only for Villa to crown his debut with an equalising goal for Spurs. I felt disappointed Forest had not started the season with a home victory, but Spurs deserved the draw and our unbeaten run was still intact.

With only one league match played Forest sold striker Peter

Withe to Newcastle United. If I had one reservation about Forest as a team, it was that we didn't score enough goals. With Peter Withe gone I could foresee that problem becoming more pronounced and so it proved. Our next three matches, against Coventry, QPR and Oldham, the last in the League Cup, were all away from home and each game ended scoreless.

One of the reasons for our inability to score the goals our play deserved was that players were being marked a lot tighter than they had been in the previous season. Opposing defenders were wise to us this time whereas previously our organisation and work rate had taken teams by surprise and we had been able to overrun them. Our goals had been spread around the side. With players being more tightly marked and opposing teams counteracting our work ethic, goals were hard to come by.

Clough and Taylor came up with an answer to our goal drought – Garry Birtles, whom they signed from non-league Long Eaton for £2,000. Having attempted to fill the void left by the departure of Peter Withe, Clough and Taylor had given young Stephen Elliott his chance in the first team. Stephen made a good contribution but the goals didn't come. Garry Birtles made an immediate impact, especially in our first taste of European Cup football.

English football had the novelty at the time of having two teams in the European Cup. Forest qualified as League champions and Liverpool by virtue of being the holders – they had beaten FC Bruges in the previous season's final. Hopes that the chances of an English team reaching the final had been doubled were dashed when Forest and Liverpool were drawn together in the very first round.

On a sultry September night at the City Ground, another capacity crowd saw Nottingham Forest make their European Cup entry in some style. Liverpool had steam-rollered virtually all opposition in their league matches while we were unbeaten but dogged by our inability to score enough goals. I always liked the big-match atmosphere. The bigger the occasion, the more I liked it. The tension in the air seemed to sharpen my brain and there was plenty of tension in the City Ground that night.

We more than matched Liverpool in every department. When Tony Woodcock made a penetrating run into the Liverpool half of the field before setting up Garry Birtles for the opening goal, I sensed Liverpool knew they had problems. They tried to slow down the tempo of the game and keep possession of the ball. I suppose they would have been content to lose by a single goal, believing they could turn around that deficit at Anfield in the second leg.

What was significant about our performance that night was our work off the ball. Over the course of ninety minutes even the busiest of midfield players will have the ball at his feet for three minutes, if that. So even the players who are dictating the play will spend something like eighty-seven minutes without the ball. In many respects, what a player does off the ball is as important as what he does when he has it. We harried and harassed Liverpool when they were in possession, and when their players did create a little space, they found the avenue for a pass denied them and team-mates tightly marked.

We were playing so well I felt we were always in with a chance of extending our lead. The second goal came when Colin Barrett won two tackles just inside our half of the field and released Garry Birtles on the left wing. Garry beat Phil Thompson and his subsequent cross was nodded down by Tony Woodcock into Colin's path. Colin had made up all the ground from inside our half and he volleyed the ball past Ray Clemence. That goal was vitally important, as there were only minutes left. We all realised it was crucial to our chances of qualifying and it served to instil greater confidence throughout the team. There was an edge to our play and at 2–0 our performance became more assured.

Clough and Taylor had surprised a lot of people in opting for Garry to lead the attack against Liverpool rather than John O'Hare or Stephen Elliott. Garry was unknown but his performance on the night justified their decision. Clough and Taylor had every faith in him and he didn't let anyone down, far from it. The following morning, Garry's name was in the headlines. Clough had unearthed another gem – a rough diamond that needed to be polished and honed but no less a gem for that.

Despite that terrific performance, many people, managers included, doubted our ability to go to Anfield and get a result. Public opinion may have favoured Liverpool but we were quietly confident and I thought we had a good chance of progressing as long as we kept our concentration for the full ninety minutes. Although still only September, the press dubbed the match 'the game of the season'.

I think Clough and Taylor detected some nerves among the players as our team bus travelled to Liverpool. To counteract this, they produced yet another unconventional technique of management. As our coach approached Liverpool, Clough stood up and asked, 'Does anyone fancy a beer?' Several players did, though I declined. When we arrived at our hotel and sat down to lunch, Clough asked, 'Does anyone fancy a glass of wine?' The offer was taken up by one or two players. Drinking alcohol before a game is anathema to many coaches and managers today but Clough and Taylor believed a social drink would prevent minds dwelling too much on the task ahead and serve to ease tension and nerves. Those who wanted a bottle of beer or a glass of wine had one. We would be getting some rest at our hotel in the afternoon and I suppose Clough thought one drink would help players get the sleep they needed.

Liverpool's physical commitment was total on the night. They laid siege but we never wavered. Frank Clark came in for Colin

Barrett, who was injured, and did a great job for us. He typified our composure under pressure and, even though he suffered a badly gashed shin, battled on to the end. I did my best to ensure we were concentrating at all times. I was determined in everything I did, hoping my confidence would rub off on my team-mates.

As the game progressed, Liverpool's frustration got the better of them and there were some niggly moments. To our credit, no one retaliated. Towards the end of the game, Kenny Burns was bringing the ball out of defence and just as he played the pass, Kenny Dalglish caught him with a late tackle. I'd known a time when Kenny Burns would have come back at that and some, but he simply eyeballed Dalglish and raised a finger as if to indicate 'no more'. There was no more. Kenny Burns' reaction to that late tackle was indicative of the composure and restraint displayed by the whole team, and was proof of what a different player he had become under Clough and Taylor.

Anfield was buzzing as only Anfield can when Liverpool are on the attack, but we had done our homework on them and soaked up all the pressure. I was very busy – I was very pleased with a couple of saves I made from Kenny Dalglish – but as the clock ticked away Liverpool's frustration turned at times to panic. I was never intimidated by atmosphere, which was just as well because the atmosphere was electric at Anfield that night. Try as they might, Liverpool could not find a way through. The game ended goalless and Forest were through 2–0 on aggregate.

To have played Liverpool twice and not conceded a goal was an achievement. At Anfield we did a superb containment job, and in a manner of which Liverpool would have been proud. Arguably, we knocked the best team in the competition out of the European Cup. I don't think the Liverpool players believed we were a better side than them but we had stood firm and proved ourselves worthy of the result.

From then on, our European adventure gained momentum. In the second round we accounted for AEK Athens and in the quarter-finals we produced a convincing 4–1 first-leg victory over Grass-hoppers of Zurich. A 1–1 draw in Switzerland ensured our place in the semi-finals against Cologne.

The first leg at the City Ground ended 3–3. Cologne were a very good side and stunned our fans into silence by cashing in on a rare irresponsible defensive performance on our part. For neu-trals, the game must have been a cracker to watch. Cologne sac-rificed their defensive strength and opted for attack. It was very rare for teams playing away from home in Europe to do that and it caught us out.

They hit us from the start and goals from Van Gool and Muller gave them an early two-goal advantage. For a time we were reeling. Then a header from Garry Birtles brought us back into the game. Ian Bowyer levelled and the ground erupted when John Robertson put us in front with a terrific diving header. It appeared that our comeback was complete. Cologne, however, wouldn't lie down. Towards the end, Cologne coach Hennes Weisweiller made a substitution, bringing on Yasuhiko Okudera, the only Japanese footballer playing top-class football in Europe. Okudera had been on the pitch for a minute only when he started and finished a move that gave Cologne their equaliser. The following day's newspapers were in no doubt. 'Forest's European Hopes Sunk By Japanese Sub' read one headline.

It was my mistake that gave them the late equaliser and I was gutted after the game. Brian Clough did his best to boost my spirits and at no time did he blame me. Some managers would have used my error to explain away the disappointing result but not Clough. When asked about it in the press conference he ignored the ques-tion and simply replied, 'We will win in Cologne.'

The common belief was that we had blown our chance of

making the final. In the event of a draw, away goals counted double, so a 0–0 or 2–2 result would not be good enough to take us through. We really had to win, or draw 3–3 at least. Few people outside Nottingham thought we could do it but we were confident of achieving a result that would put an end to the lingering doubts about our ability to compete at the highest level in Europe. I'd like to think that Brian Clough believed in my ability to keep a clean sheet because before the away leg he told us, 'All we need is one goal. That's all. One goal will see us through.'

In the interval, Clough and Taylor signed Trevor Francis from Birmingham City, Britain's first £1 million player. Trevor arrived in a blaze of publicity but he was not eligible to play in Cologne, so he had to sit out the match in the stand in his civvies.

Clough got his wish. Having soaked up early pressure, our display gradually gathered momentum and in the sixty-fifth minute we scored what proved to be a priceless goal. John Robertson took an in-swinging corner from the left and Garry Birtles, who had taken up a position at the near post, flicked it on. Cologne were wrong-footed and Ian Bowyer headed the ball into the net despite the desperate efforts of a defender to clear his lines. I jumped with joy on seeing the ball go into the net. We were ahead and I was determined we would stay in front.

In the dying minutes, Harald Konopka hit a dipping drive towards my goal, which swerved at the last moment. I was watching the ball like a hawk and I flung myself full length towards the top corner of my goal and managed to knock it away. Given what had happened in the first leg, that save gave me a great sense of relief.

The heads of the Cologne players went down and you could see they believed their last chance had gone. I shouted to my team-mates to 'keep it going' while making a calming motion with my right hand to indicate that everything was under control and no one should do anything rash.

A minute or so later the final whistle blew. Some people ran on to the pitch, to coin a phrase. They were simply celebrating our victory and I was astonished to see Forest director Fred Reacher among them. Fred ran up to me and gave me a big hug, repeating, 'Yes, yes, well done.' I'll never forget the joy and happiness Fred Reacher displayed that night. It made me realise just what our victory meant to the club and the good people of Nottingham.

Our win in Cologne was possibly the best performance by an English team abroad up until then. Yet again we had proved our doubters wrong. We had never wavered from our belief that we could beat a Cologne side studded with German internationals. Before the game, Peter Taylor had told a press conference, 'We aren't here to lay down and die.' That was never the case. After the game, a football writer from *Der Telegraf*, who prided himself on his knowledge of European players, said to me, 'Out of your entire team, your name is the only one that is familiar to me.'

'Well, you'll know us all now,' I told him.

I felt Nottingham Forest had proved a point. We had been worthy winners against Cologne. True, we were not at that time a team of internationals but we had beaten two teams who many believed were the best in the competition. Our victory over Liverpool was something of a benchmark. Even though we were League champions there were those who saw our success of the previous season as a one-off. The general opinion was that once teams had sussed out our style of play, all would revert to the status quo with Liverpool, Everton, Manchester United and Arsenal dominating domestic football. Our success in the European Cup, particularly against Liverpool and Cologne, established Forest as a force not only in domestic football, but in Europe.

Our preparations for the European Cup final were typically Clough and Taylor – professional, thorough and everything low key. From the neutral point of view, I suppose the final in Munich was not a glamour tie. Juventus, Real Madrid, Porto, Monaco and PSV Eindhoven had fallen by the way along with Liverpool and Cologne. In the final, Forest were pitted against Swedish champions Malmo, a team coached by Englishman Bobby Houghton, who one newspaper described as being 'not even a household name in his own house'.

When our party left East Midlands airport on the Monday before the final there was much press speculation about the team Clough and Taylor would field. Archie Gemmill and Martin O'Neill were key members of the team but both had been suffering from injury. There was also a doubt about Frank Clark. The injured trio all trained on the Monday and Tuesday afternoons and I think they all believed they had a genuine chance of making the starting lineup. However, when Clough and Taylor made their decision on the morning of the match after taking a long look at the Munich pitch, only Frank Clark was picked to play.

Archie and Martin were very honest professionals. I had learned when playing for Leicester Schoolboys that you can get through a game with an injury, but not with an illness, and Archie and Martin must have believed they could carry their respective injuries through ninety minutes. Being the European Cup final, their adrenalin would probably have got them through the match. As the old football saying goes, 'Nothing hurts when you are winning games.' Both players were influential figures in our midfield but Clough and Taylor were simply not prepared to risk either of them in what was the most important game in the history of the club. The pair had to be content with places on the bench. With Frank Clark fit, Ian Bowyer, whom Clough had earmarked for left-back, was given a place in midfield where he was to link with John McGovern and Trevor Francis.

The Olympic Stadium in Munich was filled to its 80,000 capacity and provided an awesome setting for our 'game of games'.

Characteristically, Clough and Taylor had instructed us not to be reckless when going forward. Malmo had not set Europe alight with their attacking play. They tended to soak up pressure and hit opponents on the break. Given the cautious approach of both teams, the opening exchanges did not produce scintillating football. We played cat and mouse with one another for twenty minutes or so before we began to seize the initiative, firing a salvo past the Malmo goal. They were the ones presented with a real chance, however, when an uncharacteristic mistake by Kenny Burns let in Jan Olaf Kindvall. Kenny read a through ball played from the Malmo midfield but in heading it back to me, he didn't apply enough weight to it. Kindvall nipped in between us and had a straightforward opportunity to lob me as I was out of my goal. To my great relief he seemed to freeze and put the ball straight into my hands. It was a huge let off.

As the first half progressed, we became more adventurous. I felt we had the mark of Malmo now. They were a dangerous side on the break but, with our work rate, their opportunities to counterattack had been rare. With the clock ticking towards half-time, it was Forest who struck.

Ian Bowyer released John Robertson and although there didn't appear to be anything on, John took off down the left wing. Two defenders attempted to close him down but John shimmied one way then the other to create the space for a cross. He produced a beauty. Trevor Francis had made ground fast from deep in our half and he arrived at the far post just in time to head the ball home.

I didn't believe Malmo were capable of producing an equaliser let alone scoring against us twice. We could have added to our lead but, in the end, that single goal from Trevor Francis was enough. Nottingham Forest were European champions. It was the third successive season in which an English team had won the

European Cup, Liverpool having won the trophy in 1977 and 1978.

We had not produced the fluid football of which we were capable but it mattered not one iota. It would have been different if we had scored a second goal. At 0–1 Malmo were content to soak up pressure still hoping to catch us on the break. If we had managed to score again, they would have had to come at us and a more open and expansive game would have developed. It certainly would have been more enjoyable from my point of view.

It had not been the best game to play in, or watch. With not much to do, I felt somewhat detached from it all. I was nevertheless elated, happy, excited and very proud of what we had achieved. Some people had raised eyebrows when I had opted to join Nottingham Forest from Stoke. A number of newspapers felt I would have been better off at Manchester United or Arsenal. When you make a career choice you never know for sure if it will turn out to be the right one. With the European Cup won, my decision to join Brian Clough and Nottingham Forest was vindicated. It turned out to be the best career decision I had ever made. I believed we were worthy successors to Liverpool. What Nottingham Forest had achieved in two years since stepping up from the Second Division was nothing less than remarkable. Even now, it almost takes my breath away to think of what we did in such a short period of time.

Our victory over Malmo was our seventy-sixth game of the season. The European Cup final had come fast off the back of our last two league matches of the season against Leeds United and West Bromwich Albion. Those had been gruelling games at the end of what had been a long, hard season. Liverpool had won the championship with some two weeks to spare. They had led the table from day one and never relinquished their hold, losing four matches only and using just fifteen players. Clough and Taylor dearly wanted us to retain the championship but when that became a mathematical impossibility, they urged us on to finish as runners-up. It was typical of them. They never settled for second best but if second best was all that was possible, that's what they aimed for, never allowing standards to drop or their disappointment to get in the way.

There was another incentive for us to finish as runners-up. The previous season when we had won the title, there had been no provision in the players' contracts for bonuses should we win the championship because no one expected it to happen. So to make up for it, for this season Clough and Taylor had negotiated for the players to receive £1,000 a point above a certain number and we had passed the points total. Forest were already assured of the runners-up spot when we met West Bromwich Albion, but the way the deal worked, if we beat Albion, every player would receive a bonus in the region of £2,000 for the game and £8,000 in total. The game was academic and the West Brom players took the field believing they were in for an end-of-season workout but we went at them like mad from the first whistle. They must have been bewildered about why we were treating the game like a Cup final. Needless to say, we all received the bonus!

Forest's success in the European Cup tended to overshadow our success in the League Cup. That's understandable but for me beating Southampton, captained by my old pal Alan Ball, in the League Cup final at Wembley was a memorable occasion. As a boy, I had watched Leicester City lose two FA Cup finals at Wembley. The first, against Spurs in 1961, I had watched on TV, but I was at Wembley when Manchester United defeated Leicester two years later. I had played in the Leicester team that lost to Manchester City in the 1969 FA Cup final. Finally to savour victory in a Cup final at Wembley laid a few ghosts to rest.

Three days before our appearance at Wembley, we beat Norwich City in the League, and the final itself was sandwiched between

European games against Grasshoppers of Zurich. Two days after winning the League Cup, Forest were in action in the League. We won every game and still found time to celebrate our success at Wembley – and managers today talk about heavy fixture lists!

Throughout the season, we used just twenty players. One of those was Peter Withe, who played in the opening game before being transferred to Newcastle. Of the other nineteen, Bryn Gunn also played just one game, so in essence the burden of the season was carried by eighteen players. John Robertson and I were the two ever presents. It is amazing to think that over the course of seventy-six games we used so few players. Liverpool's statistic of using fifteen players throughout the season was even more remarkable. Given the number of options for substitutes nowadays, a club will call on more than fifteen players for a single game! Liverpool and Forest, however, were not unique in utilising the services of so few players. West Bromwich Albion called upon sixteen players that season, Bolton eighteen and both Southampton and Leeds nineteen. Given that the league programme alone consisted of forty-two matches, I find those statistics amazing now.

The reasons for clubs using so few players in the course of a season were, in the main, threefold. Every club had a first-team squad but managers picked what they believed was the best eleven, rarely operating a policy of 'horses for courses'. A player was expected to play well irrespective of the opposition, the player he would be up against or the condition of the pitch. Changes to the team were the result either of injury or loss of form. There was no squad rotation. No manager ever rested players believing they had played too many games.

As for the players themselves, I don't think I ever came across anyone who complained of playing too many matches. Given the choice of training or playing in a game, everyone I knew preferred to be playing. The number of games there were to be played was an indication of how successful a season a team was having. It wasn't unusual for players to carry injuries because they were fearful of losing their place in the team. If a player missed a match and the team was successful without him, he might fall foul of that other old adage of football, 'never change a winning team'.

Some players were helped to play when injured by having cortisone injections. These are frowned upon nowadays but were commonplace in the seventies and eighties. The cortisone injection didn't cure an injury but masked the pain. In many respects, it did more harm than good. Apart from the alleged side-effects, a player could do lasting damage to tissue by playing with an injury he didn't feel for ninety minutes.

The plus side of using fewer players than today was that it did a lot for team spirit. Players got to know one another's style really well and, arguably, this fostered a greater level of understanding out there on the pitch. Certainly in the case of Nottingham Forest I got to know the various strengths and weaknesses of my teammates. I was aware of their ways of reading situations and could adjust my play accordingly. The same applied to every member of that Forest team. Take Trevor Francis' winning goal against Malmo, for example. When John Robertson set off on his run down the left wing, Trevor was in our half of the field. When John crossed the ball to a point just beyond the far post, Trevor had sprinted fifty yards to be on the end of that cross. The final may have been Trevor's first game in Europe for Forest but in the four months he had spent with the club he had made the effort to familiarise himself not only with the way we did things as a team, but also with the individual characteristics and styles of play of his team-mates. Such familiarity played no small part in us winning the European Cup.

Trevor and I played for England but unlike Liverpool, Cologne, Juventus or Real Madrid, Forest were not a side that was thought of as star-studded. Some of our players may not have won a place at Liverpool or Arsenal but we worked for and complemented one another. We gelled. Brian Clough's Nottingham Forest were a team in every sense of the word.

6

A TRIUMPH OF CONSISTENCY

Our remarkable unbeaten run of forty-two games eventually came to an end at Anfield on 9 December 1979, where we lost 2–0. We had created a new English League record for consecutive unbeaten matches.

Brian Clough continued to make headlines, probably because just about everything he said was eminently quotable. Before the 1979–80 season got under way Clough caused a stir when, speaking of the European Cup final, he said in an interview, 'No way would Trevor Francis have played if the others [Archie Gemmill and Martin O'Neill] had been fully fit.' For a manager to say such a thing about the player for whom he had paid a British record transfer fee and who had scored the goal that had won his club the European Cup was unusual to say the least but it was typical Clough. He was being honest. Most managers shy away from saying such things in case the player takes umbrage. Managers don't want an unhappy player on their hands. That sort of thing never bothered Clough. He didn't believe in treating players with kid gloves. If a player was upset by anything Clough said about him, Clough would simply tell the player in question to have some backbone and stop being an 'old woman'.

No one received special treatment or privileges. There were no stars. On and off the pitch we all mucked in and helped one another. Anyone who even hinted that he might have ideas above his station was quickly brought into line by Clough and Taylor, irrespective of how minor the indiscretion was perceived to be.

After training or a game, all the players took either a bath or a shower using club towels and soap. With constant use and washing, the towels had become rough and thin, and the soap was not the sort you would use in your own bathroom. It was unperfumed of the standard variety and reminded me of the blocks of Sunlight soap I would sometimes see on the shelves of my dad's grocery shop. Nobody gave a thought to the soap and towels. They got you clean and dry so they served their purpose.

When Trevor Francis arrived, he used the club's soap and towel on his first day, and on his second day he brought in his own from home. Clough made an issue of it. He saw it as a sign that Trevor was not prepared to muck in with the rest of the lads and that he didn't think what was on offer was good enough. I'm sure that, as far as Trevor was concerned, it was simply a matter of personal preference and it never occurred to him that bringing in his own soap and towel would be seen as a sign that he was not fitting in at the club. Most managers would consider it irrelevant but Clough took Trevor to task and berated him for his action. Small details were important to Clough. He seized upon a very minor incident because he wanted to preserve the status quo in the dressing room. Trevor was Britain's most expensive signing but Clough didn't want that to go to his head. He wanted Trevor to fit in at the club as everyone else had done. He saw Trevor bringing in his own soap and towel as an affront to his utilitarian approach whereby every player was treated the same and accepted what was on offer, which helped foster the 'all for one and one for all' attitude that was prevalent throughout the club.

The dressing-room atmosphere at Nottingham Forest was one of the best I ever experienced. If a manager is not careful, in a dressing room laden with testosterone, an unhealthy hierarchy can develop. A ringleader will emerge who is louder than anyone else and who can damage fragile egos with crushing one-liners. In such a situation, a tribal law develops, dictated by the ringleader and his cohorts and based on pranks, challenges and forfeits. Get on the wrong side of the ringleader and his mates and a player can find himself alienated. New, young players, and those of a quiet disposition, can fall prey to the ringleader's appetite for mickey taking, or worse. I never experienced such an unhealthy atmosphere in the Nottingham Forest dressing room. Clough and Taylor had created a great environment. As in the case of Trevor Francis' soap and towel, they were quick to seize on even the slightest incident that they felt was not in keeping with the atmosphere that existed.

That's not to say there was no mickey taking or pranks at Forest. There were plenty of both but always within the limits of acceptable behaviour. We laughed with each other but not at each other. I remember once leaving the training ground and thinking my kitbag was heavy. Glancing back, I noticed some of my team-mates doubled up with laughter and thought to myself, 'Aye, aye, what have they done?' When I opened the bag I discovered they had put two small training weights in the bottom of it. I saw the joke and laughed, too. You have to. On the odd occasion, I would indulge in a bit of horseplay as well. No one's feelings were ever hurt because everyone knew where to draw the line between what was acceptable and what wasn't.

Forest had no training ground, so we used a nearby public park. Every morning we would run from the City Ground along by the River Trent to the park. In spring and summer, tall nettles would be growing alongside the area we used as our training pitch. I remember as part of our warm-up, if results were going well, Clough would make us run through the tall grass and nettles, round a tree and back to him. The players didn't relish running through nettles but I think this was Clough's way of keeping 'our feet on the ground' and not letting a sequence of good results go to our heads.

When Forest entertained Barcelona in the European Super Cup, the Spanish club asked to use our training facilities, which of course meant the public park. We trained first and the end of our session coincided with the arrival of the Barcelona players in their team coach. I can readily recall the incredulous looks on their faces as they surveyed the scene. It was obvious that training in a public park was not to their liking. We chortled as we watched them gingerly tiptoeing their way through the nettles. I don't speak much Spanish but from the expressions on their faces I gauged that their conversation reflected their bewilderment that a team who had won the European Cup trained in a public park watched by people walking their dogs. Barcelona were defeated before the game started.

The one no-go area for players at Forest was the treatment room. At some clubs the treatment room was little more than a meeting place for gossip. Players who were fit called in for a massage and in some cases it was a haven for malingerers. At Forest, no player was allowed inside the treatment room unless he was genuinely injured and needed treatment. That rule was strictly imposed.

The policy was very different from what I had experienced in my early days at Leicester City. Given the longevity of my career, I was lucky regarding injuries but on one occasion when I did pick up an injury that required attention, I turned up at the treatment room only to be told that it was occupied. Having hung about outside for some time, I decided to go in to see who needed such lengthy treatment and, much to my surprise, there on the table was the comedian Norman Wisdom. Norman was appearing in a show at a local theatre and had injured himself while performing one of his comic falls. The club were only too happy to offer him treatment. As a young lad it was great to meet Norman Wisdom and I didn't mind waiting then. How times have changed. Can you imagine a Premier League club giving preference to a comedy actor? No, neither can I.

There was disappointment on the domestic scene in 1979–80 but more glory in Europe. Midway through the season, Liverpool opened up a substantial lead at the top of the table that, ultimately, provided insurance against a late challenge from Manchester United. We finished in fifth place, respectable enough on the face of it but given our previous successes, disappointing for everyone at the club. We had to cope with the loss of Trevor Francis, with a broken leg, but there were no excuses. Liverpool were worthy champions.

Forest actually won more home games than Liverpool but our away form cost us dear – four victories and four draws. Our final tally of thirteen defeats away from home was more than that of Bristol City who were relegated. Having developed into a team that were very difficult to break down, let alone defeat, our poor form away from home puzzled many people. In sharp contrast to our away record, Forest lost just once at home in the entire season.

Brian Clough and Peter Taylor were meticulous with new signings. Before making an offer they would look into the player's background to satisfy themselves that he had a lifestyle and character that met with their approval. Nevertheless, some of their major signings were not as successful as they hoped.

One player who never really settled at Nottingham Forest was Asa Hartford. Asa was a busy and stylish midfield player who signed for Forest in 1980 but left after sixty-three days, joining Everton for £400,000. I don't think our style of play suited Asa and he couldn't adapt. On the day Asa left, Peter Taylor told the press, 'Asa is one hell of a player but Forest are too big to change their play pattern for one player.'

Clough and Taylor wanted to strengthen the team and in the summer of 1979 Frank Gray joined from Leeds United, followed by Stan Bowles from QPR. We began the season well and, come November, when Tony Woodcock left to join Cologne, Forest headed the table but that poor form away from home cost us pole position in the New Year. The reason for it, far from being down to one single thing, was the result of a number of things happening simultaneously.

Trevor Francis played thirty games before breaking his leg but never hit a rich vein of form as a striker, and played the majority of those games on the right-hand side of midfield. He ended the season as Forest's leading goalscorer but his tally of fourteen was one of the lowest among the League's leading goalscorers. We were still sharing goals throughout the team but not in the numbers we had achieved in the previous two seasons. We lacked a twenty-five-goal-a-season striker. Our inability to score sufficient goals away from home – just nineteen throughout the season – cost us points.

In January and February, bad weather swept across Britain. In mid-January twenty-five games were postponed; a fortnight later, over thirty games were cancelled. The freeze lasted for near enough a month and caused a backlog of fixtures. Teams who were not heavily committed to Cup competitions coped better than those who were. Although Forest exited from the FA Cup in the fourth round, we were still in contention for the European, League and European Super Cups. Our involvement in three major Cup competitions, two of which involved overseas travel, took its toll when it came to catching up on league matches. Our play began to lack its usual edge and at times we looked a little jaded.

Peter Taylor may have inadvertently hit the nail on the head when he said Forest were too big to change their game for one player. Perhaps we had become too predictable.

Off the pitch, a number of players were involved in lengthy negotiations over new contracts. I don't think this really affected our performance on the pitch – it didn't affect me – but it may have had an unsettling effect on some. It was reported that I had signed a contract at Forest that would pay me £1,200 a week, making me one of the highest-paid players in Britain. I was certainly given a very good contract but I felt I had earned it. So did Clough and Taylor. In actual fact, I signed away a fair amount of money to stay at Forest. I could have earned considerably more if I had joined one of several top European clubs.

A few eyebrows were raised about my reported wages at Forest. Of course, I was aware that I was now earning far in excess of the average working person. However, my wage was nowhere near that of top players in Europe, such as Johan Cruyff and Mario Kempes; nor was it anywhere near Kevin Keegan's at Hamburg, who, word had it, earned twice as much as me. Tony Woodcock was also reportedly earning more than me at Cologne. It struck me as odd that some people in this country could criticise what I was reportedly being paid at Forest, yet at the same time be pleased that European clubs thought so highly of Kevin, Tony and others. Certain newspapers made much of the fact that Kevin and Tony were highly paid, seeing it as a benchmark of their quality as players. Yet the same papers would make a hell of a fuss about the wages of players such as me, who were being paid much less. The way I saw it, Forest were European champions and that meant we were at least the equal of the best in Europe but wages at top clubs in England were at nowhere near the level of the top continental clubs.

The double standards bugged me and once the news, if not the details, of my new contract became public, I got fed up defending it. Football is our national sport. It attracts big crowds. I had played my part in the success of Nottingham Forest who, through our success in Europe, had brought success to English football. I was earning roughly half of what a British tennis player who had never won a major tournament was earning. I don't begrudge a penny of what any sportsperson earns, but I found it hard to understand why footballers came in for criticism.

It got to the point where everyone connected with Forest benefited financially from our success. Brian Clough and Peter Taylor were awarded a joint testimonial match against Derby County, and backroom staff received bonuses. But to the best of my knowledge, the club never paid anyone anything it could not afford.

Our run in the League Cup took us to another Wembley final, where we met Wolves. We were after a hat-trick of League Cups and we should have won it but an awful mix-up led to Andy Gray scoring the only goal of the game for Wolves. The Football League introduced a brand-new type of ball for the final. Now you may well question the wisdom of introducing a new type of ball in a Cup final at Wembley and you would be right to do so. The *Daily Mail* described the match as 'a disappointing game littered with uncharacteristic errors from both sets of players'. I was of the mind that the errors were caused by the new ball and I don't think I was alone in this view. It was much lighter than the type we were all used to. Players found it difficult to weight passes correctly and the ball's tendency to bounce higher than the standard type made control difficult at times. The unpredictable flight also led to the Wolves goal.

Wolves' Peter Daniel played a long cross into my penalty area. I gauged it was going to carry through to me but it seemed to dip then suddenly drop short. David Needham and I were both thrown by this. Having expected to head the ball clear David had to rapidly adjust. I too had to adjust, and we clashed. As we staggered apart, we saw Andy Gray tapping the ball into the empty net. I had to blame myself. I never left my line unless I was sure of winning the ball, so if I had any excuse for not collecting the ball it was because it dipped early instead of carrying through, which I can only put down to the unpredictable nature of this new type of ball that had proved problematic to just about every player that day. The ball in question had a short life. It was subsequently withdrawn and never again used in top-flight football.

If the domestic season didn't come up to the standards we set ourselves, in Europe it was a different story. Barcelona were beaten over two legs for Forest to win the European Super Cup for the first time in the history of the club, but the one trophy everyone really wanted to win was the European Cup. Forest's quest to retain it in 1979–80 began with a first-round victory over Osters Vaxjo of Sweden. This was followed by victories over Arges Pitesti of Romania and Dinamo Berlin. In the semi-finals we were pitched against Ajax and Hamburg drew Real Madrid.

The first leg at the City Ground proved to be a very tight game. A goal from Trevor Francis and a penalty from John Robertson gave us a very useful 2–0 victory to take to Amsterdam, though yet again, doubts were expressed whether those two goals would be enough. I never had any doubts. Like my Forest team-mates, I was confident Ajax wouldn't score the three goals they required to progress to the final at our expense.

I had been with Forest for nearly three years and still Clough and Taylor never ceased to surprise me. The night before our return leg in Amsterdam, they summoned the squad together and informed us we were to accompany them on a 'leg stretcher'. Normally, British teams playing abroad would be confined to their hotel. All the players saw of the city was what they could see from the windows of the team coach as it ferried them to and from the stadium. Clough and Taylor, however, always liked the players to see something of the city they were visiting. 'Travel should broaden your horizons, not deaden them,' Clough once told us. In addition to having our 'horizons broadened', our walks also relieved the tedium of sitting about in hotels and provided beneficial leisurely exercise.

Like dutiful schoolboys we had followed Clough and Taylor on countless leg stretchers around the European cities we visited, with the pair pointing out various landmarks and buildings of historical significance. These walks were peppered with Clough's opinions of the cities in question. During a walk around Pitesti in Romania, a town noted for its oil and coal industry, Clough remarked, 'Pitesti is like Middlesbrough, only it hasn't got Middlesbrough's glamour.'

The Amsterdam leg stretcher was different. Clough could be confrontational, sometimes alarmingly so, and that was demonstrated within moments of us leaving our hotel. We had walked a few paces when we became aware of a group of Ajax fans on the other side of the street, seemingly on a night out. The fans, a little the worse for wear drink-wise, recognised us and began to hurl insults in our direction. Clough went over and really took them to task. He told them that when the Ajax team and their supporters had visited Nottingham they had experienced nothing but common courtesies. We were now guests of their city and they should be ashamed of themselves for the language they had used and the insults they had shouted at us. The exchanges became a little heated. I looked at Larry Lloyd and Kenny Burns and the three of us were about to step off the kerb and go to the aid of our manager when Peter Taylor barred our way with an outstretched arm.

'Hold your horses,' Peter told us.

We stood and watched as Clough remonstrated with these Ajax fans and, to my utter amazement, the fans held up their hands, apologised to Clough and quietly went on their way.

I learned something else about Brian Clough from that incident, and Peter Taylor, too. Every other manager I knew would have ignored the insults and told us to carry on walking. Clough was incensed, not only by the insults but by the fact that, to his mind, the fans were letting down their city. Clough could be bombastic but on this occasion he was forthright, making his point without inflaming the situation. Peter Taylor stopped us piling in because he knew Clough better than we did. In fact, no one knew Clough better than Taylor and vice versa.

We'd been walking around Amsterdam for ten minutes when I realised we were entering the area left of Damrak, between Warmoesstraat and Nieuwmarkt. Suddenly we found ourselves in a street lined with shop windows in which sat scantily clad young women, beckoning us to enter. This was Amsterdam's red-light district, known locally as 'Walletjes'.

'It's called Walletjes because this is where the old city walls of Amsterdam used to be,' Peter Taylor informed us. 'Also because you can't walk around here without wanting to get your wallet out.'

As we resumed our walk, Taylor continued to regale us with similar jokes. We came across a window where a young woman of some considerable size was sitting, eating a bun. She must have weighed 22 stone and her bottom and thighs were enormous. To a man, we stared at her voluptuous form in both wonder and amazement.

'I'll tell you what, lad,' said Taylor to Garry Birtles, 'if she were to sit on your face, you wouldn't hear that bloody radio of yours.'

We convulsed with laughter. On our trips abroad, Garry Birtles always took an old radio-cassette player so that he could listen to pop music or keep abreast of the football news on the BBC World Service. For some reason this old radio was a constant source of amusement to Taylor, who ribbed Garry something rotten about it. Yet in spite of Taylor's acerbic wit, Garry insisted on bringing it along, obviously believing it a small price to pay for the pleasure of listening to The Pretenders, The Jam and Dexy's Midnight Runners. Peter Taylor wound up Garry about his radio to test his character. I think he wanted to see if Garry would back down. The fact that Garry always brought along his radio was, I believe, a source of satisfaction to Taylor.

There were instances when Garry did back down when confronted by Clough and Taylor. As the team was about to leave our hotel for the European Cup final against Malmo, Garry arrived in the reception sporting stubble on his chin. This was unusual as Garry was always clean shaven. Clough took one look at him and said, in a very stern voice, 'What's that on your face?'

'A bit of stubble,' Garry replied. 'It's there to make me look mean.' Clough stared at him.

'We are leaving here in five minutes,' he said. 'If you don't shave it off, you're not playing. Get it off!'

I've never seen anyone move so fast. Garry ran back to his room and within a few minutes rejoined us, clean shaven but with his face dotted with little scraps of tissue paper, soaking up the blood from the cuts he had made with his razor.

With the players gaping and gawping at the sights of Amsterdam's red-light district, we eventually arrived at what appeared to be a cross between a striptease bar and a brothel. There were two guys on the door who were built like Coke machines and Peter Taylor engaged them in conversation, trying to negotiate a 'block deal' for entry into this place. Not for one moment did I think he was serious in his intentions, but one or two of the lads were shuffling their feet anxiously. Clough and Taylor were so unconventional, a few of the lads thought they just might be crazy enough to take us inside! Of course, we didn't go in. Taylor's heated negotiations with the two doormen were, like our walk itself, a diversionary tactic to take our minds off the big game ahead.

Along by the Oudezijds Achterburgwal canal we came across a bar that had nothing but alcohol for sale. In we went and Clough informed us that we were allowed two bottles of beer each. We sat down to talk about the sights we had seen and within minutes we were rolling about with laughter, enjoying one another's company and freedom from the tiresome routine of our hotel.

'Here we are, out enjoying a beer the night before a European Cup semi-final,' Martin O'Neill said, looking at his watch. 'It's five past ten, the Ajax players will all be in bed now.'

'Aye,' said Clough, 'but none of them will be getting any sleep!'

Our leg stretcher in Amsterdam is indicative of how football has changed over the years and, more particularly, how the reporting of it has changed. Arsenal, Manchester United or any of the other big clubs couldn't allow players to go for such a walk the night before a European Champions League match, nor can I imagine the players going out for a beer. Alcohol is anathema to managers such as Arsène Wenger. They see the odd lager before, or even after, a game as being detrimental to the life of a professional footballer, and the press are on the shoulders of the players at every opportunity.

In 1980, members of the press were in Amsterdam but they were there to report on our semi-final against Ajax and did not dog our every move. Things were just beginning to change and within two years the situation was much the same as it is today, though not as pronounced, whereby any perceived indiscretion on the part of a player would be seized upon and turned into a highly emotive story. In 1980 the press would make much of such a story if they came across it but the difference was they didn't go looking. Today some national newspapers send a few reporters to a game against foreign opposition. You have to ask the question, if one is there to report on the game, and to provide an overall view of the match, and another to cover news from training sessions, what are the others doing?

I shudder to think what the headlines and fall-out would be today if a team visited a red-light district and called into a bar for a beer on the night before a crucial Champions League game. All hell would break loose and manager and players would be vilified. I didn't think too much of it. On a Friday lunchtime we would have a team talk at Forest and quite often Brian Clough would come in and hand round beers or glasses of wine. I never partook but most people there would have one. Clough's Friday lunchtime drink struck me as a token of respect, indicating that he saw us as responsible professionals. New players attending the talk for the first time would have looks of amazement on their faces when Clough handed the drinks around. Clough's response was to say, 'Hey, young man, get it down you. It's only a glass, but it establishes a more informal spirit. It's how we do things here. It's our way and, given the success we've enjoyed, it can't be wrong.'

Instead of a lecture, those team meetings took on the air of informal discussions, which produced much more in the way of ideas. Sometimes the talk would go off on a tangent and instead of talking about the following day's game, we might end up talking about politics, a television programme or the hobbies and interests of individual players. Whatever we talked about, Clough and Taylor were always in control, happy to act as catalysts to the conversation. They knew it was good for team spirit and togetherness.

These days, alcohol is frowned upon particularly by overseas players. They have grown up in a different football culture. Many continental players think that their preparation for a match is better than that of British players who might enjoy an occasional beer. I was a dedicated professional and I don't necessarily believe their attitude is correct. The occasional beer never did us any harm at Nottingham Forest and we proved it by knocking Ajax out of the European Cup. The whole point of Clough and Taylor taking us into that Amsterdam bar for a drink was to take our minds off the big game ahead and to engender collective spirit.

That was an important aspect of the success we enjoyed as a team. When Forest took the pitch, our spirit and team ethic made us a force to be reckoned with, and our opponents had to work incredibly hard to beat us. You are better prepared for a match when your team spirit is at its zenith. Getting that right is as important as your training. Some Premier League teams have large squads with gifted players but I wonder whether they are able to generate the same cohesive spirit and atmosphere.

Sports scientists, dietitians, sports psychologists and personal trainers have a role to play in the modern game, but perhaps it isn't as important, and certainly not as crucial, as it is made out to be. By comparison, Clough and Taylor and their methods of preparing for a match and playing the game were vital to the success we enjoyed as a team. As Clough once said, 'All for one and one for all. And if you're not prepared to do that – on yer bike!'

I derived a lot of satisfaction from our 2–1 aggregate victory over Ajax. The newspaper reports were positive, especially for the away leg, one going as far as to say I now had the edge over Ray Clemence regarding the England goalkeeper's jersey. England manager Ron Greenwood was in a dilemma. He couldn't decide if Ray or I should be the regular England goalkeeper, so he had taken to playing us in alternate matches.

Obviously, I wanted to be England's regular goalkeeper, as did Ray, and I hoped that good performances for Forest would one day tilt the balance in my favour. All I could do was continue to pull out all the stops when playing for my club. I had had plenty of opportunity to do that against Ajax and even more chances in the European Cup final itself.

Our opponents were Hamburg. The German champions were hot favourites to lift the trophy and the final had the added ingredient of featuring Kevin Keegan in the Hamburg team. This was

Kevin's last game for Hamburg. He was moving to Southampton once the season had ended. Having made his name with Liverpool, Kevin had become arguably an even bigger name in Germany. When he announced that he would be quitting the Bundesliga, it was generally assumed that not even the richest English club would be able to compete with their European counterparts for his services. However, Southampton manager Lawrie McMenemy realised that an EEC regulation of the time stipulated that transfer fees between clubs from EEC countries could not go over £500,000. McMenemy actually persuaded Hamburg to accept a fee of £400,000, while at the same time persuading the Southampton board that the money they would 'save' on the fee could be used to pay Kevin's wages.

The press appeared to be torn between wanting the England captain, who had twice been voted European Footballer of the Year, to enjoy a fitting swansong and wanting an English team to lift the trophy for the fourth consecutive time. Needless to say, no such mixed sentiment existed within the Forest camp.

The final was to take place at the Bernabeu Stadium in Madrid, home of Real Madrid. As part of our preparations, Brian Clough and Peter Taylor took us to their favourite place, the Spanish coastal resort of Cala Millor. We did some light training and played small-sided games, but I was in need of some rigorous ball work. The practice pitch we were using had not one blade of grass and the sun had baked it bone hard. I was concerned that if I dived around on such a rock-hard surface, I might pick up an injury that could affect my chances of playing.

So, following a training session, the Forest trainer, Jimmy Gordon, threw a bag of balls over his shoulder and the two of us set off in search of a suitable grassed area. We walked up and down the seafront, explored the rear of countless hotels but our search was in vain. The land about Cala Millor was barren. We headed back to the team hotel, in front of which was a nice green lawn, but no sooner had Jimmy and I set up shop than the hotel manager appeared, remonstrating with us for using his lawn as a practice pitch.

Peter Taylor told me not to worry. We would soon be moving to a hotel in Arenas De San Pedro, which was a town situated in the hills of Sierra de Gredos, to the north-west of Madrid. He assured me that a pitch near the hotel would allow me all the shot-stopping practice I needed. Happy in this thought, I travelled north with the rest of the Forest squad, but when we got there my heart sank. The football pitch to which Peter had been referring was similar to a hard tennis court. Shot-stopping practice was out of the question unless I wanted an injury.

Again, I voiced my concerns to Brian and Peter, explaining there simply wasn't a suitable grassed area on which to practise.

'Well, you haven't looked hard enough, have you?' said Clough in that nasal voice of his. 'Because we know where there is a grassed area that's perfect for you, Peter me lad.'

Clough retired to the hotel and Jimmy Gordon and I dutifully followed Peter Taylor who led us to the outskirts of the small town. I thought that we must be heading for a local park although I hadn't noticed one when we first arrived.

'There you go,' said Peter. 'There's your grassed area.'

I couldn't believe what Peter was pointing at.

'Give over. You can't be serious,' I said – but he was.

Brian Clough and Peter Taylor never believed in pampering their players and I certainly wasn't an exception. We were standing in front of a traffic roundabout, and on it was a perfect circle of grass. Jimmy and I dodged the cars and climbed on to the roundabout. He put down two tracksuit tops as makeshift goalposts and I set to work. Jimmy fired shot after shot at me and I got the practice essential to my preparation for the European Cup final against a background noise of tooting horns from passing cars.

With Trevor Francis unavailable through injury, Clough and Taylor opted for just one striker, Garry Birtles. The teams lined up as follows:

Nottingham Forest: Peter Shilton, Viv Anderson, Frank Gray, John McGovern, Larry Lloyd, Kenny Burns, Martin O'Neill, Ian Bowyer, Garry Birtles, Gary Mills, John Roberston.

SV Hamburg: Rudi Kargus, Manfred Kaltz, Peter Nogly, Dietmar Jakobs, Ivan Buljan, Holger Hieronymus, Kevin Keegan, Gaspar Nemering, Jurgen Milewski, Felix Magath, Wili Reimann.

Our substitute bench included Jimmy Montgomery (goalkeeper), John O'Hare and Bryn Gunn.

Hamburg were noted for their attacking style and within minutes of the kick-off they took the game to us and we found ourselves on the back foot. The bedrock of our success had been a strong rearguard action and we soaked up pressure while always on the lookout for the opportunity of a swift counter-attack that could result in us nicking a goal. That strategy had paid off so many times, most notably in Cologne the previous season. Out of sheer necessity it was deployed against Hamburg.

Hamburg poured forward and in the first ten minutes I found myself having to produce saves from Keegan, Reimann and Buljan. There was no respite. I would throw the ball out to Viv Anderson or Frank Gray, hoping we would keep possession and gradually advance upfield, but Hamburg were buzzing. They were on to us in a flash, closing us down, forcing us into a mistake so the ball was back with them.

Keegan surged into my penalty box, squared the ball to Magath and I was airborne to palm his drive wide. The resultant corner was driven into the box and Jakobs came from heaven knows where to power the ball goalwards with the meat of his forehead. I found myself in the air again, my back arching as I reached back to tip the ball over the bar. Somewhere far away I heard thousands of voices yell 'Goa-aaawww...'

They won another corner and Larry Lloyd headed the ball clear but only as far as Nogly, who was loitering with intent just outside the penalty area. Nogly drove forwards, jinking along our defensive line, looking for the avenue for a shot. Suddenly, a voice louder than any in the Bernabeu was screaming, 'Don't foul! Don't foul! Close him down! Close him down!' I never knew I could shout that loud. Kenny Burns got a foot on the ball. 'Well done, Kenny. Well...'

Keegan was on to the loose ball and he hit it first time. Down I went, cradling the ball to my chest. I glanced up to see Kevin looking straight at me. He heaved a sigh, gritted his teeth and shook his head. I looked to my right to see if Viv Anderson had run out wide and momentarily glanced back to Kevin. He wasn't there.

The pressure had been incessant for some twenty minutes. Frank Gray, wide on the left, looked a good option. With the ball in my right hand I reached back like some Olympic javelin thrower and hurled the ball to Frank. Frank had a lovely first touch. The ball was under control straightaway and he was off down our left-hand side.

'Keep going, Frank. Keep going.' The pressure was off for the time being. The further Frank took the ball, the longer it would be before it returned. Every stride of his was a godsend and the feeling of temporary relief was wonderful.

Frank found Gary Mills inside him and Gary played the ball back out to our left, to John Robertson. With Jakobs and Buljan on to him, John's body dipped one way then the other. Talk about Houdini! He cut inside and accelerated past Kaltz, who gave chase, tugging at John's shirt. 'Keep going, John. That's it. Go!' He played the ball to Garry Birtles. 'Bugger. He hasn't got anywhere to go.' Garry laid the ball back to John, who had kept going. 'Keep going,

John. Keep going!' I could see he was going to have a go. 'Have a pop, John! Go on!'

It wasn't the best shot I've seen – a low drive that bobbled a few times across the turf – but it went to the left of Kargus. 'Aaah, hit the post, if only. . .it's there! It's there! Bloody hell. Brilliant!'

I leapt up, fists clenched, bounding across my penalty area, shouting, 'Yes! Yes! Yes!' I glanced across to our dugout to see Clough sitting calmly, his arms folded. 'Have we scored?' I thought. 'How the hell can he be so cool and unemotional?'

Taylor was on his feet, punching the air. That was more like it. He clenched his right fist and shouted to Martin O'Neill and Ian Bowyer, then he was on at Larry and Kenny. Clough, on his feet now, shouted to Viv. I was on to everybody – 'Keep it tight now. Concentrate. Concentrate. Tight.'

Hamburg were stung back into action, driving forward again. How many players did they have? We soaked it up, closing them down. 'This is OK. It's been, what, ten or twelve minutes?' They didn't have anybody like Robbo, who was capable of getting round on the outside. 'That's a good ball. Shit!' A shot from Manny Kaltz smacked against my right-hand post. Keegan was on to the rebound but I moved out to him. 'Stay upright, Peter. Upright. Now down!' The ball felt good in my hands.

In the second half, it was nearly all Hamburg. Garry Birtles battled away on his own. John O'Hare came on for Gary Mills to help hold the line. The Hamburg pressure was incessant and he must have been playing from memory. As for O'Neill and Bowyer, they covered so much ground, they had to be breathing through their backsides. Bryn Gunn came on for Frank Gray, who had been limping for five minutes.

Then Milewski was bearing down on my goal. 'Close down his vision.' I went down, heard the ball thud against my chest but then it had gone. 'Where the hell? There! Thank God.' I grasped it like a crucifix. Seventy-six minutes had been played, according to the clock, a lifetime to go.

Nogly had the ball thirty-five yards away and I just knew he was shaping up to have a go. 'My angle's good. He's going to pull the trigger...' I had its measure. 'Piledriver. Swerving.' I fingertipped it over the bar and the Forest fans roared their approval. Funny – I hadn't been aware of the crowd for ages.

It was the longest night of my life. The minutes seemed to grow and multiply. Hamburg were still buzzing. So, too, were we but we were on the back foot. It was no time for the finer things of the game. 'Get rid, Larry. Kenny, get rid. Viv, send it.' We sent the ball upfield and they sent it back as if they hated it. 'That's it, Garry. Take them on. On your own! Keep going! What a trooper!'

Clough was on his feet, arms folded, detached – unlike Taylor, who was bellowing to Martin and Ian. Clough pointed – to whom, to what? To John O'Hare. There was emotion on his face now, I could read it. 'Get in that hole. Deeper. Deeper,' Clough shouted. Then he nodded, folded his arms again and it was back to the impassive look.

The linesmen indicated time. 'We're going to do it. Nothing silly. Lord, please don't let it happen now. After all this.' There was Keegan and I was off my line like a shot for a block save. 'Maybe I'll hold...can't hold it.' The world and his wife descended on the loose ball. 'Let me at it. Keeper's! I'll have it.' Red shirts were everywhere. 'Make contact. Anybody!' Larry Lloyd didn't mess about and the ball fired away like a rocket – row G job. 'That'll do. Look at it go!'

I'd never seen such a beautiful sight as that ball sailing skywards and, as far as I know, it's still going. Referee Antonio Garrido blew a long shrill blast on his whistle and at long last I could take my eyes off the ball. It was all over. 'Yes! Yes! We've done it! We've bloody well done it!' What was I feeling? Ecstasy, happiness, joy –

all those things – but mainly relief. We had retained the European Cup. I had no idea what that really meant. The significance hadn't sunk in. The intoxication of winning the Cup was too much for that. I was flying on adrenalin, on the high of success, the joy of having the intense pressure suddenly rushing out of my body and mind. I wasn't my normal self but I had to go with the moment, be a little crazy, be unlike me. We'd won it. 'Kenny, well done!' 'Larry. Brilliant, Larry.' 'Viv. Bloody hell, tremendous, Viv.' 'Garry. Hey, Garry, tremendous, mate.'

Kevin Keegan came up to me. He was totally gutted. 'Well played, Kev,' I said. Funny how you always find yourself praising the opposition when you've beaten them.

Before the game Peter Taylor was convinced we were going to win, but despite Brain Clough's encouraging words, I detected he may have had a nagging doubt. It was understandable. There was no Trevor Francis and he had to play eighteen-year-old Gary Mills. Considering his youth, Gary had done exceptionally well in the seventy minutes he was on the pitch.

I don't think I had ever played in a match where there had been so much pressure on my goal. I'd done my job, and every member of the team had done theirs. We'd achieved what we set out to do and we had done it honestly. Hamburg had the lion's share of the possession and the game but we had applied ourselves better and gave it our all. We hadn't been lucky. Individually and collectively, we had been very good. We had been forced to defend because we didn't have any option. In the end, the team and our 24,000 travelling supporters had proved too much for Hamburg.

After the presentation we went back to our dressing room but came back out to thank the fans. At that moment they chose to put the lights out in the stadium but absolutely nothing could take away the glow of our victory. It was the most satisfying and memorable night of my career as a club player, and testimony to our ability as a team.

Hamburg undoubtedly possessed more players of true quality and people have often asked me the secret of our success. Our motivation, application, collective spirit, 'never say die' attitude and phenomenal work rate all played a part but, in essence, it was down to Brian Clough and Peter Taylor and the fact that we did things their way.

7

SAINTS PRESERVE US

Things were never quite the same at Forest following our victory over Hamburg. American football has a phrase for a team that is playing at its very best. When every player is at the top of his game and confidence is so sky high they take the field convinced they cannot be beaten, the opposition are so much in awe of them they don't believe they can win the game. When such a situation occurs, the Americans refer to a team as being 'in the zone'.

The Arsenal side of 2003–04 could be said to have been 'in the zone'. So too were Nottingham Forest during our unprecedented run of unbeaten games between 1978 and 1979. Like an old Mississippi gambler who has known better days but can still produce a winning hand in a really big poker game, in 1979–80 Forest rose to the occasion in the European Cup. I don't think it was a case of reserving our best performances for Cup competitions – we couldn't sustain our form in the other Cup competitions over an arduous league season.

The heavy programme of fixtures was beginning to have an effect on players who, in football terms, were getting on in years, such as Frank Clark and Larry Lloyd. We didn't have a great deal of strength in depth. What Forest had was a very productive youth policy, and, as Brian Clough had demonstrated, he wasn't afraid to play youngsters in the first team, even in crucial European Cup matches. Forest had some very talented young players but young players tend to be inconsistent. A seasoned professional will never have a bad game. He may produce a performance that is not up to his usual standard but rarely, if ever, will he have a stinker. Young players will be on fire one game and anonymous the next. Consistency comes with experience. The combination of some of our more experienced players beginning to show their age and the inconsistent form of younger players began to have an effect. Our performances and consequently our results suffered.

Our World Club Championship match against Nacional in Tokyo in 1980 is a case in point. Having played a league match on the Saturday we flew out to Tokyo the following day and arrived on the Monday. We did some light training on the Tuesday, played Nacional on the Wednesday and lost 0–1 to a team that had been in Tokyo for two weeks preparing for this one match. We flew home on the Thursday, arriving in London in the early hours of Friday morning. The following day we played Bristol City in the FA Cup and to say we were jaded is putting it mildly.

Our visit to Tokyo being such a short one, Clough told everyone to stay with British time to combat jet lag. The Japanese must have thought we were mad. We slept during the day and stayed awake all night. We took breakfast when the Japanese were having a drink at night and we had our evening meal when they were getting up for breakfast.

When we ran out to play Bristol City we were not sharp and it showed. With fifteen minutes of the game remaining we were trailing 1–0 but, with a Herculean effort, we managed to snatch two goals and win the tie. What won us that game was not fitness or skill, it was sheer heart. That sort of performance had been the hallmark of the Forest team in my first three years with the club but it was starting to become the exception rather than the rule.

One of our better performances came in a draw against Manchester United. It was a thrilling end-to-end match but I realised I was being called upon to produce more saves than would have been the case a couple of years previously – another little sign that the great Forest side were on the wane. The way we had been playing as a team in 1979, I doubt if United would have had half as many opportunities for shots at goal.

Forest were still up there with the best. We were still capable of producing superb performances but not with the consistency we had shown in 1978 and 1979. When we beat Hamburg to retain the European Cup, it may have been a terrific performance but Forest were out of 'the zone'.

New signings came into the club. Over a period of time, Ian Wallace, Justin Fashanu and Raimondo Ponte arrived. Individually they were good players but the collective atmosphere was not the same. Trevor Francis was sidelined, and my deputy, Chris Woods, eventually left for Queens Park Rangers. In 1980–81 Forest were European champions but I felt our performances that season did not make us the best team in England, never mind Europe.

European champions we may have been but Brian Clough was still at pains to keep everyone's feet on the ground. He always liked to treat everyone the same, from the tea lady to the club chairman. 'We all muck-in at this club,' Clough would say, but now that policy began to irk some players, myself included.

Clough used to hold a weekly press conference to announce the team for the forthcoming game on Saturday and field general questions. On one occasion, Brian asked me to attend. I thought I was there to answer questions but it turned out I was there to serve the press boys with drinks. To be truthful, I wasn't keen on the idea but I went along with it because I wanted to 'muck in'. As I began to hand round the drinks, Brian said, 'Come on, get on with it, Peter. You're not too big to serve drinks at this club.'

I wasn't angry but I was disappointed. Brian's comment was uncalled for. It appeared to me that he had me serving drinks to the press, not to indicate to them that there was an egalitarian policy at the club, but to show them that he was the boss and even England internationals did as he bade. He *was* the boss and every player had the utmost respect for him and his position. I didn't think there was any need for him to emphasise this to the press in the way he did.

My first three years at Forest had been a dream come true. Our success and the way we had achieved it gave me a great deal of satisfaction. I felt I was at the top of my game but in 1980–81, cracks started to appear in our team performances. Forest were not in the running for the title, which was contested by Aston Villa and Ipswich Town. On the final day of the season, Villa were at Arsenal and Ipswich were playing Middlesbrough at Ayresome Park. Villa lost 2–0 but it didn't matter because Ipswich also lost. Villa fans at Highbury received the news of Ipswich's demise via their transistor radios and, when the final whistle sounded, they staged a benign pitch invasion. Villa became known as the 'transistor champions'.

Spurs won the FA Cup following a replay against Manchester City, and Liverpool clinched their third European Cup and the League Cup. Forest hadn't been in the running.

My time with Forest coincided with the introduction of legalised telephone betting and I took advantage of this service more and more. I had always been interested in racing, both horses and dogs.

An abiding memory of my childhood was Dad scooping a big win on the horses when we were on holiday at Mablethorpe. Dad was never a big punter but he would have an occasional bet. He had been given a series of what he called 'hot tips' by a mate of his and placed an accumulator bet. I can clearly recall how nervous he was before each race and then the absolute delight as each horse romped home. He went to the bookies' to hear the commentary on the last race and came back some twenty minutes later, arms aloft and with a beaming smile sweeping across his face. The final horse had won and, consequently, Dad had won what for him was a lot of money. That night he took Mum, my brothers and me for a slap-up meal and he bought presents for us all. I was around eight or nine years old and Dad's success made an impression on me. From then on, I associated horses, and horseracing in particular, with happiness and good times. Of course, it never occurred to me that most people lost money on the horses. I simply saw horseracing as a means to joy.

George Dewis, my old mentor at Leicester City, had kept greyhounds and sparked my interest in them. As a young professional, I kept two and raced them on a Saturday night at Hinckley and Coalville. I was courting Sue at the time and, after the Saturday game, she and I would take off to one of the local greyhound tracks. I don't think Sue was very interested in greyhound racing but she came along anyway – we were very much in the first throes of love. After the racing we would go for a meal and perhaps to a club, which Sue was probably itching to do all the time we were at the dog track.

Looking back, the roots of the gambling problems I was to face in later life emerged during my time at Forest. Initially, telephone betting was a matter of convenience. I would finish training, arrive home just after lunch and scan the newspaper for a few minutes before turning to the racing pages where the serious reading would start. Having picked my horses, I simply picked up the phone. As time went by, the number of bets I placed each day increased, as did the amount. It was not a problem because the amount I was betting and, more to the point, losing was well within the limit I had set myself. Occasionally, I would have a really big win, a few thousand pounds, which would encourage me to bet more. It wouldn't be long before I was once again in deficit.

I suppose the first indication I had that I was losing came one Christmas when both William Hill's and Ladbroke's sent me a hamper. Sue, being an astute woman, realised that the bookies would not be sending me expensive presents unless I was a good client of theirs – that is, one who bet a fair amount and lost around the same – and for the first time we began to be at cross purposes. Every loving couple have their fair share of arguments and Sue and I had been no exception but when she took me to task about my betting, our arguments became more frequent and more heated. I was never up for confrontations with Sue. I'd state my case but when she continued to voice her concerns, I'd stonewall her and, on some occasions, I put on my coat and walk out. I'd go to a bar or a club and have a few drinks on my own. I saw it as cooling down the situation.

Immediately after one Wednesday evening game, I travelled down to Cheltenham with a friend, planning to go to the big National Hunt festival next day. The first horse of a double bet I'd placed, Sea Pigeon, had won the Champion Hurdle the day before. I was keen to see the second one, Broadsword, race on the Thursday because if it were to win, the bet would win me £10,000.

When my pal and I arrived in Cheltenham we headed straight for our hotel, the Queen's. It was quite late but the place was buzzing. There must have been about a thousand Irish people there, partying away. I had never experienced an atmosphere like it. The hotel was ringing with laughter and conviviality. Tired as I was after the game, we decided this was too good to miss and, after a few drinks, I was being treated like a long-lost brother by people from Ballybunion and Tralee.

At breakfast the following morning we were advised by our new friends to get down to the racetrack early because a record attendance had been predicted. Even though we left just after breakfast, the traffic was so bad we didn't arrive at the racecourse until the afternoon's racing was under way. Broadsword's race was about to start just as we pulled in to the car park. I asked my pal if he would mind parking the car because I wanted to be on the course to see my horse romp home and gift me ten grand. So he queued for a space while I headed for the course and, once inside, made a beeline for the winning post.

The race was over halfway through by the time I managed to push my way to a spot near the winning post and my heart began to race when I heard the course commentator announce that Broadsword had a clear lead. As they jumped the penultimate hurdle, Broadsword had a lead of three lengths and I couldn't contain my excitement. I was shouting, 'Come on, boy. Go for it,' over and over again. Then I stopped shouting. The ground was very heavy and as the horses came down the home stretch, a horse called Baron Blakeney was coming up fast. To use a punter's terminology, this horse had 'come out of the clouds'. Up to this point, Baron Blakeney had not been among the front runners. Now it was steaming past every horse and was neck and neck with Broadsword. My heart sank. My mouth was dry. Baron Blakeney pipped Broadsword at the post by a head. My head fell and I found myself looking down at a gutter drain. I could almost envisage the ten grand going down it.

My luck didn't desert me in just that race. It continued to give me a wide berth for the rest of the afternoon. I placed four hefty bets, all to win, and every horse came in second.

At the end of the day's racing, I was making my way back to my friend's car when I bumped into Peter Scudamore, the jockey who had ridden Broadsword. Peter was a youngster at the time, just beginning to make a name for himself. After exchanging initial greetings, I brought up the subject of Broadsword.

'Bad luck on Broadsword today, Scu,' I said.

'Yeah, went too early,' said Scu.

'Too early?' I said, smiling at him through gritted teeth. The pain of having just missed out on ten grand was still smarting.

'Too early,' Scu reiterated. 'Still, valuable lesson learned, eh?'

In all probability it had been for him but, ominously, not for me.

I was feeling so down and aggrieved at having been so close to winning ten grand then having four seconds that I decided to stay over at the Queen's with my new Irish friends in the hope that they would raise my spirits. The next morning my travel alarm failed to go off and I slept in. With my friend having gone home the previous evening, I was in a dilemma. How would I get to Nottingham in time for Friday training? I tried to get a taxi to take me but none was available for such a long trip. In the end, I had no option but to ring the club and tell them I would not be there for training.

I played in Forest's game on the Saturday and turned in what the newspapers said was a very good performance. Brian Clough was understanding about me missing training. He didn't tell me off and he didn't impose a fine. In fact, he made very little of it. It was the only time in my career that I ever missed a training session. Considering I was a professional footballer for thirty-two years, I would like to think that is indicative of my dedication and application. However, the fact that I missed that Friday training session, in essence because of my disappointment at having lost on the horses, may now be see as a sign of what was to come.

Our quest to win the European Cup for a third successive season ended when we were beaten 2–0 on aggregate by CSKA Sofia in the very first round. Both legs were lost by a single goal and although we dominated the second leg at the City Ground, our inability to convert possession and pressure into goals cost us dear. It was a dreadful disappointment. Having tasted European glory, I thirsted for it again.

Liverpool made sure the European Cup remained in England for a fifth successive year when they earned their third victory in the competition, courtesy of a spectacular goal from left-back Alan Kennedy against Real Madrid. Ipswich Town won the UEFA Cup with a 5–4 aggregate victory over Dutch side AZ 67 Alkmaar.

The dominance of English clubs in Europe – Aston Villa were to win the European Cup the following season – was in marked contrast to the fortunes of the national team. England had not taken part in the finals of a major international tournament since the World Cup of 1970, and we qualified for that by virtue of the fact that we were the holders. In 1966 we had been the hosts, so England had not won through the qualifying stages of a major international tournament since 1962.

England's failure in the seventies to qualify for either the World Cup or European Championship was a puzzle to me, given the success of our club sides in Europe. Perhaps the success of English clubs had something to do with the fact that teams included players from each of the home countries and Ireland. I am sure it also had something to do with the way club sides played against European opposition. The pace of the game disrupted continental sides, whereas in international football we tended to play at a slower tempo, more in keeping with how the opposition liked to play. The reasoning behind it was that, with the higher level of technique and skill, players were not easily hustled off the ball. The style of play adopted by English clubs in Europe was thought to be in-effective at international level.

Apart from the pace, the players were at least as good as those from the top Spanish, Italian, Dutch and German sides. Also, the collective spirit, which had been of paramount importance in Forest's success, seemed to bring out the best in certain players, who found they could not replicate such form at international level. Alan Hansen is a case in point. He was always outstanding at the back for Liverpool and, like all great players, was very comfortable on the ball. Alan was a wonderful club player for

Liverpool but he never consistently reproduced that form at inter-national level with Scotland.

At Forest, we looked on with appreciation and not a little envy at the success of other English clubs in Europe. It was no longer happening for us. I was still giving my all and producing good form but I could see the writing on the wall. My career at Forest no longer seemed to offer me a challenge, and I have always needed and thrived on challenges. The time was fast approaching for me to leave and accept a new challenge with another club. My last two years at Forest were happy enough but something was missing, and I don't mean medals and silverware. The spirit of the first three years, which had created the magic for me, had gone. It was time for me to go, too.

Football apart, this was not the best of times for me because of an incident that made headlines in just about every national newspaper.

Sue and I had had a few words, probably about the level of my betting, and as usual I went off on my own. I was never on my own for long. Wherever I went I would meet someone I knew, or someone who recognised me would come over for a chat. On this occasion, I went to a Nottingham club and ran into a group of friends. We had a few drinks and a few laughs and towards the end of the evening, one of our number suggested we all went for a curry. As everyone sorted themselves out, a young woman sidled up to me at the bar. She seemed to be on her own and asked where we were going. I told her for a curry and said that she could tag along if she wanted to. She said she would be happy to, but first had to make a phone call. When she came back from making the call, she joined the group and we made our way to the Indian restaurant.

It was a pleasant social occasion, with people chatting generally over the meal. When it came to time to go, I asked her how she intended to get home. She thought it would be difficult to get a taxi at such a late hour and, having established that she lived not too far from me, I offered to give her a lift.

I hadn't driven far when I became aware of a set of headlights in my rear-view mirror. The car behind appeared to be following us. I couldn't see it well enough to establish what sort of car it was, but I became concerned. I'd been stupid. I'd had a few drinks and knew myself to be over the legal limit for driving. I began to concentrate hard, making sure I indicated at every turning, ensuring I never crossed the white line in the middle of the road even when passing parked cars. Believing the car behind to be a police car routinely patrolling the neighbourhood in the early hours, I decided to turn down a country lane and wait for a few minutes before rejoining the main road.

For a moment I thought all was well but my heart started to race when headlights again appeared in my rear-view mirror, and I began to panic when the car pulled up behind me. The woman turned to look at the car, then turned to me and said, 'It's my husband.'

That was another shock to the system because I had assumed she wasn't married. Not that that really mattered, seeing as my intention was purely to give her a lift home. But her husband arriving on the scene sent shock waves through my system. I really panicked at this point. I revved the engine, thrust the car into gear, let out the clutch and sped away. I was all fingers and thumbs and momentarily lost control of the steering wheel. The car mounted what I think was a grass verge and lurched to one side. There was a thunderous crash followed by a deep, dull thud. I was thrown forward but my seatbelt prevented me coming into contact with the windscreen. I was then jerked back into my seat and I went out like a light. It later transpired that the car had hit a post with such force that the post had broken and fallen over the bonnet.

I don't know how long I was unconscious. When I came to, the police were on the scene and the woman had gone. I presumed she was not injured and had been taken home by her husband.

I failed a breath test and was taken to a police station and formally charged with driving while over the legal alcohol limit. At the police station, my prime concern was Sue. She would be wondering where I was. I wanted to let her know what had happened and that I was OK. I cursed myself for being so stupid and irresponsible as to drive when I'd had a drink. I felt ashamed. The police released me later that morning.

For a brief moment I managed to convince myself that my arrest might not be made public. I told myself there must be dozens of people arrested in Nottingham for drink-driving offences every week, yet I never read about them in the local paper or heard of them on local radio. Then I told myself, 'Who are you kidding?' I was kidding no one, least of all myself. Of course, the local media picked up the story of my arrest.

When I was released from custody I headed straight home. The first thing I had to do was explain it all to Sue. To say she was far from happy is an understatement. Though her anger and disappointment were tempered by the fact that I had survived the crash. I had been driving a Jaguar. To this day I believe that make of car saved me from sustaining serious injury, or worse. A less well constructed car would not have been able to survive the impact.

Once the local media ran the story the national press were on to it in an instant and they had a field day. The story was a scoop for the Nottingham press boys and the circumstances surrounding the crash and arrest brought the scandal writers to the city in their droves. The story made front-page headlines in the tabloid press. The broadsheets carried the story of how the tabloids had picked up on it, the way broadsheets do when not wanting to be seen directly reporting a seemingly salacious tale themselves.

From the moment I lost consciousness, I never saw the woman again. In the days following the crash both she and her husband gave their version of events to certain press. This surprised me because I thought they would have wanted to keep a low profile and get on with their life together.

I never contacted the press to offer my version of events because I didn't want to inflame the situation. The headlines, as you would expect, didn't make pleasant reading for both myself and Sue.

Needless to say, this was a very trying time for us. Fortunately, our marriage and the love we share is very strong. It had to be to endure and survive at this time.

Of course, I was concerned about what the newspapers wrote about me, and what people thought of me, but not nearly as much as I was about Sue's feelings and those of my family. To this day I am very much aware of the gravity of the situation. I had too much to drink and did something I have never subsequently done: got behind the wheel of my car while over the limit. I did something I was never prepared to do in football: I took a risk. I was in the wrong. The punishment meted out to me was justified and, without putting too fine a point on it, I paid my dues.

Sometimes in life you must face up to your mistakes. I was resolved to do this in the immediate aftermath of my arrest. Forest's very next match was away to Arsenal. On arriving at an away ground it was customary for the players to inspect the pitch, in the main to gauge what type of boots would be most suitable to wear – long studs for heavy ground, short studs for firm ground, moulded studs for hard surfaces. I always checked the condition of the goalmouths and I liked to stand around in the penalty boxes, just to get my bearings.

When the Forest party arrived at Highbury, I went out with the others to inspect the pitch. It was early and there weren't too many supporters in the ground but a fair number of home fans had already congregated on Arsenal's famous North Bank terracing. As I walked down to the penalty area in front of them, I heard some catcalls and pointed jibes. I had expected as much, but I was determined that nothing would distract me from my normal pre-match preparations, and that no amount of ribbing or abuse was going to put me off my game. Having inspected the penalty area, I was walking back to the centre spot when John Robertson came alongside me.

'Given what's happened this week, it took some bottle to do what you've just done,' John told me.

We drew and the consensus of opinion was that I had played extremely well, producing several saves to thwart Arsenal. A number of newspapers made me man of the match. My concentration and application were such that I was able to blot out all my personal troubles. Once I crossed that white line, all the pressure and emotional turmoil seemed to disappear for ninety minutes. Back in the dressing room, it all returned but I felt a strange contentment at the fact that I could blank out everything for the duration of the game and do the job I was paid to do.

Not long afterwards, I was at home one night with Sue and the boys when I received a phone call from Jon Holmes, my agent. As soon as I heard the tone of Jon's voice I knew something was up.

'Peter, you'll never guess what's happened now,' he said, agitatedly. ' You'd better get over here right away.'

I had yet to appear in court so I was still able to drive. Throughout the journey to Jon's home I felt my nerves fraying at the edges. I had no idea why he wanted to see me, but the words 'you'll never guess what's happened now' kept running through my mind. I couldn't guess what had happened but, given the lurid headlines in the tabloid press, I feared the worst.

When I arrived I could see straightaway that he was flustered. He sat me down and I tried to remain calm and collected.

'Well, I have some devastating news for you, Peter,' he said. I felt my mouth go dry. 'Jeff Pointon and I have split up. I'm going on my own.'

I didn't know whether to laugh or cry. I heard myself saying, 'I'm sorry to hear that,' but in truth at that moment I couldn't give a monkey's. Part of me was mightily relieved that the news wasn't to do with the drink-driving incident, while another part of me was cross with him for having, albeit unwittingly, subjected me to more mental turmoil.

Jon explained the situation to me and wanted to know if it would affect my business relationship with him. I assured him it wouldn't. I liked Jeff Pointon. He was the owner of Pointon–York and Jon was employed by him but Jon was the driving force as far as my interests were concerned. I was happy for him to continue as my agent. Both Jon and Jeff had done a good job for me but I'd always felt that Jon was the ideas man. To this day, I don't think he realises what turmoil he put me through that night for the fifteen minutes or so it took me to drive to his house.

In the event, Tony Woodcock and I put up guarantees for Park Associates, the sports agency business that Jon set up. He has since become one of the most successful and influential agents in sport and his achievements are well deserved.

I was eventually banned from driving and fined. I had no gripes about that. Painful as it was, justice had been fairly meted out. I had never been in trouble in my life up to this point, and I vowed to myself and to Sue that I would never be in trouble again.

Trouble of a different sort loomed at Nottingham Forest. In 1980–81 we had finished without a major trophy and seventh in the League. The following season was even more disappointing. Having scored twice in our opening game, a 2–1 win over Southampton, and played in our second match, a goalless draw with Manchester United, Trevor Francis moved to Manchester City.

It was to be the first of many comings and goings at the City Ground that season as Brian Clough tried in vain to build a team that could recreate the glory we had known in my first years with Forest. Centre-back Willie Young joined from Arsenal, the former Bayern Munich midfield player Jurgen Rober joined from Chicago Sting, Norwegian international Jan Einar Aas came from Bayern Munich, and Mark Proctor from Middlesbrough. Brian Clough introduced youngsters Peter Davenport, Steve Kendal and Calvin Plummer. These were all decent players but, whatever Clough attempted, the great spirit and collectiveness that had been so evident in our success remained elusive. He called on the services of twenty-six players in all, which on the face of it is not a great deal more than the nineteen we used in our 1977–78 championship-winning season, but it was a sign that things were not going too well on the pitch.

Forest finished twelfth, winning just seven games and scoring nineteen goals at home – a record on a par with Leeds, Wolves and Middlesbrough, who were relegated. Both Leeds and Middlesbrough managed to score more goals and Wolves won more home matches than we did. Our season's tally of forty-two goals, an average of exactly one per game, was among the lowest in the First Division. Ipswich Town and Southampton managed to score at home whereas West Ham scored as many at home as we did home and away. Our lack of goals was emphasised by the fact that Ian Wallace was Forest's leading goalscorer with nine.

We exited ignominiously from the FA Cup at the first time of asking, beaten 3–1 at home by Wrexham. Having beaten Birmingham, Blackburn and Tranmere in the League Cup, we succumbed in round five to Spurs.

Some 24,000 supporters had gone all the way to Madrid for the 1980 European Cup final, but the attendances for our final two home matches of 1981–82 were 15,000. Forest fans had seen the signs and so had I. Forest were in decline as a team.

My conviction for drink driving and the subsequent press speculation never affected my decision to move on from Nottingham
Forest. I stayed for nearly a year and a half following the incident,
but I needed to move to develop my career. Initially, I had no idea
where I might end up; I just knew I had to go somewhere else.

That somewhere turned out to be where my England team-mate
Kevin Keegan was plying his trade, a club that was undergoing a
renaissance under manager Lawrie McMenemy – Southampton.

8

ENGLAND EXPECTS

The one word to describe how I felt about playing for England is proud. To represent your country at any sport, at any level, is an honour. Irrespective of the opposition and the occasion, playing for England always filled me with a great sense of pride and duty.

I shall always remember my first appearance for the full international team in November 1970 against East Germany. Your international debut is always very special but what made the occasion auspicious for me was that I was on the way to achieving one of the goals I had set myself when a youngster – to play for England at Schoolboy, Youth, Under-23 and full international level. There aren't too many people who have done that – Terry Venables springs to mind – so when I did complete the set it gave me great satisfaction.

Following my international debut, up to February 1973 my appearances were sporadic: Gordon Banks was Sir Alf's first choice. But as the seventies unfolded I felt I was pushing for a place in the England team. Following Gordon's accident, Sir Alf was manager for fifteen internationals. Of those fifteen matches, I kept goal in twelve games, Ray Clemence twice and QPR's Phil Parkes once. Phil's cap coincided with Alf's last game as England manager, a 0–0 draw with Portugal in Lisbon. Alf had, of course, also been manager of the England Under-23 team and I had won thirteen caps with them.

Sir Alf was loyal to his employers at the FA but I feel his main loyalty was to his players. He protected us like a mother hen and every player was treated fairly. Once a game was over, Sir Alf would relax a little, more often than not allowing the Under-23 players to have a few drinks. Occasionally, he would join in. He would move about the various groups, clutching a gin and tonic and talking about international and domestic football and sometimes his own playing days. As young footballers who aspired to play for the full England team, we hung on his every word and always welcomed his company.

Alf didn't always welcome some of the company that joined us. After one Under-23 match, I was sitting with some of the lads enjoying a drink with Alf, when one of the FA's blazer brigade strolled up and engaged Alf in conversation.

'We played very well tonight, I think,' said the FA official.

'Yes, these boys did very well,' agreed Alf.

'Yes, very well,' repeated the official. 'What's his name at number nine – did very well, I think.'

'Joe. Joe Royle,' said Alf.

'Royle! That's the one. Did very well. And the goalkeeper, too. Had a very good game. Some excellent saves.'

'Peter. Peter Shilton,' said Alf.

'Shiften. Yes. Very good.' There was an awkward silence. 'So. Well done to you all,' said the official, making his exit.

When the official was out of earshot, Alf turned to us.

'Bloody silly sod,' he said. Alf took a sip of his gin and tonic and sighed. 'And there, with the likes of him, gentlemen,' he said, resignedly, 'hangs my job as England manager.'

I had established myself as the England number one under Sir Alf. I suppose the defining moment occurred during England's 1–0 victory over Scotland at Wembley in 1973, a game in which I produced a save that is remembered by many to this day. Kenny Dalglish was a formidable opponent, touched with football genius.

He was at his most dangerous when the ball was played up to him in or around the penalty box and he had his back to goal. He could turn the best defenders and was one of the best shielders of the ball I ever came across. This made life difficult for me, and for every other goalkeeper. Instead of turning and firing off a shot, more often than not Kenny would hold the ball at his feet, then suddenly force me to change position by laying the ball square for an oncoming team-mate to have a shot at goal. His ability to hold on to the ball then lay it off was one of the reasons why Liverpool midfield players scored so many goals, and why Kenny was held in such high esteem by managers and his fellow professionals.

Another part of the Dalglish weaponry was that he was very good at curling the ball around a goalkeeper. He would run towards the penalty box with defenders in front of him and, as I moved towards the edge of my six-yard box, he would fire off a shot without taking on the defenders.

Against Scotland in 1973, a corner was played into my penalty box and headed clear. The ball fell to Kenny who was lurking outside the box. As players moved out of the area Kenny hit a terrific shot across my body and to my left. I was airborne and at full stretch. It's amazing what your mind can process in a split second. I realised I wasn't going to reach the ball with my left hand, so in order to gain extra lift I brought my right arm across and over my left and managed to palm the ball to safety. Many people consider this to have been one of the great saves of my career. It is certainly one I remember well, not least because it was a crucial save in that England beat Scotland by the only goal of the game. I have good reason to remember that save from Kenny Dalglish as I believe it was turning point in my England career. The press made much of it, many football writers being given to saying I was a future England regular goalkeeper in the making. It was hailed as a great save.

I reckon about ten times a season, I would make a save that did not stem from my training but from something innate. Call it instinct if you like. On such occasions I would surprise myself. It was elation I felt then, as opposed to satisfaction.

Joe Mercer was general manager of Coventry City when he was summoned to be caretaker manager of England after Sir Alf Ramsey was so unjustly dismissed. He had been a fine player in the thirties and forties with Everton and Arsenal and, when his playing days were over, he had gone into management with Sheffield United, moving on to Aston Villa, Manchester City and Coventry.

His years in charge of Manchester City in the sixties were particularly notable. He transformed what was then a mid-table Second Division club into one that not only won promotion, but went on to become League champions and enjoy success in the FA Cup and European Cup Winners' Cup. I had cause to remember Joe because he had been manager when Manchester City beat Leicester in the 1969 Cup final.

I suppose Joe's masterstroke was to appoint the flamboyant Malcolm Allison as his assistant and coach. Joe and Malcolm were like chalk and cheese but they formed a formidable management team. Their contrasting styles complemented one another. Malcolm was brash and outspoken whereas Joe was unassuming and quietly spoken, as befitted his role as the elder statesman.

Everyone loved Joe Mercer. He had a banana grin, bandy legs and a heart bigger than his head. 'Uncle Joe', as he was referred to by some of the England players, stressed that he didn't want the England job on a permanent basis. As he told the players before his first game in charge, against Wales at Ninian Park in May 1974, 'I'm just holding the reins for a few weeks, boys. There will be no pressure on any player while I'm in charge. Just go out and play your natural game and enjoy yourselves.'

Joe Mercer was in charge of England for seven games, of which we won three, drew three and lost one (to Scotland!). I played in the first four of those games – victories over Wales and Northern Ireland, a draw with Argentina and the defeat by Scotland. Ray Clemence kept goal for the remaining three.

Joe's outlook and personality were a lot different from Sir Alf's. Alf tended to be guarded and unsmiling with the media, and somewhat defensive where tactics were concerned. Joe saw reporters as friends who were there to help him get his message across.

He wanted us to play with flourish and swagger but his laid-back approach led to some woolly team talks. Sometimes we took the field not knowing who had been assigned to take penalties. That never happened under Sir Alf although on one occasion, Alf's attention to detail led to a hilarious dressing-room incident. At the end of a team meeting before England's game against West Germany at Wembley in 1972, Sir Alf asked Emlyn Hughes to take the penalty should one be awarded. Emlyn said he would prefer not to and it would be better if someone else took it. Sir Alf homed in on Colin Bell but Colin didn't fancy the job either. Alf then asked Martin Chivers. Martin said he didn't feel right about taking a penalty. Somewhat agitated, Alf then turned to Rodney Marsh.

'Rodney, surely you have the confidence to take a penalty should we get one tonight?'

'Sure, no problem,' said Rod. 'I'll stick a penalty away any day of the week.'

'Excellent,' said Alf, beaming.

'There's only one problem,' said Rod.

'And what's that?' asked Alf.

'You ain't picked me in the team,' Marsh retorted.

Joe Mercer stepped aside when Don Revie was appointed England manager on a full-time basis. Revie was in charge of

England for thirty internationals from October 1974 to June 1977 and as I've mentioned, having established myself as the England number one, I immediately found myself 'number two' to Ray Clemence for all that time.

Following Don Revie's resignation, Ron Greenwood was appointed as England manager. One sports writer described him as 'the right man at the wrong time', which was a bit harsh. Ron was living near Brighton, blissfully happy in semi-retirement, when he received the offer from the FA to manage England.

The FA had interviewed six candidates for the England job – Ron, Brian Clough, Bobby Robson (Ipswich Town), Dave Sexton (Manchester United), Jack Charlton (Sheffield Wednesday) and Lawrie McMenemy (Southampton). Ron was originally appointed in a caretaker capacity with Lawrie McMenemy as his assistant. His first game as caretaker manager was a 0–0 draw with Switzerland. As Revie had done, Ron preferred Ray Clemence in goal to me, which may have had something to do with Ron's idea of trying to replicate Liverpool's success in domestic and European competitions. Against the Swiss, Ron picked seven Liverpool players, including Ian Callaghan, who hadn't played for England since the third match of the 1966 World Cup finals over eleven years previously.

Ron's third game as caretaker manager went a long way to landing him the job on a permanent basis. It was a World Cup qualifying game against Italy at Wembley and, inspired by Kevin Keegan and Trevor Brooking, England won 2–0. However, Italy needed a 1–0 home win over Luxembourg to qualify, and England didn't make it.

When the Home International Championship began in May 1978, Ron was established as England manager on a permanent basis, or as permanent as any manager can be. For his first five games in charge, he had played Ray four times and opted for

Manchester City's Joe Corrigan once, but I was selected for the opening game against Wales – a 3–1 victory for England. Ray played against Northern Ireland and Scotland. Steve Coppell's goal against the Scots ensured an England victory and gave Scotland a miserable send-off to the World Cup finals in Argentina.

Ron selected me for two of the next nine internationals. Then, in 1979, still unable to decide between Ray and me, he instigated his policy of playing us in alternate matches.

I had respect for Ron Greenwood. He was a disciple of Walter Winterbottom. The religious analogy is apt. Among the England players he was sometimes known as 'Reverend Ron' because of his gentlemanly ways and his tendency almost to preach when talking tactics. He was quietly strong, had some good ideas on football and his masterstroke was the appointment of Don Howe as his assistant. As manager of West Ham, Ron had advocated purist football, but often to the detriment of a well-organised defence. Don Howe brought organisation to the England defence and proved the perfect foil for Ron.

Ron was criticised for his indecision over who was to be goal-keeper. Ray and I were both disappointed not to be the regular first choice and neither of us was happy with the arrangement but we accepted it and got on with the job. But it was not encouraging to know that, should I play a blinder, I still wouldn't be selected for the next game. Not being able to establish myself as England's number one did, in a way, harm my confidence although I found some solace in the fact that I was playing in half of England's games, which was much better than being out in the cold as I had been when Don Revie was manager. For his part, Ron did tell Ray and me that if England qualified for the 1982 World Cup finals in Spain, one of us would be 'picked for the tournament and unless there was injury or loss of form, would stay in the team'.

When David Seaman announced his retirement in 2003, I read

an article that said 'Seaman was good enough to hold down the England goalkeeper's position on his own whereas Peter Shilton and Ray Clemence were vying for the position throughout their international careers.' Many people share that view but it's not true. Ray and I did compete for the England goalkeeper's jersey but not for the duration of our international careers. We more or less played in alternate games for three years, from 1979 until 1982 when I received the nod from Ron for the World Cup in Spain. After that, Ray played twice more for England, both European Championship games against Luxembourg. From 1982 onwards, Chris Woods was in competition with me for the England goalkeeper's jersey but I had by then established myself as the number-one choice. I played my last game for England against Italy in Italia '90, some eight years after Ray had departed from the international scene.

Ron Greenwood was England manager for four and a half years during which England played 55 matches, winning 33, drawing 12 and losing 10. Ron used a total of fifty players but not in such a bewildering way as Don Revie had done. In addition to Don Howe, Ron also had his old West Ham stalwarts Geoff Hurst and Bill Taylor to assist on the coaching side. He revived the England B team, which he placed under the managership of Bobby Robson. Why he felt it necessary to have a B team I have no idea. Perhaps there was an element of nostalgia in his decision; Ron had won an England B cap when he played for Chelsea.

Terry Venables and Dave Sexton were put in charge of the England Under-21s with Howard Wilkinson as assistant coach, and Brian Clough and Peter Taylor were given responsibility for the England Youth team. I think Ron was trying to get the best English managers and coaches involved in the England set-up in the hope a conveyor belt of talent would come through.

The decision to appoint Clough and Taylor was a controversial one. The Youth team already had a manager in Ken Burton. Clough was very disappointed at not having been appointed England manager, especially as he had given what he characteristically described as 'a magnificent interview'. He was convinced that he would be offered the job but I think the blazer brigade on the FA Committee were afraid that he would want to do things his way – and they were right in that assumption. I think many FA officials were afraid of Clough. They disliked him for being so outspoken. Perhaps some also feared he would shake things up from top to bottom and insist on clearing out the deadwood. In short, they feared for their positions of privilege, and with good reason.

Clough and Taylor were both very patriotic and fully behind the England cause, but I think they felt it somewhat demeaning to be put in charge of the Youth team. Under the circumstances, it came as no surprise that their involvement with Greenwood's set-up was a brief one.

It all came to a head during an international Youth tournament in the Canary Islands. An FA official ordered the young England players to board a coach that was taking them to a game. When Clough and Taylor arrived on the scene they ordered the youngsters back into the hotel. As Clough said, 'It was baking hot and I didn't want the players sitting in a stifling coach. Peter and I took them back into the hotel where we sat chatting with them and getting them relaxed before it was time to set off.' Meanwhile, the FA officials sat fuming in the coach, itching to get to the stadium. Clough was demonstrating who was boss. A number of FA officials took umbrage and words were later exchanged. The fall-out led to Clough and Taylor resigning their positions with the England Youth team.

The FA played safe in appointing Ron Greenwood. He was far less confrontational than Clough and Ron did a decent job.

England's team gradually took shape on the way to Spain '82. He opted for an orthodox back four in which, initially, Manchester City's Dave Watson was the linchpin. In midfield, Ron, or more accurately, Don Howe, asked Ray Wilkins to play a slightly defensive role while Trevor Brooking linked up with Kevin Keegan.

Following the tragic death of the trainer Bill Taylor, Ron and Don achieved their first success in guiding England to the 1980 European Championship finals in Italy, but we flattered to deceive.

The tournament preceded Ron's rota system for Ray and me and for England's opening game of the tournament, against Belgium, he opted for Ray. The game was marred by a sickening outbreak of hooliganism by so-called England fans. In my opinion, these people were not football supporters at all but criminals using football as a vehicle for indulging in violence against any foreign nationals.

Hooligans were very much in the minority at football matches. Even in this era, when hooliganism was considered to be at its height in football, the majority of domestic matches were clear of such moronic behaviour. However, when hooliganism did blight a game, its impact, especially in a high-profile match such as the one against Belgium, was colossal and the repercussions far-reaching. It would take another nine years, three tragedies and much loss of life before football's authorities were forced to put their multi-million-pound industry in order in the wake of the Taylor Report.

What had been a keenly contested match against Belgium lost its impetus following the hooliganism on the terraces and England had to be content with a draw – not an ideal start to our campaign, especially as our next game was against the host nation.

Ron recalled me for the second game and I was delighted to be back in the fold, especially against such illustrious opponents as the Italians. The atmosphere in Turin was terrific and, happily, the game passed off without incident on the terraces. A goalless draw seemed the most likely result when, ten minutes from time, Graziani swept past Liverpool's Phil Neal and played a great ball into the path of the oncoming Tardelli at the near post. Tardelli hit it first time and there was little I could do. It was a classic goal. England had dominated large stretches of the match but we were rarely productive or destructive. The nearest we had come to scoring was an effort from Ray Kennedy in the second half that came back into play off the post.

That defeat meant England needed to beat Spain by two clear goals in the final group game. It didn't happen. Goals from Trevor Brooking and Tony Woodcock were not enough as Cardenosa netted for Spain from the penalty spot. I watched from the dugout. The penalty was awarded when Ray Clemence was harshly adjudged to have pulled down Cardenosa and more controversy was to follow. Dave Watson conceded a second penalty and Dani beat Ray from the spot. The referee, however, spotted an encroachment into the penalty area by a Spanish player and ordered the spot kick to be retaken. Ray produced an excellent save from the retaken penalty but his effort was in vain. We were on our way home from a tournament that is now largely forgotten by many. Its significance lies in the fact that this was the first time England had qualified for the finals of a major international tournament since the 1970 World Cup – and we had done so then by virtue of being holders. Incidentally, I wonder how many people know or remember that the Henri Delaunay Cup is what the European Championship was called at this time.

I was recalled for England's next game, our opening qualifying match for the 1982 World Cup in Spain against Norway. Without Kevin Keegan, Trevor Brooking, Ray Wilkins, Trevor Francis and Steve Coppell, Ron Greenwood had no option but to ring the changes. A new-look midfield and attack featuring Bryan Robson (West Bromwich Albion), Eric Gates and Paul Mariner (both of Ipswich Town) and Graham Rix (Arsenal) took time to get into its stride but when Liverpool's Terry McDermott eventually gave us the lead before half-time, it served to instil more composure into our play. Prompted by Bryan Robson, we won comfortably by four goals to nil but our passage to Spain was to prove anything but smooth.

Our next game was in Bucharest against Romania and we lost 2–1, a controversial penalty deciding the outcome. Greenwood's rota system was in full swing and Ray Clemence had taken over from me in goal. In the seventy-fifth minute Kenny Sansom (Arsenal) tackled Iordanescu, who went down and rolled about on the ground like a skewered worm – a sure sign that he wasn't injured. The referee awarded the penalty amid angry protests from the England players on the pitch and on the bench. Iordanescu, displaying remarkable powers of recovery, picked himself up, beat Ray from the penalty spot and ran half the length of the pitch, jumping and celebrating his goal. As Steve Coppell later remarked, 'The words "referee" and "conned the" readily spring to mind.'

I was reinstated for England's next game, in November 1980 against Switzerland. After our defeat in Bucharest, this one was crucial to our chances of qualifying for Spain. At half-time, we were leading comfortably thanks to goals from Paul Mariner and Tony Woodock, but nerves began to jangle in the second half when Pfisyer pulled one back for Switzerland. The goal inspired the Swiss and I had to be on my toes to deny them on at least three occasions. That performance earned me the man of the match award, which, seeing England were at home, I feel says much about our performance that night. Convincing it was not.

Sandwiched between the Switzerland game and the return against Romania at Wembley was a 1–2 home defeat in a friendly against Spain. Although I was not happy with the rota system, England's performance and the manner of the defeat made this match a good one to miss.

Recalled yet again against Romania, the slippery Cumberland turf of Wembley nearly cost England dear. The game was tense and our play full of anxiety. My feet slipped from under me on the greasy turf as I went to collect a dipping header from Balaci and I was lying on the ground as two Romanian forwards homed in on the ball, which was about eighteen inches from the goal line. I hauled myself off the ground and with an outstretched arm managed to scoop the ball away just as one of the Romanian forwards was shaping to make contact with it. It was a really close thing and proved to be a crucial save as anxiety got the better of our forwards in front of goal and the game ended scoreless.

In May 1981 England suffered a 2–1 defeat against Switzerland in Basle. Terry McDermott scored what was England's first goal in five games. Ron Greenwood's honeymoon period as England manager was well and truly over. As our chances of qualifying for Spain began to look increasingly slim, the tabloid press did a hatchet job on him. Only a win against Hungary in Budapest could keep alive England's dwindling chances of qualifying – and it proved to be a famous victory. Ray was in goal. A Trevor Brooking goal was cancelled out by Hungary in the first half, but in the second period England played some inspired football. Trevor Brooking drove a rising shot so powerfully that the ball wedged between the net and metal stanchion. Kevin Keegan put the result beyond doubt when scoring from the spot some fifteen minutes from time to give England a 3–1 win and boost our hopes of qualifying for Spain.

After hitting the heights against Hungary, England plummeted to new depths in the very next game. Again, my disappointment at not being chosen to play against Norway in Oslo was tempered by the fact that this game proved to be a good one to miss. Norway defeated England 2–1 – a defeat that seemed certain to put the kibosh on our hopes of making it to the World Cup finals. The Norwegian TV match commentator went berserk. At the end of the game he screamed into his microphone, 'Are you listening Maggie Thatcher? Are you hearing me Winston Churchill? We gave your boys a hell of a beating today! A hell of a beating.'

That beating was nothing compared to the one the English media handed out to Ron Greenwood and the England players on duty against Norway. On television, Jimmy Hill compared the defeat against Norway to the humiliating defeat England had suffered when losing to the USA in the 1950 World Cup.

It appeared that matters could not get any worse, but then the reaction of that Norwegian match commentator was broadcast. When the press and a good chunk of the nation heard his ranting and raving, our humiliation was complete. The press, in particular the tabloids, slaughtered Ron and the England team.

England still had an outside chance of qualifying and while that was the case I never gave up hope of us making it to Spain. Our next game was our last group match, against Hungary at Wembley. Hungary were already assured of their place in the finals but the runners-up in the group would also qualify. However, our destiny was not entirely in our own hands. We had to hope that Romania failed to win their final group match.

Ron Greenwood made four changes from the team that had suffered the ignominious defeat in Oslo. Alvin Martin (West Ham), Steve Coppell (Manchester United), and Trevor Brooking came into the side at the expense of Russell Osman (Ipswich), Trevor Francis and Glenn Hoddle (Spurs), and I was in goal. Glenn Hoddle's omission gave the press an opportunity to display its fickleness, although I don't believe for one moment that Ron Greenwood was swayed by them when it came to picking the

England team. Before the Norway match, some quarters of the press had been campaigning for Greenwood to include Glenn in the team, citing him as England's most creative midfield player. Following that defeat, though, the same newspapers were calling for Glenn to be axed, saying he was 'a luxury at international level'. His omission for the final showdown against Hungary was generally welcomed. 'A case of horses for courses and the right decision as Glenn Hoddle was seen not to be at the races against Norway,' said the *Daily Mail*.

In the event, Romania blew it against Switzerland, which meant we needed a draw to qualify. We did a little better than that, a Paul Mariner goal giving us a 1–0 victory. A World Cup campaign that so often teetered on the brink of disaster finally ended in triumph. There was no great rejoicing in the dressing room, though; more a huge sense of relief.

I was delighted at the prospect of playing in the World Cup finals. As I drove home, I was mindful of what Ron Greenwood had told Ray and me some two years previously – should England qualify for Spain, he would choose one of us to play for the duration of the tournament. I was determined to continue my good form and in so doing help make Ron's decision a little easier for him.

9

DELL BOY

My career with Nottingham Forest was coming to a close during England's World Cup qualifying campaign of 1980 and 1981. I was still a Forest player, however, when England arrived in Spain for the World Cup finals. The press carried numerous reports about a possible move for me, citing Arsenal, Manchester United and Manchester City as possible destinations. Rumours were rife but I had not entered into any talks regarding a move from the City Ground.

The *Daily Express* published an 'exclusive' written by James Mossop that said my name was on a wanted list drawn up by Barcelona president, Jose Luis Nunez. The first I heard about this was when James Mossop rang me to ask for my reaction. I had no idea if the story was true and tried to be diplomatic, keeping my options open while not being disloyal to Forest. 'Obviously,' I replied, 'I would be interested in such a move. The prospect of playing abroad appeals to me but, at the moment, I am with some great players at Forest and for me to leave there would have to be a very good offer.'

In truth, I felt the time had come for me to move on from Forest and seek a fresh challenge. In the summer of 1981 I submitted a transfer request, despite having two years of my contract to run. I felt a move would be in the best interests of both parties. Clough and Taylor, however, didn't want me to leave. Come the start of the 1981–82 season, they persuaded me to withdraw my transfer request. More great days were in store at Forest, they said, and I decided to stay to see if that was so, but my gut feeling told me that Forest's glory days were over. Over or not, I simply hankered after new stimulation. Although I agreed to stay on, I didn't think I'd be there long term. Clough was aware of it. As England prepared for Spain, word reached me that Clough was resigned to losing me and had begun to search for my replacement.

In May 1982, Clough tried to persuade me to commit to a new long-term contract but it wasn't what I wanted. In essence, I had given Forest a year's notice of my intention to go because I didn't want to leave Clough frantically searching for a new goalkeeper. Clough wanted me to be a part of his plan to revive Forest but, seeing how determined I was to leave, he was prepared to sell me.

Clough was planning a clear-out and hoping to raise money to spend on new players by selling Justin Fashanu, Ian Wallace and John Robertson. He was probably planning to sell other players, too, but irrespective of who came and went my mind was made up. I would be one of those leaving the club.

The one person I didn't expect to leave was Peter Taylor but, on 7 May, a few days after my chat with Clough, Peter Taylor announced he was succeeding John Newman as manager of Derby County. I can only assume that Peter felt he wanted to have another crack at management on his own. He had, of course, enjoyed success at Derby with Clough but, sadly, he was not to repeat that success when in sole charge.

It had been no secret at the club that he and Clough had not been getting on for some time. Word was they'd had a fall-out following various disagreements over policy. I believe that the relationship began to crumble over differences of opinion regarding players, especially those who had been signed and were not a success, such as Asa Hartford and Justin Fashanu.

Clough and Taylor had had their differences in the past, but at

Forest for a time they really gelled. They formed a perfect double act, each complementing the other's strengths and style of management. Now the partnership was over and, sadly, they were to have little contact with one another from then until the death of Peter Taylor in the nineties.

In 1982, the newspapers were full of punning headlines to make you cringe, 'Can England Reign In Spain?' being a particular favourite. I felt we had a good chance of doing well and, with a little bit of luck, going all the way.

Ray Clemence and I were good pals and roomed together in Spain. Of course, we were both on tenterhooks, wondering which one of us Ron Greenwood would choose as his number-one goalkeeper. He told us during a training session before our opening game in Bilbao. We were working in separate areas of the training ground when Ron appeared and approached Ray. I knew then that I had been given the nod because Ron would not break the news to his preferred keeper first.

When Ron eventually came over to me, I could see from Ray's body posture that he was upset. I was elated when Ron Greenwood told me that I was to be his first-choice keeper but my heart went out to Ray. I knew how I would have felt on being told I was to miss out on the World Cup. He took the news really well and never let his obvious disappointment affect him. Throughout the tournament, he applied himself in full to the cause.

Fifa adopted a new format for Spain '82. The number of qualifying teams had been increased from sixteen to twenty-four and instead of one group stage, as in previous World Cups, there were two, with the group winners of the second phase going straight into the semi-finals. The home countries had taken advantage of the extra places, with both Scotland and Northern Ireland also qualifying. This was the first time three home nations had qualified for the final stages of a World Cup since 1958, when all four home countries had taken part in the tournament in Sweden. The new format proved top heavy and didn't improve the World Cup as a spectacle. What's more, it was ultimately to prove England's undoing.

The first phase comprised six groups of four teams, with two going through from each. England's first opponents, France, were among the bookies' favourites to win the trophy and the omens were not good when we learned that both Kevin Keegan and Trevor Brooking had injuries that ruled them out of the first group phase. In the event, we couldn't have wished for a better start.

Bryan Robson created a World Cup record for the fastest goal in the history of the tournament, scoring after just twenty-seven seconds. France recovered from this early blow, equalising after twenty-five minutes, but in the second half we regained the initiative. Ron Greenwood pulled a masterstroke when he switched Arsenal's Graham Rix to a left-sided role in midfield. Graham, playing in place of Trevor Brooking, found a lot of space and relished his new-found freedom. He linked very well in midfield with Bryan Robson, Ray Wilkins and Steve Coppell and we began to take control. Bryan Robson restored our lead with a header and Paul Mariner underlined our second-half supremacy with a close-range effort to give us a 3–1 victory.

We booked our place in the second phase of the finals in our next match, a 2–0 win over Czechoslovakia. A 1–0 victory over Kuwait in our final match was a bonus. I have cause to remember the goal against Kuwait because I had a hand in it – not in the literal sense! After about half an hour of play, I collected the ball following the breakdown of a Kuwaiti attack. Paul Mariner was well upfield and unmarked, so I cleared the ball to him and he backheeled it into the path of the oncoming Trevor Francis. Trevor set off on a thirty-yard run that culminated in him sliding the ball past the Kuwaiti keeper – not exactly route one but none the less direct.

During our stay in Bilbao, I became aware of how manipulative certain elements of the press had become. In a matter of two to three years, since Forest players were able to walk around Amsterdam's red-light district free from any intrusion by the press, the English tabloids had changed in the way they covered football.

The press were disgruntled because they felt they were not being allowed sufficient access to England players. Ron Greenwood agreed to a press call involving all the squad, saying, 'It will be better to get it done in one hit. The press boys will be satisfied and we can concentrate on our job.' The press call was held on the roof of our hotel. At one point, a reporter approached Ron and asked if he would agree to some of the players having a photograph taken with some pupils from a local ballet school. Ron readily agreed to this, saying it would be good for public relations with the local community. When the 'ballet dancers' arrived, some of us immediately smelled a rat. Six scantily clad young women appeared, each displaying a fair amount of what were voluptuous breasts.

'I know next to nothing about ballet and ballet dancers,' I said to Ray Clemence, 'but from the ballet I have seen on the telly, no way are these ballet dancers.'

Along with Ray, Terry Butcher, Kevin Keegan and others of the more seasoned players, I declined to have my photograph taken with the 'ballet dancers'. Some of the younger players, less experienced in the ways of the tabloid press, readily agreed to take part in the photo shoot, and the following day a photograph appeared in the *Sun*. The story ran along the lines of 'England players frolic with Spanish strippers'. When Ron Greenwood saw the piece he was furious. Needless to say, Ron and the rest of the squad were thereafter very wary of the press.

Some newspapers and sports writers would never contrive a 'story' but it takes only one reporter to do such a thing to make players very cautious, in some cases distrusting, of every element of the press. Spain was a watershed in the England manager's dealings with the media. Following the tournament, the FA decided to appoint a PR officer for the England team.

The team still managed to enjoy some degree of social life. After a game, Ron allowed us a drink and some time to let our hair down. We never went out but held informal parties to which we invited the couriers and interpreters, both male and female, who travelled with us. Sometimes we'd have music and there would be some dancing. Ron and Don Howe would often turn up at these gatherings and it was all good clean fun. To the best of my knowledge nothing untoward ever took place but I shudder to think what some tabloid newspapers might have made of these parties should they ever have heard about them.

We moved on to Madrid for the second group phase still without the services of the injured Kevin Keegan and Trevor Brooking. Our first game was against West Germany, who decided on a tactic of suffocating defence, and, by and large, the match was slugged out in midfield. It was far from a classic game of football and I think the Germans were happier with the final score of 0–0 than we were.

We needed to beat Spain by two clear goals to qualify for a semi-final place against France but the game ended goalless, which summed up our one deficiency – we couldn't score goals. In an attempt to pierce Spain's rearguard, after an hour Ron brought Keegan and Brooking off the bench. Both came close to scoring but it was a case of 'adios England'.

I felt gutted that we had exited from the World Cup unbeaten and having conceded just one goal in five matches. The new format and our inability to score goals proved our undoing. Apart from the three goals we had scored against France in our opening game, we had struggled to find the net.

Scotland were eliminated in the first group phase. They scored eight goals in their three matches but also conceded eight. The Scots had the same number of points as the USSR but were eliminated on goal difference. Brazil topped the group.

The surprise package was Northern Ireland. The Irish surprised everyone – I should imagine even themselves – by topping their group, which included the host nation, Yugoslavia and Honduras. With a squad largely recruited from the lower divisions of the Football League, Northern Ireland beat Spain 1–0 despite having to play with ten men for half an hour following the sending off of Luton's Mal Donaghy. Northern Ireland eventually lost to France, but their performances, especially that of seventeen-year-old Norman Whiteside, lived in the memory.

Italy triumphed in the tournament, beating West Germany 3–1 in what was a highly entertaining final. Striker Paolo Rossi, Italy's star player, had returned to football after a two-year ban following allegations that he had been involved in a bribery scandal. Italy's triumph was very much that of a restored Italian master.

Our elimination heralded the departure of Ron Greenwood. Enter Bobby Robson, who had been named as Ron's successor while we were in Spain.

Some people criticised Bobby, believing him to be indecisive, but I found him to be positive and strong. His first big decision – one that belied the criticism that he was indecisive – was to omit Kevin Keegan from the squad. Bobby is a great football man. As England manager he was a terrific organiser and always wanted us to play enterprising football. Bobby told the players, 'When you get the ball, look forward first, then square second.'

In his first game in charge – a European Championship qualifier against Denmark – I was kept very busy against what was a lively

Danish attack and I think my performance in that game went some way to convincing Bobby that I should be his first-choice goalkeeper. Also, over the years I'd enjoyed a number of good performances against Ipswich Town and perhaps that played a part in his decision. As I mentioned, Ray Clemence played two more games for England but I don't think he wanted to sit it out on the bench and so he decided to retire from international football. With Ray no longer a part of the England set-up, my competition for the goalkeeper's jersey was to come from Chris Woods and a young player by the name of David Seaman!

After the World Cup in Spain, I took stock of my future in the game and the inevitable move from Forest. A number of clubs had made enquiries. Arsenal were tipped as favourites for my signature but Sue wasn't keen on living in London and neither was I. The thought of living in Hampshire appealed to me, as did the thought of playing in a Southampton side that included Kevin Keegan and Alan Ball. I had spoken to the manager, Lawrie McMenemy, and been impressed with him and what he had to say, and so I opted for Southampton. Financially, it was a good deal for me and I genuinely felt that the club had the players to achieve success. Leaving Nottingham wasn't easy but it was the right decision.

In the event, I never did play many games alongside Kevin or Alan. Kevin left at the end of our 1982–83 pre-season tour to join Arthur Cox at Newcastle United and Alan also left the club. Looking back, I think Lawrie signed me knowing that Kevin and Alan were finishing, seeing me as adding some experience to his side.

At the time, Southampton were a mixture of seasoned professionals, such as Chris Nichol, David Armstrong and Nick Holmes, and promising youngsters, such as Mark Wright and Danny Wallace.

I liked Lawrie because he had stature. His backroom boys, Lew

Chatterely and John Mortimore, were football men through and through. I got on with all three, related to them and trusted them. Lawrie was a football man but he left the training and coaching to Lew and John. Occasionally, Lawrie would appear on the training ground in a neat tracksuit and his involvement would largely consist of blowing a whistle, much to the amusement of Alan Ball, who would rib Lawrie mercilessly. He would say such things as, 'If managing doesn't work out, you could always get a job on Southampton station.' Lawrie took all of Alan's light-hearted mickey taking in good part.

Lawrie McMenemy created a very good team at Southampton. The club enjoyed the most successful period in its history although we were never to win a major domestic trophy.

The former Sunderland, Bury, Blackpool and Carlisle manager, Bob Stokoe, once said, 'It's easy to be a good manager. All you have to do is sign good players. You don't have to tell good players what to do because they know. The difficult part of management is signing the good players.' It could be said that Lawrie McMenemy adhered to Bob Stokoe's philosophy of management. In essence, Lawrie built that Southampton side around experienced players, at a later date adding the likes of my ex-Leicester team-mate Frank Worthington and the left-back Mark Dennis.

Lawrie sometimes picked out young, inexperienced players for criticism following a below-par performance, but he was equally prepared to lock horns with the more seasoned pros. Lawrie had never played the game even at league level, but he still took internationals to task if he felt they were doing something not in the best interests of the team. For instance, Kevin Keegan's depart-ure from the club was preceded by a fall-out with Lawrie Mac. It seemed they disagreed over the role Lawrie wanted Kevin to perform in the side, and to the best of my knowledge the matter was never resolved. Likewise, Lawrie also had differences with

Alan Ball and Mick Channon, albeit ones that were resolved quickly. One one occasion Lawrie was engaged in a heated debate with Mick Channon about his role in a game, only for Mick, who was establishing himself as a racehorse owner of some note, to respond: 'That's all well and good, gaffer, but you have to remember football, for me, is now a hobby!'

That said, Southampton did very well under Lawrie. I enjoyed my football immensely at Southampton. We were up there challenging in the First Division and reached three Cup semi-finals. In addition, while at Southampton I became the most capped player in the history of the club, with forty-nine.

Having finished in mid-table in 1982–83, my first season at the club, things really took off for Southampton in the following year, our most successful in the League. Throughout the season, we mounted a serious challenge to Liverpool but, in the end, fell three points short. Ironically, the other team involved in the race for the championship was Nottingham Forest, who finished in third place.

As runners-up, Southampton qualified for the 1984–85 UEFA Cup but the closest we came to winning any major trophy was in domestic competitions.

A lot of people remember the Southampton of the early eighties for the famous trio of Ball, Keegan and Channon, but the most successful days were achieved without the services of those three great players. In my opinion, that side was fantastic when it came to playing entertaining football, but they were in essence a home team. The records show they rarely got a result away from home. The Southampton team I played for was capable of achieving results both home and away, as indicated by our final placings in the First Division. The one thing that prevented us from winning the championship or a major Cup competition was that we lacked the killer instinct up front. We were also, for some time, denied the services of Steve Moran, who sustained a back injury that was to plague him.

Steve had made a great impact at the club and was being talked of as another Kevin Keegan. He was similar in both height and style to Keegan and, if anything, was proving a more prolific goalscorer. Since coming in to the first team, Steve had averaged a goal every other game. His predatory instinct and livewire play had earned him England Under-21 honours and, when injured, his presence in the team was sorely missed.

The 1983–84 season was very much a case of 'nearly' as, apart from being runners-up in the First Division, we reached the semi-finals of the FA Cup. As fate would have it, our Cup run began with a 2–1 victory at Nottingham Forest. I was a little apprehensive about what sort of reaction I would receive from the Forest fans on my return to the City Ground but any anxieties I may have had proved unfounded and I was given a warm reception by the home supporters before and after the game.

We accounted for Portsmouth in round four in a hard-fought derby game at Fratton Park, and were drawn away again in round five at Blackburn Rovers. This was another tight game but a 1–0 victory pitched us against Sheffield Wednesday in the quarter-finals. Sheffield Wednesday, along with Chelsea, were on course for promotion from the Second Division and we needed a replay to account for them. The initial encounter had been yet another close-fought affair but we comfortably accounted for Howard Wilkinson's side in the replay, winning 5–1.

The other three semi-finalists were Everton, Watford and Plymouth Argyle. I suppose part of the allure and magic of the FA Cup is that it invariably produces a surprise package. Plymouth were in the lower reaches of the Third Division and had done remarkably well to reach the semi-finals under the management of Dave Smith. We were hoping to draw them or, failing that,

Watford but when the draw was made we got Everton, the bookies' clear favourites to win the Cup.

Managed by Howard Kendall, Everton had a very good team, including Peter Reid, Andy Gray, Neville Southall, Graeme Sharp, Adrian Heath, Gary Stevens and Kevin Ratcliffe. Although we could have asked for a more kindly draw, we were nevertheless confident of beating Everton but you need a bit of luck in Cup competitions and luck was what Southampton didn't have.

The game was played at Highbury and Southampton created the lion's share of chances, but after ninety goalless minutes extra-time beckoned. I felt we had the edge but we were left to rue our missed chances when Everton made the breakthrough with just over a minute of extra-time remaining.

The pitch was in a typical end-of-season state for those days. It had been heavy and the groundsman had at one point used a lot of sand to soak up the water. The spring winds had dried it out and what we were left with was a hard, sandy and, in some places, bumpy surface. The ball was crossed into my penalty area. Adrian Heath had made a run and, in normal circumstances, I don't think he would have connected, as the ball was coming in at midriff height, making it almost impossible for good contact. But the ball bounced on a part of the penalty area that was particularly sandy and spun up into the air. Adrian flung his head to one side and the ball skimmed off his head and into the top corner of the net.

We were gutted to lose the semi-final at such a late stage, but that's football. Adrian got a break when the ball hit the sand and didn't bounce as normal, but we'd created enough chances to win half a dozen semi-finals. As it turned out, it would not be the first time that Southampton's lack of killer instinct in front of goal proved to be our undoing. It's my belief that, if Southampton had possessed more of a potent strike force, the team could have been among the honours in the eighties.

As it was, Southampton were never again to achieve such lofty heights in the League. In a decade largely dominated by Liverpool and Everton, Southampton often occupied a mid-table position. In 1984–85 we finished fifth; the following season it was fourteenth. In 1986–87, in what proved to be my final season at the Dell, Southampton were twelfth.

The closest we came to winning silverware was in both the FA and League Cups. In 1985–86, having beaten Middlesbrough, Wigan, Millwall and Brighton, Southampton once again reached the semi-finals of the FA Cup where our opponents were Liverpool.

Self-appraisal is no guarantee of merit, I know, but I felt I had a terrific game against Liverpool. We'd been under the cosh from the start but had battled valiantly and were on equal terms with fifteen minutes to go when we were presented with a chance to wrap up the tie. George Lawrence snapped at the ball and a gilt-edged opportunity to make it to the final was gone. People remember that miss but tend to forget that George's efforts in previous rounds had played an important role in Southampton reaching the semi-finals. You have to take your chances in football because you'll be punished for not doing so. Liverpool punished us, winning the tie in extra-time.

Southampton's other Cup foray took place in the League Cup in the following season. Having disposed of Swindon Town, Manchester United, Shrewsbury Town and Aston Villa, we were once more up against Liverpool in the two-leg semi-final. We drew 0–0 at home but at Anfield were turned over to the tune of three goals to nil.

By the time of the Anfield match, Chris Nichol had taken over as manager from Lawrie McMenemy, who had, in turn, taken over at Sunderland. Sadly for Lawrie and Sunderland, his tenure as manager with the Wearside club was not a happy one. When he arrived at Roker Park, Lawrie promised to take Sunderland out of the Second Division. He did, in fact, keep that promise – in 1987, Sunderland were relegated to the Third.

While I was at Southampton I felt I was playing as well as I had done at Forest. I was established as England's number-one goalkeeper and played in the finals of the 1986 World Cup. Southampton never featured among the honours but we played attractive and enterprising football and I felt on top of my game. Career-wise I was happy at Southampton but financial troubles were beginning to bubble-up. At the time, I could never have envisaged just how critical the situation would become.

When I was at Leicester City, I had an interest in two racehorses. Jockey Red Weaver had called into the treatment room for some physiotherapy on a shoulder injury and I got chatting with him. He told me that a local trainer, Alan Jarvis, had a horse for sale and suggested it might be a decent investment. To cut a long story short, I ended up as a part-owner of this horse, along with a few other Leicester players. We often went along to watch it race although it always seemed to flatter to deceive. Of course, the day none of us went, it was a 10 to 1 winner!

The other horse, Admiral Jersey, was purchased through my company, Peter Shilton Limited. I wouldn't go so far as to say I nearly lost my shirt on Jersey, but it turned out not to be a good investment.

The lack of success of those two horses put me off ownership for a number of years but at Southampton my interest was rekindled. When Mick Channon and I had been members of the England Youth team in the 1960s, Mick owned a filly by the name of Cathy Jane for which he had paid £400. She won the Brown Jack Stakes at Ascot. Mick and I went to a betting shop to listen to the race commentary – the only place you could do so in those days – and Mick was delighted at her win. From her he eventually bred Janesmead, which he owned in partnership with Kevin Keegan.

Mick's love of horseracing continued throughout his career as a footballer. While I was at Southampton Mick selected and bought a horse for me, for which I paid ten thousand guineas. I named it Hard To Catch and it did rather well for us. That fuelled my enthusiasm and I bought a horse myself, Between The Sticks, through trainer Richard Hannon, to whom I'd been introduced by Mick.

Richard trained at Marlborough, which is not that far away from Southampton. I would often drive over and spend a pleasant hour or so watching the horses on the gallops, harbouring dreams of one day owning a string of horses and perhaps even a stud.

I paid around twenty-three thousand guineas for Between The Sticks and had high hopes for her when she won her first two races. Before the first one, at Newmarket, I asked Richard Hannon if she had a chance. Richard said she had a decent chance as there were only eight runners and advised me to place an each-way bet. I was rather nervous and, not wanting to jinx Between The Sticks, decided not to put any money on her. Perhaps the fact that the owner didn't place a bet helped boost her odds. The bookies were offering her at 33 to 1. In the event, she romped home. As the owner, I was asked to give an interview for television. Richard told me to say that I did have a little flutter on her but I felt uncomfortable telling a lie so admitted on camera that I hadn't placed a bet on my own horse in her maiden race. To this day, punters come up to me and remind me of the day I never had a bet on my own horse at 33 to 1.

Between The Sticks did well for me and the success of my first two horses encouraged me to purchase others. With the benefit of hindsight, that was to prove a costly mistake.

At the time, Sue and I had our house in Southampton and a holiday home in Devon. However, the costs of training and stabling my horses, together with the fact that I had begun to bet more regularly and heavily, started to eat into our finances. I had no real money problems because, although my outgoings were considerable, my income from football more than covered them. Now I can see how the seeds were being sown for the financial trouble I would soon encounter.

The problems really hit me in the late eighties, following my transfer to Derby County in 1987. One newspaper described the move as 'Britain's most successful entrepreneurial publisher lands British football's most successful goalkeeper – it's the dream team!' In time, the 'dream team' were to be living out their respective nightmares.

10

HAND OF GOD

When it came to winning major trophies, my career with England was to be similar to my career with Southampton – a case of 'nearly'. With England, though, exits from major tournaments were invariably accompanied by pain and angst.

Bobby Robson was not the popular choice to succeed Ron Greenwood as England manager. Many fans still wanted to see Brian Clough in the job and Bobby had to face flak from certain quarters of the press before his first game in charge. It was not long before the *Sun* was giving away 'Robson Out – Clough In' badges and holding a national phone-in poll in a bid to undermine Bobby. That was very tame stuff in comparison with what he had to endure later, before eventually being hailed as 'the best England manager since Sir Alf Ramsey' by, you've guessed it, the *Sun*.

It's the mark of the man that Bobby Robson exhibited nothing but grace and dignity in the face of stinging criticism in his early days in the job. The attitude changed as England started to produce good results and performances, particularly in major tournaments.

I played in the finals of three major competitions under Bobby Robson – the 1986 World Cup in Mexico, the 1988 European Championship in Germany and Italia '90.

I liked Bobby Robson as both a manager and a man. He was upfront with me, not afraid to speak his mind; he also encouraged enterprising football. And his man management was very good. When he left a player out of the team, more times than not he sat down with him and explained the reasons for his omission.

I remember an occasion on tour with England when Joe Mercer was manager. Joe came to me and said, 'I'm going to give Ray a game. You're not dropped. It's not because you've played badly or anything like that. I'm just resting you for the one game.' I had no problem with that at all. In the event, Ray stayed in the team for the rest of the tour. I was very disappointed, not only to be left out of the team but at the way Joe handled the situation. He never told me why he was continuing with Ray; he simply ignored me. For him not to speak to me again for the remainder of the tour I felt was poor man management on his part, and I lost a lot of respect for him over it. I thought he should have been honest with me. I'm a reasonable guy. If Joe had told me I was being left out for the rest of the tour, I would have been disappointed but I would have respected his decision. As it was, I felt Joe had bottled it.

Bobby's decision to omit Kevin Keegan from the squad was highly controversial. Kevin had sixty-three caps and had twice been voted European Footballer of the Year. No one could doubt his contribution to England and Kevin was upset. Bobby was mindful of the role Kevin had played in the England set-up but he was looking ahead to Euro '84. As far as I could gather, he believed Kevin's career as an international had reached the 'tipping' point.

Right from the start, Bobby Robson chose me as his number-one goalkeeper, and stuck with me, and I will always be grateful to him for that. His first game in charge was the European Championship qualifier against Denmark in Copenhagen in September 1982. A Jesper Olsen goal twenty seconds from time gave the Danes a 2–2 draw. Bobby gave a first cap to Luton's Ricky Hill, who came on as a substitute for Aston Villa's Tony Morley. On the face of it, a draw in Denmark was not a bad start for Bobby as England manager, nor our quest to reach the finals of the 1984 European Championship.

Unfortunately, England never did make it to the finals. A 0–0 draw against Greece and a 1–0 defeat against Denmark, both at Wembley, proved our undoing. In our penultimate group game we beat Hungary 3–0 at Wembley to keep alive our chances of qualification but before we played our final group game, in Luxembourg, news came through that Denmark had beaten Greece 2–0 to clinch the one qualifying place from the group. Bobby Robson played Ray Clemence in goal and England beat Luxembourg 4–0, but the result was academic. Bobby Robson was left to turn his attention towards the 1986 World Cup.

While Europe partied in the summer of 1984, England embarked upon a tour of South America. Few people gave us much chance of doing well against Brazil, Uruguay and Chile. According to the press, the result of our game against Brazil was a foregone conclusion. England had not beaten Brazil in the last eleven encounters, our only victory coming in the first-ever meeting of the two teams, which was in 1956 at Wembley. Stanley Matthews inspired England to a 4–2 victory.

When Bobby Robson announced his team to play Brazil, it raised a few eyebrows. Bobby included the youngsters John Barnes (Watford), Mark Hateley (Portsmouth) and Mark Chamberlain (Stoke City). England surprised everyone. John Barnes set off on a corkscrew run that took him past five Brazilian players before he slid the ball past goalkeeper Roberto Costa. John's effort was hailed as one of the all-time great England goals and went a long way towards making his name in football. John's goal was a tremendous boost to our confidence.

Brazil reacted as only Brazil can. They attacked. Time and again I was called upon to make saves but, for all their pressure, Brazil couldn't produce an equaliser and in the sixty-fifth minute we added to our lead. A cross from John Barnes met Mark Hateley's head and the electronic scoreboard displayed the unbelievable scoreline – Brazil 0 England 2.

Another youngster, QPR's Clive Allen, came on for his international debut in place of Tony Woodcock. Having seen us establish a two-goal lead, I did everything in my power to preserve it and when the final whistle sounded, I felt a mixture of joy, pride and relief. It was Brazil's first home defeat for twenty-six years. Bobby Robson's much-criticised policy of preferring youngsters to experienced heads at international level, and of sticking to a 4–2–4 formation, had been largely vindicated.

Some months later, in October 1984, we couldn't have wished for a better start in attempting to qualify for the 1986 World Cup in Mexico. Finland were beaten 5–0 at Wembley and three weeks later we were in Istanbul to take on Turkey. Many people were saying that Turkey was a very tough place to play and the night before the game Turkish supporters assembled outside our team hotel, banging drums and blowing horns to keep the players awake. We did manage to get some sleep, but it was fitful.

At the stadium the next day, we walked out to inspect the pitch and although there was over an hour to kick-off, one section of the stadium was already jam-packed with Turkish supporters. As soon as they saw the England team emerge form the tunnel, they gave us some terrible stick. The verbal abuse they hurled at us was just for starters. Within a minute we were being pelted with fruit, coins and what I took to be offal. This part of the ground was where the cheaper seats were allocated and was known as the 'popular stand'. Needless to say, it wasn't very popular with us.

The tirade of abuse followed us as we left the field and met us when we re-emerged for the start of the game. Come half-time, however, with England leading 4–0, as we went in for the interval, the stadium was silent. Then, suddenly, the Turkish supporters broke into spontaneous applause in recognition of our first-half performance. I had to laugh at the fickle nature of their support.

The final result was unbelievable. We thrashed Turkey 8–0 and Bryan Robson became the first England captain to score a hat-trick since Vivian Woodward in 1908.

The spirit of the team under Bobby Robson was very good but the change in the way the tabloid press reported football continued. Under Don Revie, when England had a midweek game at Wembley we would report to our team hotel in Cockfosters on a Sunday afternoon. Having played a league game on the Saturday, our time was more or less our own on a Sunday and all the players would go down to the local pub on the Sunday night for a couple of beers. This continued under Ron Greenwood and never at any time was it an issue with the England management. The press didn't dog your every move and there were no reporters hanging about outside the hotel, hoping for a sniff of a scurrilous story.

There was one occasion, however, when some of the players moved on from the pub to a nightclub in Tottenham Court Road. The following day everyone trained well but the newspapers had got to hear about the visit and the story made front-page news. I remember the *Sun* had a cartoon that showed some England players leaning against goalposts with bottles in their hands. The relaxed relationship that top footballers had enjoyed with the press for many years was becoming a thing of the past. Not only were certain elements of the press becoming more interested in the personal lives and off-the-field activities of England players, some were not beyond manipulating the truth in order to create a tit-illating, or even scandalous, story.

One time, when Bobby Robson was manager, I reported to the England team hotel in High Wycombe on a Thursday in preparation for a match taking place the following week. On the Saturday afternoon, Bobby told those players who were within reasonable travelling distance of their homes that they could spend

Saturday night with their families and report back to our hotel on Sunday teatime. I stayed at the hotel, as did Trevor Francis. Trevor told me that a family friend of his who lived near by had invited him for Sunday lunch and extended an invitation for me to join them. We went to a lovely pub-cum-restaurant, enjoyed a fabulous Sunday lunch, and at a quarter to three were on the point of paying the bill when the other 'bill' arrived on the scene. It was made out that the reason for the police's presence was because we were drinking outside the licensing hours. The police saw that we'd had a drink as part of our meal and nothing was made of the situation. The following day, however, a tabloid newspaper ran the headline, 'England Players Caught Up In Drinks Raid'. How this had all come about I don't know. I can only assume someone wanting to make a few bob had seen Trevor and me, telephoned the police saying the pub was serving drinks after hours, then tipped off the newspaper in question. To my mind, it was a story as unmerited as it was unsavoury.

The two convincing victories over Finland and Turkey appeared to provide the perfect platform for England's quest to qualify for the 1986 World Cup finals but a series of drawn matches against Romania (home and away), Finland and Northern Ireland contrived to put us under pressure. In the event, an earlier single-goal victory over the Irish and another convincing win over Turkey (5–0) meant we were Mexico bound. As runners-up in the group, Northern Ireland also qualified. Despite stuttering along the way, England went to Mexico as the only European team unbeaten in the qualifying stages. Nevertheless, as far as the tabloids were concerned, the jury was still out on Bobby Robson as England manager.

Bobby had endured a rough ride from the press. In May 1985 following the draws against Romania and Finland, England travelled to Hampden Park to contest the Sir Stanley Rous Cup. It was a very open and evenly contested game, as the match statistics of twenty goal attempts by England and fourteen from Scotland testify. There was only one goal, however, scored by Scotland's Richard Gough. At the time, England were still on course for Mexico, but we awoke to screaming headlines that read, 'Robson Must Go' and 'Sack Robson Before It's Too Late'.

Just before the World Cup, the papers refrained from giving Bobby a tough time but in the back of my mind I thought, 'Should our World Cup campaign get off to a bad start, the tabloids will have the daggers out for us.' Our start was such the press didn't get the daggers out – it was more like sabres and lances.

Our World Cup preparation was first class. The England team spent a month in Colorado in the United States, training and acclimatising. Our hotel was one of the best I have ever stayed in. The grounds and gardens were fantastic, the centrepiece being a lake so big you couldn't see from one end to the other. There was a superb golf course and, of all things, an ice rink.

Once again, a member the press contrived to make his presence felt. A tabloid journalist approached the manager of the hotel and allegedly offered him a sum of money if he would inform the reporter in question of any 'indiscretions by any members of the England team'. The reporter was given short shrift and asked to leave the hotel. That incident made us all even more wary of the media – as I say, one bad apple...

The training facilities were among the best I had ever come across. We trained at the sports complex of a nearby US Air Force base with superb sports fields, a 5,000-seater indoor basketball stadium, an Olympic-standard swimming pool, saunas and steam rooms, most of which we utilised. Everything was laid on and all went to plan. Bobby even arranged for our wives and girlfriends to fly over and stay for a week. It was the best preparation for a major tournament I had ever known.

The training was also probably the toughest I had known – two hours a day in temperatures that were in the high nineties. It was designed to help us adjust to the heat and the altitude. A ball travels quicker through rarefied air than it normally would. After a week or so, I was confident that the quicker ball wouldn't cause me any problems.

After our month was up, we flew down to Monterrey in Mexico, where it was even hotter than Colorado had been and the training facilities were nowhere near as good. The training pitches were baked hard. I had to wear a tracksuit at every session to protect my legs. Throwing yourself around while wearing a tracksuit in temperatures in excess of 110 degrees was hard work. I shed pounds, but Bobby Robson and his staff were meticulous in their monitoring of the well being of every player – so much so that not one player was ill in the entire time we were in Mexico.

The Monterrey stadium, where we played our first game, against Portugal, was a big letdown, on a par with a bad Third Division ground. It held about 5,000 people, the pitch was poor and the changing facilities basic. The pitch was so bumpy the groundsman had been instructed to let the grass grow. He had done what he could – where there was grass, it was much longer than it would normally have been.

In fact, though, the Mexican government and footballing authorities had done remarkably well. The original venue for the World Cup had been Colombia but when it became apparent that the stadiums, facilities and infrastructure of that country were not going to be ready in time, FIFA switched the finals to Mexico. Then, a few months before the first game was due to kick off, Mexico City suffered a devastating earthquake. Many people lost their lives and the destruction was considerable. Given the short notice and that terrible tragedy, it's to the credit of Mexico that the 1986 World Cup was staged at all.

England should have beaten Portugal but we just never got going. The facilities, the hard, bumpy pitch with its long grass, and the lack of atmosphere all contributed to our mindset. Gary Lineker played with a sprained wrist strapped up and Bryan Robson suffered a recurrence of a shoulder injury and was substituted, but really the story of our 1–0 defeat was one of missed chances. We created enough opportunities to have won the game comfortably but poor finishing let us down.

It went from bad to worse when we drew 0–0 with Morocco in our second group match. Bryan Robson's shoulder let him down again. He had to be substituted and this time he was out of the tournament. To compound our problems, acting captain Ray Wilkins was sent off for throwing the ball in the direction of the referee in frustration at an offside decision. Uncharacteristically, Gary Linker missed a few chances, but our overall performance against Morocco was poor.

After all the meticulous preparation, we just couldn't seem to lift ourselves. It wasn't for lack of trying but it appeared to me that the harder we tried the more we came unstuck. I'm sure it had something to do with the small stadium and the lack of atmosphere. We should have been able to deal with those things but for some reason, in our opening two matches, we didn't.

All changed, however, when we switched to the larger stadium in Monterrey for our final group game, against Poland. For the first time we felt as if we were involved in a World Cup and raised our game accordingly. The bigger stadium with its superior pitch and atmosphere gave us a mental boost. I believe another reason why we suddenly started playing better was that we reverted back to a 4–4–2 formation.

Bobby Robson placed a lot of importance on the role of his namesake, but following Bryan's injury and Ray Wilkins' suspension, Bobby had to rethink his tactics against the Poles. Peter

Beardsley replaced Mark Hateley up front as Gary Lineker's strike partner. Chris Waddle was replaced by Trevor Steven of Everton, and Steve Hodge and Peter Reid replaced Robson and Wilkins. It was not unusual for an England manager to change the formation of the team in mid-tournament. Alf Ramsey did it during the 1966 World Cup and although Bobby Robson's change of tactics was not to have the monumental effect of Ramsey's in '66, our performance against Poland was one of considerable improvement.

Gary Lineker, who was a lot more comfortable playing in the 4–4–2 system, suddenly found space and a rhythm to his play. He scored a hat-trick, the only goals of the game, in the first half and we enjoyed a convincing victory, the result of which ensured our progress to the second round.

It could have been a totally different story, however. In the first minute of the game, a defensive lapse allowed a Polish player to break with a clear run on goal. I managed to make a decent save. I beat out his effort and Terry Butcher mopped up the loose ball and played it back to me. I thought to myself, 'If that had gone in, we could really have been in the mire.' In the event, we put our game together and some clinical finishing from Gary earned a crucial victory.

I was pleased for Bobby Robson. In the wake of our disappointing start, he had, as expected, come in for some terrible stick. One tabloid called for him to be sacked, which I thought was harsh and unfair, if not ridiculous. England still had a chance of qualifying for round two, yet there was a newspaper calling for the manager to be sacked mid-tournament!

From Monterrey we moved on to Mexico City and a comfortable 3–0 win over Paraguay. The game took place in the Azteca Stadium, which is one of the best stadiums I ever played in. The facilities are superb and the Alp-like stands generate an electric atmosphere. The pitch is not one of the best, though, and against

Paraguay it was patchy. Divets had not been replaced but filled with sand and the midfield in particular was hard and bumpy. Two goals from Gary Lineker and one from Peter Beardsley helped England to qualify for the quarter-finals where our opponents were the favourites, Argentina.

Goalkeepers tend to remember their crucial saves but sometimes the goals scored against you stay with you for ever. In England's quarter-final match against Argentina, I unwittingly found myself playing a key role in one of the most infamous goals in the history of World Cup football.

The pre-match hype bordered on the hysterical. This was the first football match between the two countries since the Falklands War and, with so much at stake, not only the British but the world's media focused attention on the game. Four years earlier the two countries had been at war and, in some quarters, this match was portrayed as something of a sporting rerun of that conflict. I didn't see it that way but the gravity and the importance of the occasion were not lost on me. We were playing one of the best teams in the world, one member of which was the greatest player in the world. Along with the rest of my England team-mates, there wasn't much I didn't know about Diego Maradona. He was the finest player of his generation, touched with football genius. Small and squat, he possessed a big heart. A player of immaculate technique, out-standing distribution, rare vision and consummate skill, he was a tempestuous football idol whose brilliance was such that it was said he was capable of winning the World Cup on his own. I thought he could be stopped.

The Italians had stopped him dead in his tracks in the previous World Cup in Spain although to accomplish that involved them kicking him up hill and down dale whenever the opportunity arose to lay a boot on his passing figure. Bobby Robson would not ask his players to resort to such shabby tactics. There was no need. As a team, we felt we had enough about us to stop the threat of Maradona.

The sports pages were filled with derogatory remarks about the Argentinian team and Maradona in particular. The tabloids had gone from bingo to jingo. For their part, the Argentine press were equally volatile. In the days leading up to the game, it all served to create a disturbing atmosphere of malice. I tried to detach myself from it and I think Maradona did, too. In countless interviews with the press, he refused to be drawn into saying the game had to do with anything other than football. 'I am here', he said, repeatedly, 'to play football, not politics.'

Following an unhappy spell with Barcelona, Maradona had joined Napoli as a mature twenty-five-year-old. In Italy, he had recaptured the bewitching form that had made him an idol. He enjoyed a free role with Argentina and was the hub on which every move turned. He could size up a situation in an instant and, to go with his complete mastery of the ball and great powers of acceleration, he had the cunning to veil his intentions and the patience to bide his time before making his strike. He loved the ball to be played to his feet. When he peeled off defenders, he preferred to turn away to his left. For a small guy, his immaculate timing made him good in the air. I knew all that and more about Maradona. What I didn't know was that he was also a cheat.

In the absence of Bryan Robson and Ray Wilkins, I had been made captain and admit to having harboured thoughts of captaining England in the final. I felt the team Bobby Robson had created had as good a chance as any of winning the World Cup. The main stumbling block was Argentina but we thought if we could keep Maradona quiet, Argentina would struggle to score, and Gary Lineker was always likely to get a goal for us.

The first half was how I expected it to be – very tight with nothing much between either side. Argentina enjoyed marginally more

LEFT: A proud day for me. In my England Schoolboy blazer prior to making my debut for England v Republic of Ireland at Northampton's County Ground. The delivery bike in the background I used to cycle to and from Filbert Street for training.

BELOW: England Under 23s v West Germany at Filbert Street in 1971. Colin Todd is captain and behind me is John Robson (Derby), Larry Lloyd and Brian Kidd.

TOP: I have had the (doubtful?) privilege to sing on four hit records. This was the first
the England 1970 World Cup squad singing 'Back Home' on *Top Of The Pops*. Even t
England trainer and doctor got in on the act.

ABOVE RIGHT & LEFT: Training with Sir Alf prior to my full international debut agai
East Germany at Wembley in November 1970 - a game in which I like to think I show
them how to organise a wall (*Popperfoto*).

Signing autographs after an England training session in Prague. These were the days when England players did have contact with supporters at training. I was an avid collector of autographs as a boy so never refused a request for my signature unless I could help it (*Foto Ivoaclk*).

ABOVE: An ITV poster to promote their coverage of England's crucial World Cup qualifier against Poland in 1973. The colours on the poster are fantastic but not so the artist's depiction of me. I am featured four times and not one looks like me – I hope.

RIGHT: Attending an England post-match dinner. On my left are Colin Todd, Emlyn Hughes, Martin Peters and Roy McFarland. Opposite are Norman Hunter and Paul Madeley. Norman is about to get tucked into his starter of fish, whereas in the background an FA official tells the story of the one that got away.

Equal but different:
e man who followed
Banks of England

BY JEFF POWELL

ON will get up early this morning,
o the clamouring recognition for his
ng saves and go through an army
ne which ensures Her Majesty's
be found wanting
ave to scale 100-
cannons on their

acy may have come
d's newest leading
it has not come

self-inflicted torture
ult course near his
side Leicester gym-
dicated preparation
nce Hannibal made
hants across moun-

lieve England's foot-
r time between in-
o another night club
with Shilton pain-

ive to excel is ama-
was 14, it was clear
ine short" of total

Scenes of utter dejection
following the disastrous
World Cup qualifier
against Poland at Wembley,
October 1973 - a match
that was to have a great
impact on English football
(*Popperfoto & Empics*).

Keeping Scotland
at bay. Action
from Hampden
Park, the Home
Internationals,
18 May 1974
(*Mirrorpix*).

TOP LEFT: With Trevor Brooking and Mick Channon prior to England's crucial World Cup qualifier against Italy in 1976.

TOP RIGHT: With Ray Clemence, England's other no.1. Ray and myself were the best of friends throughout our England careers, and remain so to this day (*Sporting Pictures*).

ABOVE LEFT: In action against France in England's opener in Spain in 1982. Bryan Robson scored the fastest goal in World Cup finals history, England won the game 3–1, but we flattered to deceive. Our inability to score goals would see us undefeated but eliminated (*Mirrorpix*).

ABOVE RIGHT: Surely a unique moment in the history of international football: an England goalkeeper wearing a Scotland jersey . . . and while playing against Scotland (*Sporting Pictures*).

TOP LEFT: With my England room-mate, Gary Lineker, celebrating the victory over Turkey that meant we'd qualified for the World Cup in 1986 (*Popperfoto*).

TOP RIGHT, ABOVE, TOP AND BELOW LEFT OPPOSITE: Maradona, Mexico '86. We felt we could handle him . . . but that was before 'The Hand of God' . . . (*Mirrorpix, Getty Images, Empics*).

ABOVE RIGHT: Stepping out for my 100th cap, against Holland, the European Championships, 1988 (*Popperfoto*).

TOP: . . . and breaking Bobby Moore's record number of caps, Copenhagen in 1989 (*Getty Images*).

ABOVE LEFT AND RIGHT: Thwarting Oman Biyik of Cameroon in Italia '90 in the opening minutes with a one-on-one save (*Empics*) . . . and with the gaffer, Bobby Robson, following our qualification for Italia '90, after a 0–0 draw in Poland (*Popperfoto*).

The semi-final against Germany. There was little I could do once the ball had deflected from Paul Parker . . . but the scenes of celebration on our welcome home at Luton were something that will stay with me for ever (*Popperfoto, Sporting Pictures, Mirrorpix*).

TOP: A warm hug from Pele prior to playing for the Football League against the Rest Of The World at Wembley.

ABOVE: Flanked by two greats of the game, Franz Beckenbauer and Bobby Moore at my 'farewell game' against an International XI at White Hart Lane.

RIGHT: All the lads together, during my time at Derby. Left to right: myself, my brothers Tony and Graham, and my dad . . .
BELOW: in action for Derby, a tough but very enjoyable time (*Sporting Pictures*) . . .
MIDDLE RIGHT: and the view from the dug-out against Marlow Town in the FA Cup first round, November 1993. Life at Plymouth gave me my first taste of management – who knows if it will be my last? (*Getty Images*).

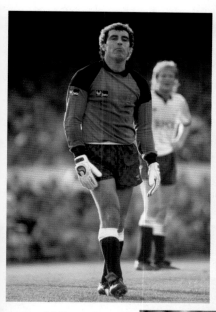

RIGHT: 22 December 1996. My 1,000th League match. The occasion was Leyton Orient v Brighton and such was the interest that the match was live on Sky and the gate at Brisbane Road was more than twice the average. Here I'm presented with a commemorative edition of the *Guinness Book of Records* (*Getty Images*).

TOP: A very joyous and happy day for Sue and myself, the occasion of our wedding in 1970. I still have the suit.

ABOVE: Eamon Andrews and Jon Holmes, and (right) Glenn Hoddle, Kenny Samson, Tony Woodcock, Viv Anderson and Chris Waddle surprise me at Waterloo Station for the *This Is Your Life* programme. They were pretending to be porters, but my suspicions were aroused when one of them offered to carry my bag . . .

. . . along with
Peter Bonetti
and Lev
Yashin, Gordon
Banks was one
of my boyhood
heroes. He also
turned up as a
surprise guest
on *This Is Your
Life*.

Another very proud day for me. With Sue, Michael and Sam at Buckingham Palace to receive my OBE.

possession but they never created anything in front of goal and, to be honest, I felt very comfortable. What chances were created in the first half were created by England. Gary Lineker headed narrowly over following a cross from Glenn Hoddle, Peter Beardsley fizzed a shot just wide of a post and Trevor Steven fired into a thicket of legs. On the balance of play, the goalless scoreline at the interval was, to my mind, a fair one. Everything was to change dramatically in the second half.

A mish-mash of a ball came upfield. Maradona made ground from midfield and, from a point some twenty yards from my goal, chipped the ball towards the angle of my penalty area on my left-hand side. Years of experience had instilled in me an intuitive sense of when danger was about. Whenever play unfolded around the edge of my penalty area, I always knew if there was danger or not. I'd been a professional goalkeeper for twenty-one years. In addition to working tirelessly at my craft, I had evolved a sixth sense, so I knew whether to hit my toes or not. When Maradona chipped the ball towards the angle of my penalty area I was relaxed. There was no adrenalin rush, no need for me to take evasive action, because there was no danger to my goal. Maradona was looking for a one–two but I knew it wasn't going to happen. That ball was not going to be played back into his path.

The ball bounced off an Argentinian leg like a pinball. Steve Hodge threw his left leg behind him and made contact with the ball with an upward movement. It spooned into the air. My brain immediately went into action – red alert.

I immediately took to my toes. The ball arced in a parabola, descending to a point a yard or so from my penalty spot. I never left my goal area unless I was certain that I would win the ball. I knew I had to leave my line to win this ball and, what's more, I knew I would win it. Out of the corner of my eye I saw Maradona on the run. My senses again took command. He had too much ground to make up. Even allowing for the fact that he was free to take off on his favoured left foot, I knew, all things being equal, I was going to make it to the ball first.

As I took off from the ground, I wasn't so much reaching for the ball as over-reaching, but I knew I was going to make contact. I also knew, given his height and the trajectory of the ball, Maradona could not get his head to it. That just wasn't going to happen. I was aware that Maradona was airborne but all was well. He hadn't made sufficient height. It was my ball and I flung out my right arm, ready to punch it clear. I was really stretching so I knew I wasn't going to achieve the ideal height and distance, but it was good enough to avert danger.

After that, my mind's all a fuzzle. Adrenalin rushed to my brain. I punched thin air! Maradona had made contact with the ball but there was just no way that could have happened. For him to have headed that ball was impossible.

The Azteca Stadium erupted. An almighty roar swept down from the massed tiers of seating. Maradona was bolting across my penalty area, jumping and punching the air with his left hand. It came to me then. That's it! He used his hand! He must have. There's no other explanation, no other way he could have beaten me to that ball. 'Ref! Hey Ref! Ref-er-eeee!'

Maradona knew he wasn't going to get his head on that ball, so he did what a lot of centre-forwards would do in such a situation – he used his hand, expecting to hear the referee blow his whistle for hand ball, as would happen ninety-nine times out of a hundred. He gambled.

The odds of both the referee, Ali Ben Naseur of Tunisia, and his assistant not seeing his hand ball were stacked against him. Maradona took those odds because there was nothing left open to him. Luck, fate, call it what you will, was on his side that day. The match officials didn't see Maradona's hand ball and England's

World Cup fate was sealed. Later, Maradona claimed it was the 'Hand of God'. Maradona knew I was going to win the ball and that's why he stuck up his left hand. I was horrified when I saw the referee and his assistant running up the field, ready to take their places for the re-start. My stomach felt like an empty pit.

Maradona's goal affected England. We stuck doggedly to the task in hand but it took the edge off our game. From that moment on, although we were a match for Argentina in terms of ability and effort, we were suddenly not as mentally strong.

Maradona's second goal was a fantastic solo effort, now acclaimed as one of the greatest goals ever to have been scored. Four minutes after his infamous opener, he picked up the ball on the halfway line and, with a deft flick, beat both Peter Beardsley and Peter Reid and accelerated into our half of the field. After the two Peters came the two Terrys, Butcher and Fenwick. I came off my line to narrow Maradona's vision of goal. He was moving the ball forward with his left foot and my position offered him a wide gap through which to fire off a shot. Terry Butcher was breathing down his neck. I would say that 99 per cent of players finding themselves in that situation would opt to shoot into the gap. I was expecting him to do that and was ready for him. Suddenly, Maradona switched the ball from his left to his right foot and jabbed it goalwards just as Terry Butcher made the tackle. I hit the ground but was a split second too late. Maradona's shot evaded me. I was so near to getting a touch but didn't make contact and the ball carried on into the net. Cue stadium eruption.

Countless people have asked me if Terry Butcher got the decisive touch on the ball. I don't think so. It was all Maradona's own work. In scoring that solo goal, he had proved to the watching world that he was one of the all-time great footballers.

It was a great goal but it should never have been allowed. We contested the legitimacy of this goal as well but, again, our protests fell on deaf ears. Before Maradona had collected the ball in the centre of the field, we had been in possession. Glenn Hoddle had the ball at his feet but was scythed down by a tackle that took him out at thigh height. Why the referee didn't blow for what was an obvious foul I'll never know. The loose ball broke to Maradona and the rest is history.

As expected, Gary Lineker scored but England were out of the World Cup. My dream of captaining my country in a World Cup final was to remain just that, a dream.

Back in the dressing room we were all devastated. Bobby Robson came in.

'He didn't handle that ball, did he?' he said.

To a man, we all replied, 'He did.'

Bobby looked forlornly at the floor for a moment.

'Then we've just been flippin' cheated,' he said.

We were all so gutted no one could bring themselves to mention the foul on Glenn Hoddle that preceded Maradona's second goal. Bobby turned about and left the room.

I felt embittered. To be honest, I was so disappointed that England had been eliminated from the World Cup, that, at the time, I didn't dwell too much on the controversy surrounding Maradona's hand ball. It hasn't gone away, though. It has accompanied me through life to this day.

What amazed me was that no one from the press asked me about Maradona's 'Hand of God' goal. I found it unbelievable that no one from the media sought my point of view. I have never really publicly given my version of events until now. The one question I have been asked repeatedly is, 'Why didn't you go straight through him?' The answer is simple. I couldn't have gone straight through him because I was over-reaching for the ball. It wasn't my style to go through a forward, although I did so unwittingly on occasions when the player arrived so late I hadn't seen him. In over-reaching for the ball, and given Maradona's position, even if that had been my intention, it would have been physically impossible for me to have taken him out. Besides, as I've explained, all things being equal, I knew I would win the race to the ball without having recourse to the man. As it turned out, all things were not equal.

Given the highly controversial circumstances of both Maradona's goals, particularly the first one, I find it interesting that, to the best of my knowledge, neither the referee nor the assistant referee involved in the incident ever officiated in an international match again.

One final point may have something to do with the British psyche and the way we view ourselves. For decades, various people in this country have been at pains to prove that Geoff Hurst's second goal against West Germany in the 1966 World Cup final never crossed the line. So-called boffins have spent countless hours on computers, trying to prove the ball never crossed the line. I wonder how many people you would find in other countries expending all that effort trying to prove that one of the goals that won their country the World Cup should never have been allowed. I don't suppose any Argentinian has ever devoted any time at all to proving that the goal that effectively secured victory for Argentina over England in the '86 World Cup and subsequently helped them win the trophy should never have been allowed.

11

THE AGONY AND THEIR ECSTASY

Sue, quite rightly, wasn't happy about the amount of money I was gambling. She was also concerned that my business interests, mainly the horses, were not flourishing and were proving a drain on our finances. Sue and I loved each other but pressure was mounting and our relationship was, at times, strained.

On one occasion we had a particularly heated argument. It was verbal but very volatile and in the heat of the moment, Sue picked up the telephone and called the police. The police duly arrived at our home and I was taken away to the police station. I wasn't charged with anything. I think they removed me from the scene simply to allow the situation to calm down and to prevent it escalating. It was, as one person later described it, 'a minor category domestic'.

The next morning the *Sun* ran a story along the lines of 'Shilton Is A Wife Beater'. I was shocked when I read this and thought it disgraceful. To set the record straight, Sue and I gave an interview to the press. Sue said the story was not true, and while there had been a heated argument between us, that was the extent of it. The incident was a private matter. She had called the police in the heat of the moment but nobody had been hurt or assaulted. The following day she regretted having telephoned the police. I was full of regret for having fuelled our differences.

On the morning the story appeared in the *Sun*, the Southampton chairman called on Sue. She was at home with our boys, Sam and

Michael, and told him that the incident was most regrettable and should never have happened. She told him that the story in the press was untrue and we were both deeply upset about its content. The chairman accepted Sue at her word and the club made nothing else of the matter.

The incident had occurred after a game. I was not relaxed and it didn't help that when I got home I had a couple of drinks. Fortunately, the press conference Sue and I called defused the matter and the story quickly disappeared from the newspapers but one or two ugly rumours persisted. One in particular suggested I was a heavy drinker. Looking back, I can understand how this rumour came about. The car crash in Nottingham and the argument at home in Southampton had both taken place when I'd been drinking. I was never a regular drinker but on one or two occasions, few and far between, I did indulge in more than was good for me. I could not have been a professional footballer for over thirty years if I had also been a heavy drinker – no human body would have been up to it. When I did have a good drink, though, it really was a good drink, and on a couple of occasions it got me into bother.

I think this was basically because, when I did hit the booze, my system wasn't used to it. That's my take on it. I knew players who went out regularly and would drink quite a lot with no effect. They would turn up for training the next day and train as hard and as well as the next man. Perhaps their systems had become attuned to alcohol in quantity. All I can assume is that because I was not a regular drinker, when I did binge, it really did have an adverse effect on me. I was naïve not to have realised it at the time but it didn't affect my training and I was always in optimum shape for games.

Sue and I really enjoyed living in Hampshire. In fact, it was the best place we lived during my playing days. For the vast majority of the five years I spent with the club I was very happy there. When Lawrie McMenemy went to Sunderland, he asked if I would like to join him at Roker Park. I declined because at the time I had no thoughts of leaving but, by the summer of 1987, I believed I had gone as far as I could with Southampton. My career needed a fresh impetus and when Derby County enquired about my services, I was a ready listener.

The chairman of Derby County was Robert Maxwell. In addition to owning the *Daily Mirror* and other publications, Maxwell had once owned Oxford United. The club had achieved unprecedented success during that time, securing promotion to the First Division and winning the League Cup in 1986. Robert Maxwell had taken over at Derby because he felt the club had more potential than Oxford United. With all due respect, Derby are a bigger club than Oxford with a much greater fan base. Maxwell believed he could take the club onward and upward, and recapture the glory days of the early seventies when Derby had won the First Division championship and were foraging in Europe.

I, too, believed Derby were on the point of achieving success. Maxwell had invested heavily in Oxford United and it had paid off. I was assured that his investment in Derby County was to be far greater. He was backing manager Arthur Cox to the hilt. I trusted Arthur Cox's judgement and believed he would bring top-quality players to the Baseball Ground and turn Derby into a top-quality team. In short, I was convinced that a move to Derby would provide me with the new challenge I was longing for.

Arthur Cox travelled down to my home in Southampton with director Stuart Webb. They told me about Robert Maxwell and the plans he had for Derby County, and I was suitably impressed by all that I heard. I was impressed by Arthur Cox, too, who struck me as a football man and very down to earth and honest. Arthur wasn't charismatic in the mould of Brian Clough or Lawrie

McMenemy, but I had been in the game for over twenty years and never heard a bad word said about him. His stature and reputation among players were high. Southampton accepted the fee of £345,000, the deal offered to me by Arthur Cox was a good one and so I eventually agreed to sign on the dotted line.

I had to go to the *Daily Mirror* offices in London to complete the deal with Robert Maxwell in person. The meeting took place in his apartment in the Mirror Building. I had heard stories about what sort of man he was but, on this occasion, he was perfectly charming. Having agreed the deal and signed the papers, Maxwell had smoked salmon and champagne brought in and asked a *Daily Mirror* photographer to take some pictures of us together, including the classic one of the chairman standing over his new acquisition as he signs for the club. Maxwell seemed more concerned about the *Daily Mirror* getting the exclusive story of me signing for Derby than he did about the cost of the deal.

At first, I really did think Maxwell was going to be as good as his promises. Mark Wright made the same journey as me from Southampton. Dean Saunders was bought from Oxford United and Ted McMinn from Glasgow Rangers. I had been instrumental in the signing of Mark Wright. A number of clubs were interested in him but I sold him the dream I had been sold and talked him into signing for Derby. The club had just been promoted from what was then the Second Division to the First. They had a good, honest team but in order to realise Robert Maxwell's dreams, they needed more top-flight players than Mark Wright, Dean Saunders and me. Unfortunately, for all his promises, Robert Maxwell was not to oversee any more big-name signings.

In my first season with Derby, 1987–88, we found life tough in the First Division, finishing in fifteenth place. The following season we showed a marked improvement to finish fifth, but we were eighteen points adrift of Arsenal and runners-up Liverpool.

These two clubs had conjured up the most dramatic finish to any championship. Arsenal travelled to Anfield for the last game of the season needing a two-goal victory to wrestle the title from Liverpool. Having taken the lead, Arsenal scored the crucial second goal when Michael Thomas netted a minute into injury-time. In all probability, that was the most sensational climax to a title race in the 101-year history of the Football League.

Arthur Cox persuaded Robert Maxwell to go the extra mile and provide money for the players that would enable Derby to launch a serious challenge for the championship in the following season. Unfortunately, Arthur was unsuccessful in his attempts to bring many of the players he wanted to the club. Robert Maxwell was beginning to be the subject of some unflattering stories. There were doubts about him carrying out all the promises he had made and a lot of the players Arthur Cox wanted opted to go elsewhere. As the stories about Robert Maxwell gained momentum, his investment in the club became less.

One of Arthur's targets was the Manchester City utility player Paul Warhurst. Arthur told me that he had agreed what he believed was a very good fee for Warhurst – 'a steal', as Arthur described it.

'The only problem', Arthur went on, 'is he won't let me have the money.'

It was frustrating. I had gone to Derby wanting to do really well for the club and with high hopes of winning honours. Maxwell was beginning to renege on the promises he'd made, not just to me but to everyone connected with the club. As a team, we weren't good enough to challenge for honours and we had come to a point when we weren't signing players. In 1989–90 Derby finished a lowly sixteenth, just three points ahead of relegated Sheffield Wednesday. In all my time at the club we had never looked as if we would win anything and that season was, in essence, a fight against relegation.

My increasing frustration with the fortunes of Derby County was fuelled by my financial problems, which were becoming more acute. At one point, I went to see Arthur and told him I was not at all happy. Like most football clubs, Derby's answer to a disgruntled player was to offer a new contract.

Arthur Cox, Stuart Webb and I travelled down to London for a meeting with Robert Maxwell in a penthouse in the Mirror Building. We were sitting in an anteroom when we heard the sound of a helicopter landing on the roof. Suddenly, Robert Maxwell appeared in a somewhat agitated state. He said, 'Good morning, Arthur. Morning, Stuart,' and beckoned me to follow him into his office. I sat opposite him and he proceeded to take off his watch and place it on his desk so he could see the face. I took that to mean he wasn't going to give me very much time.

'Arthur and Stuart tell me you are not too happy,' he began.

I said that, in the light of our previous conversation, I had been led to believe the club would be signing a few more players and that this had not happened.

'Well, that's between me, Stuart and Arthur. But obviously I would like to keep you happy because they have told me you are irreplaceable.'

I told him what I wanted. Maxwell eyed me for a moment.

'OK, you can have that,' he said, 'no problem. I'll see Arthur and Stuart and it'll be sorted. Just keep up the good work.' Time up!

The deal involved a large signing-on fee to be paid in three instalments and a wage increase. It made me one of the best-paid players in the country, but even that was not to solve my financial problems.

When I joined Derby, I bought a small house in Leicestershire. Sue was still living with Sam and Michael in Hampshire because we were undecided whether the family should move permanently to the Midlands. A few months of commuting brought it home that this wasn't to our liking or to the benefit of family life. So I decided to buy a larger house in Leicestershire, and keep both our home in Hampshire and holiday home in Devon.

Now I saw our home in Hampshire as an investment and decided to rent it out. This proved to be a big mistake. House prices fell and kept on falling. Many people found they could not move house even if they wanted to because their properties had negative equity. In the late eighties, interest rates went through the roof and I found myself owning four properties the market value of which was less than the purchase price. At the same time, I was being financially crippled by soaring mortgage repayments.

If it had just been a matter of the properties, I could have weathered the storm, but my unsuccessful racehorses, their training and stabling costs, coupled with my gambling, began to put a severe strain on my finances. I couldn't sell the houses because of the negative equity and, with money tight, nobody wanted to buy unsuccessful racehorses.

My release was no release at all. My gambling increased and my losses added to the problem. I kept reading in the financial pages that the housing slump would eventually bottom out and the market would pick up. I reasoned that what I had to do was hang on in there. There would have to be a turn about in the housing market sooner or later and when that did happen, I would have tidy investments on my hands that I could sell at a handsome profit. Only the housing market continued to dip.

When I received a large payment from my football pension, I made another big mistake – or rather, two big mistakes. I bought another two racehorses, one for 30,000 guineas, the other for 35,000 guineas. I had high hopes for these two, and I thought, in time, they would be valuable breeders. How wrong I was. The first horse proved to be useless as a racehorse, and the second wasn't even that good.

By this time, Robert Maxwell had been succeeded as chairman of Derby County by Lionel Pickering. The club had got wind of the fact that I was sliding into financial difficulties and asked Jon Holmes and me to attend a meeting. As my agent, I don't think Jon liked the idea but he came along in the hope that we could agree a plan that would help me out of trouble. The gist of the advice was that I should sell my properties. Lionel Pickering even offered to speak to the building societies in question in the hope of coming up with some sort of scheme whereby I could do this without incurring heavy losses. Jon offered some suggestions regarding the horses.

I didn't want to hear what they said. I felt I was earning enough money to keep the ship afloat, and I was still hopeful that the housing market would soon pick up so that I could sell the houses at a profit. My pride wouldn't allow me go along with the solutions offered. These people had my best interests at heart but I was convinced matters would soon improve, which was yet another serious error of judgement. I should have accepted their help and advice and cut my costs. I may have ended up owing a lump sum but I could have paid that off in time. As I say, my pride got the better of me.

With hindsight, I can't believe I didn't do the sensible thing and accept the advice and help offered to me. I had been successful in football since I was sixteen years of age and I felt I could get out of anything by my own efforts. I still had a good relationship with Jon Holmes but it wasn't what it had been. I was increasingly negotiating deals on my own behalf, in part, I suppose, because I realised our relationship was coming to an end and in part because I felt confident doing it. Jon was representing Gary Lineker and it appeared to me, rightly or wrongly, that Gary's success and lifestyle were more appealing to him as an agent. If that was the case, I can understand it. Jon knew I had a real problem with money, as did Derby County.

I raised money from the bank by using the three signing-on payments of my new contract. The arrangement was that when the payments were due, the club would pay them to the bank instead of to me. Of course, I had to inform the club, which immediately alerted them to the fact that my financial problems were getting worse. I think Jon was feeling I was getting myself into a right mess. He did his best to help me but I think the fact that I was not taking 'best advice' worried him.

When Lionel Pickering took over from Robert Maxwell he ploughed a lot of money into the club. Jon and Lionel Pickering both continued to argue that I should sell my properties but I stood my ground yet again in the belief that the market was set to improve. So I made yet another error of judgement. It was all becoming very messy, and my relationship with Jon began to deteriorate when he discovered I had negotiated a loan with a close friend of his and not told him about it.

Trevor Bennett is a big Leicester City supporter. To ease my immediate financial problems, I borrowed £50,000 from him and didn't tell Jon about it. When I attended the meeting at Derby County, they told me they needed to know the extent of my financial commitments in order to help me. I just couldn't bring myself to tell them I had borrowed £50,000 from Trevor Bennett.

Again it was a matter of pride. In time, I paid Trevor back what I owed him. Thanks to his benevolence the loan was interest free. When Jon found out about it, he was far from happy that I had concealed it from him and Derby County, and I can understand why Jon was annoyed. He told me, 'I feel you have gone behind my back. As such, I have no alternative but to inform you we have to sever your connection with my company.'

I could fully understand Jon's position and even saw it coming. The end of my business relationship with Jon Holmes came when I was at Plymouth Argyle. Given my circumstances, I am amazed that it had lasted for so long.

I never allowed my financial problems to affect my performances for either Derby County or England. I may not have been focused on the reality of my financial situation, but I was totally focused where my football was concerned.

Between the infamous defeat by Argentina in the 1986 World Cup and Euro '88 in Germany, England played seventeen matches, losing just two. But the fact that we had drawn seven of the other fifteen made one or two sports writers question Bobby Robson's credentials as England manager. Robson selected me for twelve of those seventeen games. For the other five he opted for Chris Woods of Rangers. Chris had left Nottingham Forest in 1979 and arrived in Glasgow via QPR and Norwich City. He was pushing me hard but I felt I was at the top of my game and believed I was Bobby Robson's number-one choice because when it came to European Championship qualifiers, I always received the nod.

England qualified from a group that included Northern Ireland, Yugoslavia and Turkey. Yet again, we enjoyed a resounding 8–0 victory over the Turks, this time at Wembley.

In the late eighties, football woke up to the commercial potential of replica shirts. There was a time when a team wore the same strip all season, and by that I mean the same clothes. Nowadays, Premier League clubs wear new kit for every match. When I played for Leicester City and Stoke City in the sixties and seventies, a club might have new kit, and change the design, every three or four years. Wear and tear took their toll. It wasn't unusual for shirts and shorts to be darned, or for a player to wear two pairs of socks, the outer socks covering holes in the ones underneath.

A team's change strip was usually as far removed from the regular kit as it was possible to be. At Leicester, our change strip was white as opposed to blue. With the realisation that they could make a lot of additional income from the sale of replica kits, many clubs began to change the designs every year. With the away kit, some clubs introduced up to three new kits in a single season.

To the best of my knowledge, the very first commercial tie-in involved the shirts the England team wore in the 1966 World Cup. Inside the shirt was a label with the instruction 'Always wash with Lux soap'. Replica shirts were not sold in the sixties, so the Lux name was seen only by the players and those who did the washing – what you might call a very limited market.

In the eighties, marketing and design people were brought in and football shirts began to convey not only club or country identity but brand values and a trendy image, in keeping with the notion that football shirts were leisurewear. This led to some ridiculous designs as the kit designers tried to ape current fashion trends, and clubs tried to cash-in on what was a burgeoning market. Who can forget the Arsenal away shirt of the late eighties, which looked as if it had been designed by the artist Jackson Pollock when he had a migraine? I was a victim of this trend when England were about to play their opening match of the 1988 European Championship against the Republic of Ireland. England kitman Fred Street came to my room.

'Peter, you'd better come and take a look at this,' he said. I accompanied Fred to the kit room and when he produced the jersey I was assigned to wear against Ireland, my eyes nearly popped. The jersey Fred held up was predominantly green with black and yellow zigzags.

'What on earth is that?' I demanded.

'The new England goalkeeping strip,' replied Fred. I usually wore a grey top with blue shorts and socks. The strip, which I liked, had been introduced for the 1986 World Cup and I felt very comfortable wearing it.

I took one look at this zigzag strip and told Fred, 'You're joking. I'm not wearing that. It's ridiculous.'

He told me that this new green shirt with black shorts and socks was the only goalkeeper's strip that had been packed for the tournament.

'I can't wear it,' I said.

'You'll have to,' said Fred.

'Nobody has thought this through,' I went on.

'How do you mean?'

'I can't wear a green top. Ireland play in green!'

I couldn't believe we had arrived for a major international tournament and the FA had changed the goalkeeper's top without asking if I would be happy wearing it – and without bringing an alternative strip. Fred went to see the England phsyiotherapist, Norman Meadows, to explain the problem. Norman brought out an old grey England jersey which had been packed somewhere, for use in training.

You will have gathered by now that I was meticulous in my preparation for games. Even as a schoolboy I had taken great care that my kit was immaculate, even going as far as to wash and iron my bootlaces. For England's opening match of the 1988 European Championship finals, I walked out at the Stuttgart stadium, ready to face the Republic of Ireland, wearing an old, faded grey goalkeeper's training top, black shorts and socks. I felt it very unprofessional.

Oddly, that was not the only instance of me being issued with a jersey that was the same colour as the opposition's shirts. In 1984 I played for England against Scotland at Hampden. Arriving in the dressing room an hour or so before kick-off, I was taken aback to see the kit that I had been issued contained a dark blue jersey. I pointed out to Bobby Robson that I couldn't wear it because Scotland would be in their traditional shirts of dark blue. No alternative jersey could be found and so, in the end, I had to borrow one from the Scotland kitman. I walked out at Hampden alongside the Scotland goalkeeper, Jim Leighton, the pair of us sporting yellow goalkeeper's jerseys complete with Scotland badge on the breast. That must be the only instance of an England goalkeeper wearing a Scotland shirt when playing against Scotland. It was pointless me swapping shirts with Jim after that game!

As with the 1986 World Cup, England got off to a bad start in Euro '88 – but this time we were not to get out of jail. A Ray Houghton goal after only six minutes was enough to give the Republic victory. Ireland defied all our attempts to save the game. Gary Lineker missed a number of gilt-edged chances before Pat Bonner in the Republic goal produced a fantastic save to deny him an equaliser.

Jack Charlton's team were 25 to 1 outsiders for the championship and considered by many to be the weakest in the group. With Holland and Russia to come, it was seen as essential for us to beat them. Now we faced a monumental task.

We played Holland, widely tipped as potential champions, in Dusseldorf, and Marco Van Basten demonstrated to all that he was a world-class striker. Van Basten gave Holland the lead a minute before half-time, and struck again in the second half after we had equalised through Bryan Robson. Ruud Gullit was running the show and at times we found ourselves chasing shadows. Van Basten finally ended any hopes we had of salvaging something from the game when he made it 3–1 to complete a terrific hat-trick.

I was very disappointed with the result and the performance in my one hundredth game for England. Soon I was to be devastated. When Bobby Robson announced the team for England's final group match, against Russia, I had been replaced by Chris Woods.

I always felt a striker had to produce something special to beat me and Marco Van Basten had done that on three occasions. Holland had been so dominant, I was also of the opinion that our margin of defeat could have been greater but for me making several saves.

I was therefore totally nonplussed by Bobby Robson's decision to drop me. England had been outplayed by the Dutch and Bobby made two outfield changes, too: Mark Wright was replaced by Everton's Dave Watson and Steve McMahon came in for Peter Beardsley. Given England's general performance against Van Basten and co, I felt my omission for the Russia game was unwarranted.

Russia compounded England's and Bobby Robson's misery, also winning by three goals to one. Gary Lineker's uncharacteristic lethargy was later explained when he was diagnosed as suffering from hepatitis. Gary and myself had been room-mates for years. His hepatitis resulted in me receiving the precautionary measure of a very painful injection in my backside.

In the wake of another convincing defeat and England's consequent exit from the tournament, the tabloid press got their teeth into Bobby Robson. To his credit, Bobby rode out the storm as if he were some single-handed around-the-world yachtsman.

Three months later, Bobby was still England manager and I was again his number-one choice keeper when we played Denmark at Wembley. This was England's first match since our elimination from Euro '88 and the public voted with their feet. When the teams walked out of the Wembley tunnel I was shocked to see so many empty spaces in the stands. The official attendance was 25,000, among the lowest ever for an England international at Wembley. Those who did turn up, however, were treated to the sight of a young, beefy player who would become a star during the next major tournament England were to be involved in. Against Denmark, Bobby Robson brought on Paul Gascoigne as a substitute for Peter Beardsley. Gazza was introduced with only four minutes of the game remaining. I'm not even sure if he managed to get a touch of the ball. What I do know is, no one that night could ever have envisaged what an impact Paul Gascoigne was to have on English football two years on.

England played a total of nineteen games between Euro '88 and the 1990 World Cup in Italy and lost just one. That was against Uruguay at Wembley in May 1990 in our final home match before the start of the World Cup. Qualification for Italia '90 and an undefeated run of seventeen matches, including a victory over Brazil, did much to ease the pressure on Bobby Robson. Nevertheless, the tabloids were still quick to attack Bobby for any performance they saw as being below par.

England arrived in Italy with a squad that had changed much since Euro '88. Stuart Pearce, Paul Gascoigne, Des Walker, David Platt, Steve Bull and Paul Parker had broken into the squad. Some seasoned internationals were still there, including Terry Butcher, Bryan Robson, Gary Lineker, John Barnes, Peter Beardsley and me. All in all, I felt Bobby Robson had chosen a well-balanced squad and I was hopeful that we would do well.

BBC TV's coverage of Italia '90 introduced opera to many football fans. The theme for their coverage of the tournament featured Luciano Pavarotti singing 'Nessun Dorma' from Puccini's *Turandot*. It was an inspired choice and sales of the opera reached an all-time high as the nation warmed to Pavarotti's version of a classic and immersed itself in the fervour of the World Cup.

As in Euro '88, England's opening match was against the Republic of Ireland and, although we didn't get off to a winning start, fears of history repeating itself proved unfounded. The game ended in a draw and I was given the right jersey to wear. In this game, I equalled Pat Jennings' world record of 119 caps. I was very proud, and more so when I walked out for our second group match, against Holland, to claim the new world record.

Bobby Robson opted for a sweeper system against the Dutch, a system he had virtually ignored in all his time as England manager. Bobby chose my Derby team-mate Mark Wright for the job in what was Mark's first international appearance since the debacle against Holland in Euro '88.

England produced a world-class performance against world-class team. The game ended goalless and Paul Gascoigne came of age on the international stage. Paul was outstanding in the England midfield. His passing and his forward running were exceptional. At one point, he twisted and turned three Dutch players in a display of skill of which the great Johan Cruyff would have been proud.

David Platt, who replaced the injured Bryan Robson, demonstrated that he was a highly competent international player, and I thought we had won the game when Stuart Pearce drove a free kick into the net in the last minute. My celebrations were short-lived. The referee reminded everyone that he had awarded an indirect free kick and thus disallowed Stuart's effort. Although happy enough with the draw, I felt we had deserved to win the game. As it was, the way the other results had unfolded, we were still in with a very good chance of progressing to the next stage.

We achieved it in our final group match, beating Egypt 1–0, thanks to Mark Wright's first international goal. It's funny how your memory often recalls totally insignificant details. During this match, I remember looking up and seeing what appeared to be an entire crew from an Egyptian naval ship sitting in the stands, resplendent in their white uniforms. Why that image should have stayed with me, I don't know, but it has.

In the second round, we came up against Belgium in what proved to be a really tight game. The match was played at a furious pace from start to finish. Enzo Schifo and Jan Ceulemans both smacked shots against my right-hand post, and just before half-time John Barnes netted from a Gary Lineker cross but the goal was disallowed for offside. The referee waved away John's and Gary's protests. Later, the television cameras showed John was onside when Gary played the ball to him.

With the game goalless and well into injury-time, I was mentally preparing myself for extra-time and a penalty shoot-out when Paul Gascoigne floated a free kick deep into the Belgian penalty area. David Platt had his back to goal but as the ball dropped over his shoulder, he suddenly spun around and volleyed it into the far corner of the net. The subsequent celebrations provided two more abiding images of Italia '90 – the England players falling on top of David Platt, who had ended his celebratory run by dropping to his knees near the touchline, and Gary Lineker turning to look across to the referee with an expression of sheer surprise and delight.

David Platt's last-gasp winner set up a quarter-final against Cameroon. Bobby Robson made the mistake of telling us this would be our easiest game to date. In fact, it was our toughest.

I remember, as we left the dressing room, hearing singing. In the tunnel, we discovered its source. The Cameroon team were already in line and singing what I took to be their national anthem at full volume. I had never come across such a thing before and was somewhat in awe of their patriotism and collective spirit. Bobby Robson had other ideas: he thought it was a tactical ploy and said, 'Come on, lads, let's sing our World Cup song.' Unsurprisingly, he got little response. As the teams began to walk out, one of the Cameroon players turned to Gary Lineker and said, 'Mr Robson is a nice man. But he is wrong. We will not be easy. We will give you a very hard game, and we will beat you.' He was wrong only where the final result was concerned.

I have no idea why Bobby thought that this was going to be our easiest game. Cameroon had caused the upset of the tournament in their first game when they had beaten the holders, Argentina. They topped their group and had beaten Colombia in round two. Their cavalier approach had also won over a lot of the Italian fans, who would be rooting for them on the night.

Cameroon started well, and I recall making a terrific save early on in a one-on-one situation, and it was against the run of play when David Platt scored with a header. Cameroon didn't fold, as Bobby Robson had expected. They kept coming at us but at the break our single-goal lead was still intact. For the second half, Cameroon's Russian manager, Valeri Nepomniachi, played his trump card. He brought on their talisman, Roger Milla, who at 38, 39, 40 or 41 years of age – depending on which newspaper you read – produced a performance that belied his age, whatever it was.

On the hour, Milla was hauled down by Gazza as he ran on goal, and the referee had no hesitation in pointing to the penalty spot. I dived the right way and got my fingers to the ball, but not enough to keep Emmanuel Kunde's spot kick out of the top corner. He levelled the scores. Four minutes later, Milla drew our defenders towards him before threading a slide-rule pass into the path of the on-running Eugene Ekeke. Ekeke sprinted clear, I came out of my goal to narrow the angle but he slipped the ball past me. The alarm bells were ringing and they kept on ringing until the final six minutes of the game when Gary Lineker turned in the penalty area and was brought down. Gary dusted himself off and prepared to take the penalty himself. If he felt the pressure, he never showed it. Gary calmly planted the ball in the back of the net, to everyone's relief. The game went into extra-time and a minute before the break Gary won another penalty when he was pulled down by the Cameroon keeper Thomas N'kono. N'kono decided to dive to his right but it wouldn't have mattered which way he went because Gary's spot kick went straight down the middle. Our relief at the final whistle was clear for all to see.

Bobby Robson came into the dressing room after the game and complimented us on the way we had stuck to our task. Then, with an impish smile on his face, Bobby turned to Gary Lineker.

'What did I tell you?' he said. 'Didn't I tell you all it would be your easiest game to date?'

There was a large glass of water next to Gary and how he resisted the temptation I'll never know.

We took the business of the World Cup very seriously but it did have its lighter moments. Mobile phones were a relatively new phenomenon in 1990. A lot of the players had them but they were not the chic, minimalist instruments we have today. Bobby Robson, for one, seemed to find difficulty in coming to terms with this new technology. As we were preparing to leave the dressing room after the Cameroon game, Bobby was continually fiddling with his mobile phone and holding it up to his ear. Stuart Pearce asked Bobby what the trouble was.

'This damn mobile phone,' said Bobby, all of a fluster. 'I was expecting a lot of calls after the game, but I'm not sure it's working.'

'There's a surefire way of finding out,' said Stuart, casting a wicked grin in the direction of the remaining players. 'Dial your own number. If it rings, you'll know it's working.'

'That's a good idea,' said Bobby, who proceeded to punch his own number into the phone before holding it up to his ear.

'No good,' said Bobby, in all sincerity. 'It's engaged!'

Bobby stood there nonplussed, wondering why we had all fallen about laughing.

But for Cameroon's indiscipline when defending against a player of Gary Lineker's quality, the outcome of our quarter-final might well have been a different story. Some newspapers said we had been fortunate to win, but penalties are all part of the game and we were through. That's all that mattered. We were the first England team to reach the semi-finals of a World Cup on foreign soil. Our old football adversaries West Germany provided the opposition and what took place between us was a game as epic as any of its predecessors.

A number of criteria are critical to winning the World Cup. A team must not only comprise top-class players, it must also have a number of world-class players. In Gary Lineker and Paul Gascoigne, Bobby Robson could call upon the services of world-class players. Given the quality of the opposition at Italia '90, I felt we had a team that stood a good chance of winning the World Cup.

Another important factor can be termed 'peaking'. In a World Cup, the players are asked to play in a series of high-pressure games in a short space of time. Some teams start off like a house on fire. They post good performances and results in opening matches, but lose their momentum and impetus as the competition becomes more demanding. Ideally, what you're looking for is to build momentum with each match with a view to peaking in the final. Players do not require too much training during a World Cup because you're playing so many games within a short period of time. Fine-tuning is the key. Like athletes in the Olympic Games, the idea is to prepare in such a way that, come the day, you're at your peak both physically and mentally, as individuals and as a team.

England got the preparation right for Italia '90. We started in unspectacular fashion against the Republic of Ireland and our performances improved with every game so that we arrived at the semi-final stage unbeaten. So did West Germany, who had achieved a fantastic result when beating Holland in round two. West Germany were now favourites to win the World Cup, but we were confident of beating them.

One other thing is essential to winning not only the World Cup but any Cup in football. No matter how good or great a team is, they will never win a Cup competition unless they have a little luck. A team may possess the perfect blend of players, they can get their preparation spot on, they can peak at the optimum time but what a manager cannot legislate for is luck, or the lack of it. Against West Germany we had everything right. What we didn't have was luck.

England started the game as underdogs, but emerged from the tunnel raring to go. From the first whistle we took the game to the Germans and in the opening three minutes won three corners in succession. Gazza was at his most mercurial, dominating the midfield and often making Lothar Matthaus look an average player. Gazza was brimming with confidence. At one point he nutmegged Matthaus, much to the chagrin of the German captain and the delight of the crowd.

As the game unfolded, I felt comfortable, confident of our chances of making it to the final. We were working and playing as a cohesive unit, creating chances and, to my mind, looking as good, if not better, than the much-fancied Germans. West Germany were a very good side, however, and it wasn't long before they began to take a grip on proceedings. For a time we were on the back foot. I had to get down quickly to save from Thon and minutes later just managed to fingertip away a blistering free kick from Augenthaler. Just before the interval, Jürgen Klinsmann bulleted a header at my goal from only eight yards. My response was purely instinctive, a reaction save, but, to my mind, one of the best I ever made. At half-time there were no goals, honours shared.

Bobby Robson didn't say much during the interval. He complimented us for the way we had applied ourselves in the first half. He was encouraged by the fact we had created chances and told us to maintain our efforts in that department because he was convinced a goal would come.

'You're playing well as a unit. Your shape is good and you look solid in defence,' Bobby told us. 'I can't see where they're going to get a goal from. To be honest, I think they must be thinking that as well.'

West Germany upped it a gear in the second half. They came at us in determined mood and started to boss the game. I still felt very comfortable. Germany enjoyed a lot of possession but they never created an opening that I found troublesome. Then, on the hour, luck, call it what you will, sided with the Germans.

Germany won a free kick just outside my penalty area to the left of centre. I shouted to Mark Wright and David Platt to form a wall and manoeuvred into the correct position on my goal line to cover a direct shot at goal or a chip over the wall. I also told Paul Parker to take up a position from where he would be able to block a secondary shot. The ball was played square to Brehme, making the wall redundant, who then hit a shot towards goal. As soon as I saw the ball being played to Brehme, I made my move to narrow the angle. I reacted as if it was a straight shot at my goal from the edge of the penalty box, which initially it was. Paul Parker did the job he was supposed to do, advancing to close down Brehme's shot, only for the ball to hit his outstretched leg and deflect skywards. My momentum suddenly had to change. From narrowing the angle for a straightforward shot at goal, I now had to back-pedal as the ball spooned goalwards through the air. This all happened in a split second. I felt I'd made a good job of readjusting quickly but the ball suddenly dipped between my outstretched fingers and the crossbar and into the net.

Many match reports asked serious questions of me, saying it was a soft goal and suggesting if I had jumped another inch or so, I would have tipped the ball over the bar. The journalists who wrote such things revealed just how little they understood about goalkeeping. In similar circumstances, I have seen the majority of goalkeepers rooted to the spot in no man's land. They are never criticised for it because TV commentators and a good many supporters think, 'He had no chance of getting that.' In fact, they do have a chance if they react quickly. I did react quickly to the deflected shot but I didn't make the save. If I had remained rooted to the spot and looked on helplessly as the ball sailed over my head, I'm sure not a word would have been said.

In the light of the criticism I received from some quarters, I was pleased when, in an interview for *World Soccer* magazine, Brehme said, 'When my shot deflected off Parker and I saw the way the ball looped, I was certain it was going to be a goal. But Shilton reacted like no other goalkeeper I had seen. He covered ground very quickly and I was relieved to see the ball evade his fingers and go into the net.'

That night luck was with Brehme. As I have said, luck plays an important role in football. Sir Stanley Matthews said, 'No team enjoys success without having a slice of luck.' I go along with Stan on that. I also firmly believe that over the course of a season, or a career, luck tends to even itself out.

In our second-round tie against Belgium, I had looked on as two shots rapped against my right-hand post. I felt luck was on my side then but not when facing Brehme's shot in the semi-final. Neither was luck on my side when jumping with Maradona in the 1986 World Cup quarter-final.

For me, the difference between our defeat by Argentina in '86 and by West Germany in 1990 was that we did get back into the game. Ten minutes from time, Paul Parker crossed from the right and found Gary Lineker on the edge of the German penalty box. Gary was surrounded by German defenders but showed just what a world-class striker he was by finding the room to place a shot past Illgner for the equaliser.

Gary's goal took the game into extra-time. Both sides rattled the woodwork in the extra period. Then, as the clock ticked down, Gazza dived into a tackle on the halfway line. The Brazilian referee reached for a yellow card. Having been cautioned earlier in the tournament, Gazza realised that if we were to go on and beat West Germany, he would miss the final. Gazza was distraught, overcome with emotion, and for a few minutes he appeared detached from the game.

Gary Lineker signalled to Bobby Robson on the bench to 'watch the lad'. There was no need. Gazza gathered himself together and applied himself to the task in hand. There were no further goals and, as in the case of the other semi-final between Argentina and Italy, we went to penalties.

I had never been involved in a penalty shoot-out before and neither had England. The Germans had when they lost to Czechoslovakia in the 1976 European Championship final. After 120 minutes of pulsating football, it now boiled down to ten minutes of high drama. Gary Lineker was first up and put us in pole position with a typically confident spot kick. The thing about penalties is that the marksman is always expected to score. I never liked to move too early when facing a penalty as I felt the pressure was always on the taker, and often the ball can be hit straight at the keeper. Brehme matched Lineker's strike, then Peter Beardsley and Matthaus both succeeded, followed by David Platt and Reidle. I moved the correct way and as early as I could but every penalty was struck well and into the corners.

When Stuart Pearce stepped up to take England's fourth penalty, given his record of penalty taking, I think most people were confident he would put it away. Stuart drove the ball too near to Illgner and the German keeper blocked with his legs. I felt the pressure was on me when facing Thon. Thon's penalty was in keeping with Germany's previous efforts. He drove it hard and into the corner. I again guessed right but couldn't get a finger on his kick.

With West Germany now in the driving seat, the pressure switched from me to Chris Waddle. I don't think anybody who was there or who watched it on TV has ever forgotten the expression on Chris Waddle's face when he saw his penalty kick sail over the bar. His eyes closed and it was as if he was wanting the earth to open and swallow him up, to remove him from that place and the mental pain that had suddenly gripped him.

The German players ran to Illgner to congratulate him. Chris had ballooned his shot over the bar but the Germans had to have a focus for their celebration and it was instinctive that it should be their goalkeeper. Illgner had, after all, saved from Stuart Pearce. I thought it a nice touch that the German captain, Lothar Matthaus, rather than immediately joining his team-mates in celebration, walked over to Chris Waddle, put a comforting arm around him and offered words of consolation. In what was a moment of contrasting emotions, Matthaus' gesture was indicative of the sportsmanship in which the game was played.

I think most of my team-mates were in a state of shock. Paul Gascoigne openly wept and, in so doing, won the hearts of the nation. Having watched the drama unfold on their TV screens, most people empathised with Gazza. His performances and his heartfelt display of emotion not only endeared him to the nation and the media, but afforded him celebrity cult status. On his return to England, he found he was a star and all manner of commercial opportunities came his way. As I was to tell him, 'You made more money out of tears than Ken Dodd.'

I was bitterly disappointed but in time overcame my disappointment. I felt a great sense of pride at the fact that we had become the first England team to reach the semi-finals of a World Cup on foreign soil. In football there is often a very thin line between success and failure. In the case of England and Italia '90 I believe that line was very thin indeed.

Although we had been eliminated, we still had another game to play, against the other beaten semi-finalists, host nation, Italy. The match took place in Bari to decide who would take third place in the competition. It is one of the curiosities of the World Cup that they should have such a match. The players don't want it and it has little interest for supporters. After the heartache of a semi-final elimination, players just want to go home to their families. The last thing they want to do is stay and play a meaningless match.

I was made captain for the game because it was my 125th for England, a world record for international appearances. Italy won 2–1 but the game was a triumph for sportsmanship. Both sets of players had it in mind to produce an exhibition match and it was played in a very sporting manner, in sharp contrast to the final itself. West Germany and Argentina produced what I can only describe as a squalid final. The game was full of vitriol and dissent, and Monzon and Dezotti of Argentina became the first players ever to be sent off in World Cup final.

The media warmed to the way England and Italy approached their play-off game. England had failed to win the World Cup and we lost to Italy, but our pride and dignity were still intact. After eight years as England manager, during which time he had been subjected to some horrendous attacks by certain elements of the media, Bobby Robson's star was in the ascendancy. He picked up the newspapers to find he was being hailed as the best England manager after Sir Alf Ramsey, but our game against Italy was Bobby's last as England boss. He had accepted the role of chief coach at PSV Eindhoven, where he was to enjoy considerable success. The nation also appeared to be appreciative of our efforts. When the England party arrived back at Luton airport thousands of supporters gave us a tremendous welcome home. The sight of so many well wishers voicing their appreciation of our efforts is a sight that will remain with me for ever.

The Italy game was a fitting finale to our World Cup campaign and Bobby Robson's tenure as England manager. The match marked another finale, too. I was now over forty years of age. After a career with England that spanned twenty-one years, I decided to retire from international football. I had won 125 full caps and 11 Under-23 caps. I had featured in the final stages of four World Cups, playing in three of them. My international career had begun in the sixties and I made my final bow in 1990. I had known agony and ecstasy but I could have no regrets.

12

PILGRIM'S PROGRESS

I had taken my decision to retire from international football prior to England's game against Belgium. I think I could have carried on at international level for another two years but it seemed fitting to bow out during Italia '90.

I had been mulling it over ever since England qualified for Italy and during the tournament I told Bobby Robson I was finishing at international level 'no matter what'. I told him that the European Championship in two years' time would be a tournament too far. I was content to commit myself to Derby County and see how things turned out there.

Bobby was full of understanding. He thanked me for my efforts and loyalty to both him and England and complimented me on the way I had applied myself at international level over the years. He went on to say he was saddened that I had 'called it a day' but, given my age, understood the reasons behind me making 'what must have been a very difficult decision'. He wished me luck in my future career and, seeing as he too was bowing out, I reciprocated by wishing him every success in Holland. I wouldn't exactly say it was a meeting of minds but, given our particular circumstances, there was empathy and not a little sympathy that both our England careers were coming to an end.

When Graham Taylor succeeded Bobby Robson as England manager, the word was that he wanted me to return to the international scene but my mind was made up. Graham still wanted to tap into my experience and asked if I would join his backroom staff as the England goalkeeping coach, which I did. The role never rested comfortably with me, though. I had been in competition with Chris Woods and David Seaman and now to be their coach felt awkward. After seven months in the post, I said 'Thanks but no thanks' to Graham Taylor.

When the late John McGrath was coming to the end of his days as a player with Southampton, the Saints' manager, Ted Bates, asked John if he had any plans for when he retired.

'Well, I have been giving it some thought,' said John, 'and I've half a mind to be a manager.'

'That's all you'll need,' replied Ted.

Ted had been manager of Southampton for eighteen years and can be forgiven that little bit of cynicism on the prerequisite of football management.

I had been giving my future some thought and had come to the conclusion that management was the next logical step. I always felt that I could become a good manager. I had played for some of the all-time great managers in English football and had learned a great deal about the game from them. The knowledge I had gleaned from Sir Alf Ramsey, Brian Clough, Bobby Robson, Ron Greenwood, Tony Waddington and Lawrie McMenemy, together with my own experience and ideas, would stand me in good stead.

The season immediately following Italia '90 proved disastrous for Derby County. Robert Maxwell made his exit, presumably to concentrate on his problems away from football, and his sons carried on as chairman and vice-chairman, but I realised that the aims outlined to me when I first joined the club were long gone. Rather than Derby being a force in Europe, in 1990–91 we were, once again, forced to battle against relegation.

Throughout the season, Derby struggled to score goals. Our final tally of thirty-seven was the lowest in the First Division, while our tally of seventy-five against was the highest. Derby's inability to score goals and penchant for conceding them was the perfect relegation recipe. We won just five games that season. Ironically, one of those was a 6–2 victory over my old club, Southampton.

We made a very poor start to the season, not winning one of our first nine matches. Again, there was a touch of irony about Derby's first victory, a 1–0 success at Southampton in late October. That Derby should achieve the double over Southampton in what was a disastrous season was, I must point out, not a case of me pulling out all the stops when playing against my old club. I gave it my all in every game but we were always on the back foot and the defence just wasn't up to the job in the First Division – not that they were alone in that. Derby still had quality players in Mark Wright, Dean Saunders and Mick Harford, but not enough of them for the top flight. When we suffered a 7–1 home defeat at the hands of Liverpool in March, it was our thirteenth game without a win. I was a professional so I kept going, producing the best I could in every game, but I felt like I was trying to plug holes in a sieve. In the end, Derby finished bottom and were relegated along with Sunderland. (Only two teams were relegated that season.)

It was essential that Derby should bounce back at the first time of asking because a revolution was due to take place in English football in 1992–93 – the formation of the Premier League. Everyone at the club was hell bent on achieving promotion, including me. I wanted the club to be a part of the newly formed League, but I was also seriously considering my own future in the game.

One day Arthur Cox pulled me to one side and informed me that Hull City were interested in talking to me about becoming their manager. I was delighted to be seen in that light and Hull is a fine city, but I just didn't fancy a move there. So I carried on doing my best to help Derby's quest for promotion while keeping an eye open for a managerial vacancy that was more appealing to me.

Derby were doing well, one of eight clubs with a real chance of automatic promotion, when I heard that Plymouth Argyle were looking for a new manager following the sacking of David Kemp. Plymouth appealed to me. I had a holiday home in Devon, knew the area and loved it. I had always thought of Plymouth Argyle as having tremendous potential. The club enjoyed a good bedrock of support, and history showed that when the team had done well, attendances in excess of 20,000 were not uncommon.

While Derby were involved in the battle for promotion, Plymouth were embroiled in a battle against relegation, second from bottom of the Second Division. Although the odds seemed against them, I didn't think it was impossible for them to haul themselves to safety. The new manager's immediate task of preserving the club's Second Division status would be difficult, though. The team appeared to have only one player, Dwight Marshall, who was capable of scoring goals. Some cursory research yielded the information that the club's second-highest goalscorer had netted two. Scoring goals wasn't the only problem. As with Derby in the previous season, Plymouth were leaking goals in every game. I didn't expect anything else. Clubs rarely, if ever, want to appoint a new manager when things are going well. A new manager always inherits problems, and it appeared to me that Plymouth had plenty of those, but I was up for the challenge.

I didn't know anyone at Plymouth Argyle so I sought the advice of an FA official I knew, Mr Smart. Mr Smart was connected with Swindon Town but he told me he knew one of the directors at Plymouth, Mr Bloom. Mr Smart telephoned Mr Bloom, who, in addition to being on the Plymouth board, was an associate of Mr Smart's at the FA. It all sounds like something out of *Reservoir Dogs* but Mr Smart got back to me and told me that Plymouth would be 'very interested in talking to you about their vacant manager's position'.

I received a telephone call asking if I could drive over to Ipswich to meet with the Plymouth board prior to the club's game against Ipswich Town. We met in a hotel and I was immediately informed that the composition of the board was 'fairly new'. I was introduced to Mr Bloom, Mr Angilly, Mr Jones and the chairman, Dan McCauley. The interview went well and they seemed impressed with what I had to say and my ideas for the team and the club. I gained the impression that no one individual was a power broker and that the directors were very much a board. Looking back, I do recall McCauley making a few comments that were not in common with those of his colleagues. He made one or two remarks that, in the circumstances, I felt were uncalled for, one being how few goalkeepers had made successful managers. I didn't think this was aimed at me because he was right. I never attached any significance to McCauley's quips and left the interview in an upbeat mood, thinking I had a very good chance of landing my first job as a manager.

The board had asked me, should I be offered the job, the nature of the deal I wanted. The idea was that I would be a player–manager and my experience as a goalkeeper would help Plymouth stave off relegation. The club had a good goalkeeper in Rhys Wilmott, who had joined from Arsenal, and, from the conversation, I got the idea that the board felt they could finance my deal by selling Rhys Wilmott, whose value in the transfer market was around £300,000. Part of my role as manager would be to sell players to raise finance, not only to broker my deal but to strengthen the team as 'there will not be a lot of money available'. From that I knew the Plymouth job was going to be tough, but nothing I heard had dimmed my enthusiasm and I was absolutely delighted when I was subsequently offered the position.

I left Derby County with the club riding high in the Second Division and with a very good chance of achieving automatic promotion back to the top flight. I drove down to Devon knowing I had a big job on my hands. I could see the club and the team were in a mess. I didn't realise just how big a mess. I had fifteen matches left in which to save Plymouth Argyle from relegation.

Initially, I didn't want to make big changes because I thought that would have an unsettling effect. My first dilemma was the goalkeeper. Rhys Wilmott was playing well but, as the player with the most value on the transfer market, I had to sell him. I found myself in a 'Catch 22' situation. In order to sell Rhys I had to play him in the first team. How else could I convince any interested managers that he was a good goalkeeper capable of doing a job for their club? I couldn't ring up another manager and say, 'I have a terrific young goalkeeper who is doing the business. He'd be a great asset to your team,' and then, when asked where he was playing, say, 'In the reserves.'

In 1992, most players had an agent but it was still possible for a manager to get on the telephone and sell the virtues of a player to another manager. This had been part and parcel of the manager's job throughout the history of football, although not all attempts to unload a player were successful. When Tommy Docherty was manager of Manchester United, he wanted to move Jim Holton from Old Trafford. Sunderland boss Bob Stokoe had been forced to sell Dave Watson to Manchester City. Docherty knew Stokoe was looking for a replacement centre-half and had Watson's size-able fee at his disposal, so he rang Bob in the hope of persuading him to buy Holton. Stokoe didn't appear that keen on Jim.

'He's a terrific centre-back. A top-class player. Big and strong. Fantastic in the air. Very good on the ground. A great team player,' said Tommy, building up Holton as much as he could. Stokoe was not convinced Jim was for him. 'I'm telling you, Bob,' said

Docherty, giving it one final throw of the dice, 'a quarter of a million wouldn't buy this lad.'

'I know,' said Stokoe, 'and I'm one of them!'

I had to continue playing Rhys Wilmott in the first team in order to keep him in the 'shop window', which, of course, meant I couldn't play. So I kept fit, ready to come in to the team as and when.

At Derby, like most players, I didn't go to watch a lot of games. At Plymouth, I knew that I had to get out and about every night in order to find promising players who could do a job for me. Reserve-team and non-league football were my best bets. There was no time to lose but the nearest place to watch players of a decent standard was Bristol, an hour and three-quarters' drive away. Going to the Midlands involved a six-hour round trip. Having to be at the club bright and early the following morning to take training, I found the scouting trips ate into my time. I had to do it because the team had to be strengthened, so I devised a plan. I would drive to London, take in a reserve-team game in the afternoon and a game in the evening, stay overnight, repeat the process the following day and drive back to Plymouth. The travelling was tiresome and I had the added burden of trying to keep physically and mentally fit to play when Rhys Wilmott was eventually sold.

I got off to a reasonable start as a manager. In my first home game in charge, Plymouth drew 1–1 with Derby. Given that Derby were riding high and Plymouth were near the bottom of the league, it was a good result.

I had been quite nervous before the match, although I was at pains not to relay any nerves to the players. I was also filled with optimism. This was a new chapter not only in my career but in my life. I did my best to pass on my optimism to the players by concentrating on their individual strengths and telling them that, collectively, they were strong and capable of beating not only

Derby but every other team in the division. We bossed the game for lengthy periods and, when it was over, I emphasised to the players what a good performance it had been and that they should consider this to be just the start of better days ahead for both them and the club.

I was sincere in what I said, but the Derby match and subsequent games showed me there were certain parts of the team that needed to be urgently improved. We badly needed a decent forward, someone who could not only score goals but hold up the ball. We needed someone to link play who would be consistent in performance. That said, I was pleased to have got the team playing with more verve and confidence and felt I was doing something right when McCauley rang.

'Things are picking up,' he said. 'Have you any other player in mind that you might want?'

I was pleased to receive this call because, during the interview, I had been led to believe there was no money available for new players. I was also pleased because it implied I was doing a good job. I was told that money was available for team strengthening on the proviso that I would 'get it back by selling players'.

Kevin Nugent of Leyton Orient was a striker who fitted the bill – I had seen him on one of my trips to London. I thought his goals and his style of play would be considerable assets to us in our quest to avoid relegation but, unfortunately, Kevin had been at the club for just a week or so when he broke a toe and was sidelined.

It was a hell of a blow to lose his services, especially as the board had pushed the boat out in sanctioning a fee in the region of £200,000 for him. We just had to buckle down without Kevin and, happily, performances did pick up.

Rhys Wilmott was sold to Grimsby Town but for a lot less than anticipated. With Rhys gone, I stepped up into the first team with seven matches remaining. Our form had improved but so, too, had that of the other clubs involved in the relegation dogfight. I found myself scanning the table for their results. I read their fixtures and tried to be realistic when working out what points they might conjure up as opposed to what I believed we were capable of achieving. Never before or since have I taken such an interest in the fortunes of Port Vale, Oxford, Brighton and Newcastle United. Newcastle's fight against relegation was being spearheaded by Kevin Keegan and Terry McDermott. If one of those teams had a midweek game, I found myself constantly tuning in to the radio to see how the match was progressing. Management was changing me and my habits. My mindset and hopes went up and down in accordance with results.

In the end, it went to the last game of the season, against Blackburn Rovers. Under their new manager, Kenny Dalglish, Blackburn needed a win to ensure a place in the play-offs for promotion to the new Premier League. I could have wished for an easier finale. There was much at stake for both teams and while I was operating on a tight budget, Kenny Dalglish had benefited from the financial clout of Blackburn's owner, the steel magnate Jack Walker. Kevin Nugent returned for the game but really he shouldn't have played because he was still in some discomfort.

Blackburn proved too strong. Although we took an early lead, their two late goals sealed our fate. Other results went against us and Plymouth were relegated along with Brighton and Port Vale. We were two points adrift of Oxford, who finished fourth from bottom.

Blackburn, who had finished in sixth place, progressed via the play-offs to the Premier League and within two seasons were runners-up for the championship. The following season, 1994–95, Blackburn won the Premiership. From 1992 to 2004, Blackburn have been the only club to break the Arsenal–Manchester United stranglehold on the title. For the record, in 1991–92 Derby County finished in third place in the Second Division, but, like so many teams who finish third, failed to gain promotion via the play-offs.

While Blackburn went on to rub shoulders with the big boys, I set about preparing Plymouth to face Chester, Wigan and Hartlepool. Although I was very disappointed, I consoled myself with the thought that the real damage had been done before my arrival. Many people had seemed resigned to the fact that the club would go down but I believed we had a chance of escaping. I was upset that all our efforts had been in vain but, in a strange sort of way, the commitment most had shown made me optimistic for the future. I was confident I could turn things around and win promotion back to what was now Division One. First I had to do what I couldn't do when I arrived at the club – instigate a big clear out and make some changes.

I unloaded several players whom I didn't think were good enough and felt vindicated when the majority of them found clubs in non-league football. In addition, I sold two decent players. Nick Marker and 'Jock' Morrison were saleable assets and I needed money to strengthen the team. They both went to Blackburn Rovers and the deal involved two Blackburn players, Craig Skinner and Keith Hill, moving to Home Park. Kenny Dalglish felt Skinner and Hill would be fringe players for Blackburn in the Premier League but I knew they would do a good job for Plymouth.

Jock Morrison's departure resulted in my first run-in with McCauley, who didn't want Morrison to go. I pointed out that my brief was to finance new signings with sales. Morrison's transfer would generate money and was a good move for the lad himself. McCauley thought otherwise. I reiterated that in order to strengthen the team I had to sell players. From McCauley's response I was now of the opinion this meant certain players only, and as this seemed to imply those whom no other club wanted to buy, I was left to wonder how on earth I could make money in the transfer market.

When I first got the job as manager, I needed an assistant and turned to my old pal and former Nottingham Forest team-mate, John McGovern. John had a reasonable job but I managed to persuade the board to offer him a decent salary and was delighted when he accepted. Following our relegation, I was looking for a new youth-team coach and John thought that another former Nottingham Forest team-mate, Ian Bowyer, might be suitable. Ian accepted the position and I felt I had a good backroom staff around me, which further fuelled my optimism for the future of the club.

I was very busy in the close season. In addition to selling players and hiring backroom staff, I made what for Plymouth were two big signings – Steve Castle from Leyton Orient and Paul Dalton from Hartlepool United. I also brought in Dominic Naylor from Barnet and – the player I considered my best buy – Steve McCall from Sheffield Wednesday for £25,000. From Derby County I purchased Mark Patterson and a young centre-back, Andy Comyn.

I also managed to get a young goalkeeper, Alan Nichols, from Cheltenham Town, at the time a non-league club. Alan showed a lot of promise and eventually played for the England Under-21s but, tragically, a few years after I'd left Plymouth he was to lose his life in a motorbike accident.

There were others I had my eye on but I found that Plymouth's geographical location was sometimes an obstacle. Many northern- and Midlands-based players are reluctant to move to Devon because of the cost of housing and a different way of life. What they make in increased wages is gobbled up by the higher house prices. Clubs such as Mansfield and Scunthorpe find it easier to sign players than Plymouth or Exeter. That's simply because a player who is based in the Manchester or Birmingham area does not necessarily have to move house to play for them. For lower-division clubs based in the Midlands or north, the catchment area for players is much wider than it is for Plymouth, which is why I felt a great deal of satisfaction in signing the players I did. In persuading Dalton, Castle and McCall to sign for Plymouth, I adopted a similar philosophy to the one Lawrie McMenemy applied when he was manager of Southampton. I told the players that Plymouth was a great club to play for and the area was a fantastic place for them to bring their families to live, which I believe to be true.

The pre-season went well. The new players gelled and with my backroom staff in place I had high hopes that a good season was in store. My preparations as a manager were as meticulous as they had been as a player. However, luck, fate, call it what you will, was to deal me a blow.

Steve Castle was the first player to pick up an injury, which necessitated a lengthy spell on the sidelines. Then Paul Dalton sustained an injury that put him out of action for a good few months, and so it went on. At one point in the first three months of the season, I had twelve first-team players injured and thus unavailable for selection. The injuries were not the usual training-ground strains and pulls, but were of a more serious nature – a broken leg and a back injury to name a couple. Needless to say, performances and results were affected.

Getting key players back to fitness was crucially important but there was a problem regarding their rehabilitation and recovery. When I was overhauling my backroom staff, I felt we needed a good physiotherapist at the club. John McGovern knew just the person – Mark Leather, who was with Preston. John volunteered to speak to Mark about it, Mark joined us and in no time at all he found himself very busy indeed. I thought everything was going well but after three weeks Mark came to see me.

'I'm sorry, Peter, but I can't stay at this club,' he said.

I was completely taken aback and asked him what the problem was. Mark told me that he didn't think his relationship with the chairman was working out. He was not prepared to move his family down to Devon and, after giving the matter considered thought, had decided to leave Plymouth and return to the north-west, which is exactly what happened. Mark eventually became the physiotherapist at Liverpool, which says much for his expertise.

I was very upset to lose Mark Leather, whom I considered to be an integral part of my backroom staff, especially with so many injured players. I went to see McCauley. The chairman made a lot of excuses and, at one point, questioned the need for a full-time physiotherapist. I pointed out that we had a dozen injured players. That situation would resolve itself in due course but, as a progressive club with ambitions, we did need someone full-time. I don't think McCauley felt the cost could be justified.

However, with our injury list, we needed to do something quickly and we appointed an Australian lady who was working locally for the NHS. She came to the club twice a week to treat the players. The situation was far from ideal.

When I first joined the club nobody had complete control although I gained the impression that McCauley was the main money man. In the short time I had been there, that situation appeared to have changed. It seemed to me that McCauley was now in control of the board and, therefore, the club. It was again intimated that I had to raise money by selling players to compensate for the money that had been spent on the new recruits.

As the 1992–93 season began to unfold, my dealings with McCauley became more strained. I resolved the physiotherapy problem to a degree by appointing Paul Sumner, who had been working locally for the NHS. The salary we could offer was not enough to attract an experienced physiotherapist from another club. Paul was a super lad but he hadn't had a lot to do with sports injuries, until now. Paul had been at the club for just a week or so when one of the players went over on his ankle in training. I was concerned about losing yet another player.

'How long is it going to be? A week? Two weeks?' I asked.

'About eight weeks,' he said.

'Two months for a turned ankle? You must be bloody joking.'

That prognosis may have been acceptable in the NHS but in football you want your players back as soon as possible. Eight weeks was ridiculous. I'd known players return quicker from a broken leg. Paul wasn't wise to the ways of football, so I had to put him right. His expertise lay elsewhere in physiotherapy. He did well for us in time but it must have been a steep learning curve for him.

I was desperate to get the injured players back and gelling together as a team. Halfway through the season we were mid-table and immediate promotion wasn't on the cards. One of the office staff came to see me brandishing a copy of a local newspaper and said, 'I think you had better read this, Peter.' 'This' was an interview with McCauley in which, to my mind, he slaughtered not only me but the players. His overall view seemed to be that things weren't good enough and matters had to change. I couldn't believe what I had read, but thought that perhaps a local reporter had caught him after a game and his reaction was of the knee-jerk variety.

When I confronted McCauley about the interview he dismissed it as being of no consequence. It seemed to me that there were a few things McCauley didn't understand about football clubs. A club needs continuity and cohesion in order for it to progress. It also needs proactive leadership from the top. I was really put out by McCauley's comments in the press, especially in light of all the injuries that had blighted our season thus far.

Some weeks later a situation occurred that made me question further my relationship with McCauley. There had been four or five days of incessant rain before a home game and the Home Park pitch was waterlogged, to the extent that the groundsman had to place boards across it to walk on. Usually, the only time I spoke to McCauley was at board meetings or on the telephone and I received a call from him.

'Look, we need this game on Saturday,' he said. 'You've got to get this game on.' With that, he put the phone down.

There was no way the game could take place but on the Friday I called the referee, who agreed to come to look at the pitch. The referee was in no doubt. He informed me that he shouldn't have been called in because there was no possibility of the game going ahead, given the state of the pitch. I knew this but had asked him to come to cover my back. I suspected McCauley wouldn't be best pleased when he learned the game was postponed.

Just as I was leaving the ground, McCauley arrived, accompanied by his wife, and began ranting and raving at me.

'You got this game called off,' he said at one point.

'I'm sorry, but have you seen the state of the pitch?' I replied.

'I don't have to. You got the game called off.'

I reiterated that he should take a look at the pitch, bade him a respectful 'goodbye' and left. The whole situation was ridiculous. I thought that McCauley didn't want the game postponed because of the catering and other costs that would be incurred. I didn't want the club to lose financially but there was just no possibility of that game going ahead.

What had begun as a taut relationship between McCauley and me was beginning to become acrimonious. Other board members tried to ease my anxiety by saying, 'The chairman is still behind you.'

Plymouth finished the 1992–93 season in mid-table. I was far from satisfied but, taking into account the horrendous injury list and the small squad, I felt we had done well to finish midway. With a fully fit squad, I still believed I had assembled a team capable of mounting a serious challenge for promotion, and there-fore was confident of a significant improvement in 1993–94.

Manchester United had become the first champions of the money-led Premier League. United's talisman was the enigmatic Eric Cantona, signed from Leeds for a mere £1.2 million. The effect that the Premiership, or, more pertinently, television, was to have on the game can be discerned by the fact that Cantona's weekly wage in 1992 was £4,000. A little over a decade later, Premiership players with nowhere near the talent of Cantona are earning over ten times as much.

Our main problem was that we couldn't score goals, but with Castle, Nugent and Dalton fully fit, I believed that problem would be solved the following season. Alan Nichols, the young goalkeeper I had signed from Cheltenham, had a really good pre-season. My first full season as a manager had been a real learning experience. I had played twenty-three games for Plymouth in 1992–93 but with Nichols doing so well, I decided to play him in the first team and concentrate on management.

The season started well and it got better. Free from injuries, come mid-season Plymouth were top of the Second Division. As the season progressed, Reading, Port Vale, Stockport and Plymouth played leapfrog at the head of the table. This relative success had another bonus as far as I was concerned. The good results meant there were no run-ins with McCauley about the team. Lack of goals was a thing of the past and we now had a side that was free-scoring. Plymouth were to end the season as the highest-scoring team in the Football League.

The promotion chase went to the wire. On the final day we went to Hartlepool needing a win and for Port Vale to lose at Brighton in order for us to gain automatic promotion. I couldn't have asked for more from my players. They produced an outstanding per-formance to beat Hartlepool 8–1 with goals from Richard Landon

(3), Paul Dalton (2), Steve McCall, Steve Castle and Dwight Marshall. To everyone's great disappointment, this terrific effort proved insufficient. Port Vale won at Brighton and secured automatic promotion along with Reading.

Plymouth went into the play-offs along with Stockport County, York City and Burnley. Our opponents were Burnley. Plymouth had finished twelve points ahead of them and, when we secured a 0–0 draw at Turf Moor, I felt they wouldn't relish coming to Home Park. Their strength was really their home form. Though confident, I said to McCauley, 'Let's not get carried away. Let's keep it all low profile. There is still a job to do.'

In the run-in to the end of the season, little snippets had appeared in one of the local newspapers that I thought undermined the good work we had been doing. On the morning of our second-leg game against Burnley, an article appeared in the said newspaper, the gist of which was that Burnley weren't a particularly good team and, should we beat them, it could not be considered a great achievement. I thought this was a putdown and was annoyed that such an article should appear on, of all days, the day of the game.

I could see when Burnley ran out they were fired up. We took the lead but so well did they play in defence we couldn't add to our advantage. The Burnley goalkeeper, Marlon Beresford, was in inspired form. We kept up the pressure but Burnley hit us with two breakaway goals just before the interval and from being in pole position we now found ourselves chasing the game. We pounded Burnley in the second half but couldn't find a way through their resolute defence. Ten minutes from time, Burnley went on a rare attack. Alan Nichols, uncharacteristically, dropped a cross and we gifted Burnley a third goal. That was the killer blow. Burnley were through. They went on to win the play-off final and promotion to the First Division.

I was devastated – so near yet so far. After the game, I curtailed my disappointment and offered my congratulations to their manager, Jimmy Mullen. What I heard made me angry. Burnley had stayed overnight. On the morning of the game, Jimmy Mullen had bought a copy of the local morning newspaper and had read the article suggesting his side were not much of a team and that for Plymouth to beat them would not be much of an achievement. Jimmy had pinned the article up in the away dressing room. It had the desired effect. Jimmy told me that when his players read it, they were determined to prove that they were a good team.

After the defeat by Burnley, it all went downhill. When I first signed for Plymouth, part of the deal involved three payments in return for the club using my image for commercial purposes. I received the first of these up front. During the early part of my contract, my personal financial situation became strained again and I phoned McCauley to ask if he would let me have the remaining two instalments. I offered to pay interest on them so, ostensibly, I negotiated an advance. This was quite common in the game. I was peeved when some time later an article appeared in a national tabloid, in which McCauley revealed he had loaned me money. I was aggrieved because it was a personal matter and also because the piece read as if the money were a straightforward loan as opposed to an advance of what was contractually due to me.

Following Plymouth's defeat in the play-offs, I had a meeting with McCauley to discuss a new contract – I had initially signed for two years with a one-year option – and was surprised when he told me that unless I took a pay cut I would not be offered a new contract. Whether this was simply a negotiating ploy I don't know, but I found myself in a dilemma. However, my circumstances were such that I didn't want to be out of work, so I had little option but to agree. After the meeting, McCauley and I posed for press photographers, smiling and apparently in unison, but I was thinking, 'This isn't going to last.'

I must have been doing something right because money was made available to spend on new players for the 1994–95 season. I wanted two, one who could provide a little more pace at the back, and one who could add pace up front. I was very interested in Gillingham's Nicky Forster, to play up front, and a centre-half from Burnley. Another alternative, for the money I'd been given, was Port Vale's Peter Swan, who could play either in the heart of defence or as a striker. Nicky Forster decided he wanted to stay in the London area, so I went for Peter Swan, whom the board seemed very keen on seeing at the club. Unfortunately, Peter and his family didn't settle in the area and he didn't do himself justice on the field. He proved to be, in football parlance, 'an expensive signing'.

To add to my woes, another dose of injuries befell key players. Before the start of the season, Steve Castle reported to me, complaining of the symptoms of flu. I'm no medic but I could tell from looking at Steve that he wasn't well at all and so referred him to a doctor. The doctor confirmed that Steve was suffering from yellow jaundice, which would sideline him for some considerable time. A few days later, Paul Dalton sustained an injury to his back and I was horrified when told Paul was going to be out for some six months. Losing my two main goalscorers was a blow. Peter Swan didn't produce the performances I knew he was capable of, and with quite a few other players injured as well, we had a very indifferent start to the season.

I felt under pressure in my job and, with the immense pressure of mounting debts, I remember thinking, 'This is like a festering boil and there will come a day when it bursts.' That day was not long coming.

Damage limitation was the name of the game. With things going well on the pitch in the play-off season, I didn't want my financial situation to be made public for fear it would affect my situation at the club, so I tried to shore things up, but I suppose, deep down, I knew my efforts were going to be futile. I thought I was in desperate need of a short-term solution in order, as I believed, to buy time, so I turned to my pal and assistant manager, John McGovern. I told John I had a 'few slight financial problems'. John was understanding and offered to loan me £7,000. He also suggested that Ian Bowyer might be in a position to help and Ian offered to lend me £5,000.

During the contract talks, McCauley had told me that the club were not prepared to offer John a new contract on his current terms. I didn't want John to leave Plymouth, as he'd said he would unless offered at least the same salary, because he was an integral part of the set-up and we worked very well together. I had already agreed to reduced terms but I asked McCauley to pay John the same and take the difference out of my salary. As it turned out, the board felt John was a good assistant and the directors were willing to pay him the same as before so there was no need for any part of it to be deducted from my wages.

Some time later I received a bombshell. We were in the office and John asked, 'Do you mind if I get away a bit earlier today?' It was lunchtime and I said that would be OK. I was planning to catch up on paperwork that afternoon and would field any calls. Later on, I was driving home when my phone rang. It was Mr Jones, one of the directors, and what he had to say stunned me.

'Have you heard the news?' he asked. I hadn't, so he told me that John McGovern had resigned as my assistant manager, citing that he couldn't work with me any more, that I owed him money and we now had an untenable relationship. I was shocked and gutted. He had mentioned to me on a couple of occasions that he was not happy with me owing him money. I assured him that he would be paid back and, if necessary, I would speak to his solicitor and tie-up a proper payment agreement.

I drove straight to John's house to talk things over with him, to find out what was going on. John refused to open the door to me. We had a brief talk via the intercom system, in which John told me that he didn't want to speak to me. A few days later, he joined Archie Gemmill at Rotherham United.

In time, I did repay both John and Ian. Losing John was a great blow to me, but it was the manner of his going that hurt me most. We had been through all manner of things together at Nottingham Forest and battled to achieve the success we did. We had won the League championship and the European Cup. I had always felt John and I were kindred spirits.

After I'd repaid the money I owed him, John gave an interview to a national newspaper that was less than flattering to me. I was very disappointed to read this piece, as John must have known what effect it would have on me and my family, and though it's all water under the bridge now, I knew things could never be the same between us.

Following John's departure, I promoted Ian Bowyer to my assistant, but the seeds of my own departure as manager of Plymouth Argyle were now well and truly sown. Ian Bowyer never revealed to anyone that I had borrowed money from him. I was indebted to Ian in more ways than one.

Word was beginning to circulate of my financial plight and that my job as manager at Plymouth was under threat, and I received a call from former England team-mate, Steve Coppell. Steve spoke to me in confidence. Initially, Steve had rung to discuss a PFA matter, but went on to say that he knew I had one or two problems at the club and advised me to seek the help of a Manchester-based lawyer, Mike Morrison.

Rumours were circulating around Plymouth that my time at the club was about to end. We won our next game 3–2 but nothing could save me. A meeting was held. Discussions were conducted in legal language that was beyond my ken, but I understood enough to know my tenure as manager of Plymouth Argyle had come to an end.

I was only a few months into a new contract. Mike Morrison handled the details but there was to be no financial compensation. Mike also helped me with my response to the many stories that were circulating in the press. In a perverse way, my departure from Plymouth came as a relief. At least I had been relieved of one big problem in my life.

To this day, Argyle supporters tell me that the Plymouth team I managed played some of the most attractive and attacking football they have ever seen at Home Park. Who knows what might have happened had it not been for injuries to key players? But I have been around in football long enough to know any manager could say the same.

I didn't feel a sense of failure. I had guided Plymouth to the play-offs in the previous season and, to the best of my knowledge, balanced the books in terms of buying and selling players. The team played open, attractive football but a combination of factors had conspired to produce indifferent results. Then there was the strained relationship with Dan McCauley, who had effectively assumed control of the club. I found him difficult to get on with. Seemingly, I wasn't the only Plymouth manager to experience this. Following my departure, Plymouth had five managers in the space of five years.

Given time and backing, I felt I could have guided the club to promotion. It was my first and, to date, only experience of management and, under the circumstances, I felt I had done a very good job.

However, the disappointment of leaving Plymouth was overridden by the anxiety I was now feeling regarding my financial situation. Mike Morrison had told me the time had come to 'face up to the realities'. He meant my perilous financial situation. Now he gave it to me straight. I was to attend a meeting at which those present would try to structure a plan to enable me to meet my creditors. If matters continued, I would be on the verge of bankruptcy. I didn't want the stigma of that. More importantly, I wanted to pay back the money I owed and get myself straight. Mike told me that simply agreeing to this meeting would buy me a little extra time. Should I decide not to take his advice, I would face the toughest penalty I had ever faced.

13

FOR THE RECORD

I was at the lowest point of my life. Still living in Plymouth, I went about the city aware that I was being talked about. I have never been one to wish my life away, life is too precious to me, but there were times when I wished I could project myself two or three years forward to a time when the mess I had got myself into had been resolved.

I wanted to stay in the game and the one thing that energised me was that I needed four games to become the first player in the history of English football to play 1,000 league matches. The game being what it is these days, I didn't think anyone else was ever likely to play 1,000 league games. I believed I could still play at club level and the thought of achieving this milestone spurred me on to make a comeback as a player.

Sue and I wanted to return to the Coventry area to live. My son, Sam, was on the books of Plymouth Argyle and, although he was carving out a career for himself there, in light of what had happened to me, he didn't want to stay at Home Park.

There are times in life when you feel everything is going against you and that fate is never going to deal you a decent hand again. Leaving Plymouth Argyle was such a time for me but fate did take a hand in the shape of a call from Wimbledon.

Wimbledon had a Cup match at Liverpool. Their goalkeeper had picked up an injury and was by no means certain to be fit for the tie. As I wasn't cup-tied, would I sign for Wimbledon as cover?

In the event, the goalkeeper was passed fit but I did travel to Anfield and sat on the Wimbledon bench as the substitute goalkeeper. I felt fit, the pre-match warm-up went well and I thought that, should I be called upon, I could do the job. As it happened, the Bolton Wanderers manager, Bruce Rioch, was in the Anfield crowd and, a few days later, Bruce invited me to join his team.

There were three months remaining of the 1994–95 season and Bolton were on course for promotion from the First Division. They were also in the Coca-Cola Cup final against Liverpool. Bruce wanted me as cover, too, but, as opposed to my brief spell with Wimbledon, I did get to play for Bolton Wanderers. I played one full game for Bolton and made one appearance as substitute, ironically against one of my old clubs, Stoke City.

I was on the bench at Stoke when the Bolton goalkeeper, Aidan Davison, was sent off after only ten minutes following a foul on the Stoke striker, Paul Peschisolido. I was plunged into what, even at this early stage, was a tempestuous game. Following the sacking of Joe Jordan, Stoke City had been rejuvenated under the management of Lou Macari. The first thing I had to do was face the penalty that had been awarded for Davison's foul on Peschisolido. I wish I could say it was a fairytale return but it wasn't. Orlygsson sent me the wrong way and I conceded a goal seconds into my 998th league game. John McGinlay equalised and although Stoke pressed hard, Bolton held out for a 1–1 draw. I was kept busy and made a number of telling saves. When the final whistle sounded I felt I had done a good job for Bolton.

At forty-six, I was not the oldest footballer to have played at the Victoria Ground. Stan Matthews had played for Stoke in the First Division, then the equivalent of the Premiership, at the age of fifty!

Bolton missed out on automatic promotion to the Premier League and so had to endure the play-offs. First-choice keeper Keith Branagan had sustained an injury and, on the strength of my performance at Stoke, Bruce Rioch picked me for the first leg of Bolton's play-off match against Wolves at Molineux.

Molineux was packed to the rafters and, as with every play-off game, the atmosphere was tense and taut. The game ended in a 2–1 win for Wolves but Bruce Rioch was full of compliments for my performance. He said he was content with the scoreline because he thought Bolton could turn them over in the home leg. He was right. Branagan was passed fit and Bolton progressed to the final at Wembley against Reading.

So there I was, back at the famous old stadium that held so many memories. I was on the bench and although I took no part in the game, I felt great pride in the fact that Bolton triumphed 4–2 to clinch a place in the Premier League. My contribution had been minimal, but being involved in the game at that level and being a part of a successful team raised my spirits at a time when they had been at rock bottom.

Of course, I knew I wouldn't feature in Bolton's plans, but come the start of the 1995–96 season, thirty years after I had first joined Leicester City, I found myself in the Premiership. After my stint at Bolton, I signed as cover for Ron Atkinson and Coventry City and on the opening day I was on the bench at Newcastle United.

Coventry was to feature again in the lives of the Shilton family because Sam joined them from Plymouth and eventually played for them in the Premiership under the management of Gordon Strachan. Sam has since played for Hartlepool United, Kidderminster and is now at Burton Albion in the Conference. A little bit of history is repeating itself because the Burton manager is Nigel Clough, son of Brian. Sue and I have followed Sam's career very closely. He is a midfield player and in many ways I'm glad he never took up goalkeeping. Some sons of famous fathers have played in the same position. Danny Greaves, for instance, was a decent forward with Southend United but hardly a match report was written without the words 'son of the goalscoring legend, Jimmy Greaves' appearing somewhere. That proved a big millstone around Danny's neck. It was unfair constantly to compare him with his father, one of the greatest goalscorers of all time. Happily, with Sam being a midfield player, he has never had to endure comparisons and has been free to create his own name in the game.

After Coventry, I went to West Ham at the invitation of Harry Redknapp. Harry asked me to coach his goalkeepers and keep fit, again, as cover. I played a few games in the West Ham reserve team and remember being impressed by a couple of youngsters in that side, Rio Ferdinand and Frank Lampard junior. The fact that I was old enough to be their father never bothered me, or them, at all. I enjoyed my time at West Ham but I was itching to play the couple of games that would take me to the 1,000 mark. So when Leyton Orient called and said they were interested in me not only as cover but for their first team, I was delighted. Orient were a Third Division side but that mattered not one iota to me. A league game is a league game, irrespective of the division.

Alvin Martin and goalkeeper Les Sealey had joined Leyton Orient from West Ham but, apparently, things hadn't worked out for them in the way they had hoped. As far as I know, Les Sealey had said that he wanted to return to West Ham as cover. I couldn't see myself playing in the West Ham first team and so said I was quite happy to go to Brisbane Road. I think Orient chairman Barry Hearn was trying to reduce the club's wage bill. Les Sealey was one of Orient's best-paid players and, as I was willing to join Orient for less than they were paying Les, the deal went through.

I had a meeting with Barry Hearn, who struck me as a decent guy with the best interests of his club at heart. Barry told me he didn't want to break the club's wage structure in order to have me playing for Orient. For my part, I told Barry I wasn't looking for a fortune but the prospect of me making my 1,000th appearance could be a money-spinner for the club and bring them a lot of publicity. The deal we struck was, I believe, a good one for both parties. I was to be paid a little under the standard wage at the club but would receive a 'signing-on' payment of £8,000, which the club would more than recoup when I played my 1,000th league game. I made my 999th appearance for Leyton Orient at Fulham.

Fulham were on course for promotion from the Third Division and I had a lot to do in that game. I played well and was confident of being included in the side for Orient's next match at home to Brighton. In the days leading up to the match, Leyton Orient found themselves the subject of media attention the like of which they had not experienced for many years. I felt very proud at the prospect of achieving the milestone and gave countless interviews to television, radio and the press. I even gave interviews to foreign TV stations and football magazines and, in so doing, provided unlikely publicity for a Third Division match between Orient and Brighton. The fillip for Orient came in the form of SkySports deciding to make the game one of their live broadcasts. I was delighted, not only for myself, but for Barry Hearn and the club. The money from Sky would more than compensate for my signing-on fee.

Barry Hearn is a showman. He knows how to promote a sporting event and he went about promoting the Brighton game with gusto. I had let him know that I would appreciate it if he didn't turn the game into a carnival and he was at pains to impress upon me that this would not be the case.

'It'll be low key, just a few touches to mark the occasion as being different from a normal league game. In fact, you probably won't notice them. It'll be like a normal league match,' he assured me.

Normal league match? In that case, I must have been missing out for all those years with other clubs!

SkySport's Andy Gray interviewed me in the dressing room

before the game and TV cameras filmed me getting changed. I came down the tunnel to find a red carpet laid across the pitch, leading to my penalty area. As I trotted along the carpet and waved in response to the applause from a crowd twice the size of the normal Brisbane Road attendance, balloons were released and fireworks boomed and sparked at either side of me. As I took up my position in the penalty area for the warm-up, photographers ringed me. I noticed many young supporters on the terrace behind the goal were brandishing photographs of me, which I later learned had been on sale in the club shop at £1 a time. I remember thinking, 'If this is a low-key affair, I'd love to be at a sporting event that Barry Hearn really gets his promotional teeth into.'

Before the kick-off I received a presentation from the Football League to mark the occasion and was filled with a mixture of pride and happiness, yet also sadness, for I knew my long career was finally coming to an end.

The game was something of an anticlimax. I had hoped to produce a good performance but I hardly had a shot to save. On the other hand, I kept a clean sheet and was relieved not to have spoiled the occasion by making a mistake.

I played nine games for Orient. My last was in a defeat at Wigan. I had always set myself targets and my final one as a player was to achieve that 1,000 league-match record. I had done it, and played most of the games in the top flight. Afterwards, I realised I hadn't set myself any more targets. That was it. It really was over.

I spoke to Barry Hearn, told him I was calling it a day and thanked him for the opportunity he had given me. Barry was great. He thanked me for my efforts on behalf of his club and team and agreed to pay up what remained of my short-term contract.

This was 1997, thirty-two years after I had first signed for Leicester City. In that time, I had seen unbelievable and irrevocable changes. When I started out, football in this country was still a leisure pursuit, the preserve of the working class. Now the game, at the top at least, was a cult-celebrity, multi-million-pound industry. Football always had drama, colour, excitement and passion, and it was good that the game had changed so much. Without change it would be grey and sterile.

Change – that was exactly what my life was about to do. I faced the prospect of finding another career and the crucial meeting with Mike Morrison and his financial people was looming. What change would that bring? In the event, it was to change me and my life as irrevocably as I had seen football change over the last three decades.

They looked decent folk to me, which of course they were. They sat across from me on the other side of a large oak desk, as if I had come for a job interview. It was an interview and my future was in their hands, but there was to be no job forthcoming. I had been asked to bring along all my outstanding bills and the paperwork for all my debts. When I opened a briefcase and all the bills spilled across the desk, their jaws dropped. This was the first time I had really faced up to my problems.

One of the people Mike Morrison had asked to attend the meeting was Chris Slater, who worked for an insolvency company. Chris told me that I had considerable earning potential but because I couldn't meet my debts, I would have to subject myself to an invoked voluntary agreement, known as an IVA. Rather than be declared bankrupt, I would have to adhere to this IVA. As I understood it, should my creditors be in agreement, I would commit myself to paying the lion's share of what I owed them over a period of five years. Some 80 per cent of my earnings would go towards paying off my debts and the remaining 20 per cent would be mine to live off.

I was desperate to get myself straight and put matters right with those to whom I owed money, so I readily agreed to what had been suggested.

I still had to attend a bankruptcy hearing and as my financial problems and debts were laid out before me, I came face to face not only with my situation, but with myself. It was not a pleasant experience. I was one of the best-known footballers in the world, supposedly of above-average intelligence, and yet I had made such a mess of things. Like everyone else, I thought I knew myself. I'd always considered myself to be a fair guy, who never wanted to hurt or upset anyone. I found that how you view yourself isn't necessarily the way you are viewed by others. I didn't want to bear the stigma of being a bankrupt for the rest of my life, but more importantly, I wanted to pay everyone back to prove that the view they had of me was wrong.

In many respects, facing that bankruptcy hearing was a blessed relief. I found solace in the fact that I had hit the bottom and couldn't go any further down. I had escaped bankruptcy by the skin of my teeth, thanks to the help and advice of those present at the meeting. I knew it would be tough to pay off all my creditors, but having agreed to the IVA, I felt that from now on, the only way for me was up.

It was not going to be that simple, of course. I was about to embark on the most difficult journey of my life, but one I was determined to make. On the plus side, I knew I could actually do something. Many people faced with the prospect of bankruptcy do not have the wherewithal to get out of the situation. At least my name still carried some weight and credence. With my experience and knowledge of the game, appearances on television and radio were likely, and the after-dinner and promotional circuits were possibilities. Likewise, my expertise as a goalkeeper could open doors to coaching. It would not happen overnight, far from it, but I told the hearing that, given time, I could earn enough money to meet my financial responsibilities. To my everlasting relief, I was told I would be given that time and it was noted 'for the record'.

An IVA is by definition voluntary and I was a willing volunteer. I had to get myself out of the mess I had got myself into.

The following years were a chastening experience. I worked hard. For two years I coached the goalkeepers at Middlesbrough for two days a week. I worked the after-dinner circuit and became involved in corporate speaking. I do not have sole representation with an agent, but one, Essex-based David Davies, provided me with a lot of work for which I am most grateful.

Rumour had it that I had run up a lot gambling debts but my gambling debts were small. My main debts were to building societies, banks, the Inland Revenue and individuals I had borrowed from in the hope of 'buying time' in the mistaken belief that my financial situation would eventually right itself.

Mark Morrison and his colleagues had come up with a structured plan that was right for all concerned. I stuck to that plan and the experience changed me. I had always thought of myself as a sensible and responsible person but over the years of the IVA, I found out what responsibility really is. I became more thoughtful, more objective, in everything I did. I wasn't proud of the way I had handled my financial affairs but I was proud when the IVA was finally lifted. My creditors had received the money as per the agreement. The slate had been wiped clean and I was free to start again. Whatever I earned would be mine, with the exception, of course, of the wee amount the Inland Revenue demands of us.

While I was subject to the IVA I had several offers to commit the story of my life to a book. I declined to do this for one reason. I didn't want the story to end with me still owing money and my problems unresolved. I have always liked a story with a happy ending – happy endings make for happy beginnings. In 2003 I embarked upon a new life, older, certainly wiser and happier than I had been for many years.

14

THEN AND NOW

I began my career with Leicester City when Sir Stanley Matthews was still playing First Division football and played my final game in the Football League in the era of David Beckham. I was a professional for thirty-two years and played a total of 1,400 first-class matches, which included a record 1,005 games in the Football League. In that time, I'd like to think I learned more than a little about goalkeeping.

One of the questions I am most often asked is, 'Why aren't the great British goalkeepers around any more?' The simple answer to that is, 'They still are around. It's just that they're in their fifties and sixties now.' Seriously though, when I started out, such excellent British goalkeepers as Gordon Banks, Peter Bonetti, Tony Waiters, Jim Montgomery, Peter Grummitt, Bill Brown, Gordon West, Gary Sprake, Ronnie Simpson, Ron Springett and Alan Hodgkinson were playing. Banks and Bonetti were the outstanding keepers of that era.

Later, when I had established myself in the game, there were two greats, Ray Clemence and Pat Jennings, but there was also a bevy of first-class goalkeepers, such as David Harvey, Phil Parkes, Bob Wilson, Alex Stepney, Joe Corrigan, Ian McFaul, Mark Wallington and Paul Cooper.

When I retired from international football in 1990, there were two overseas goalkeepers on the books of clubs in what was then the First Division, and neither could be said to have been first-choice keepers. In 2003–04, there were thirty-six overseas goal-keepers with Premiership clubs. Of the twenty first-choice goalkeepers in the Premiership, just eight were English or Irish. The quality and impact of goalkeepers such as Antti Niemi of Southampton and Tomas Sorensen of Aston Villa are not in doubt. What of the contribution of goalkeepers such as Jurgen Macho (Chelsea), Shwan Jalal (Spurs), John Karelse (Newcastle United), Jeremy Bon (Bolton Wanderers), Martin Herrera (Fulham) or Jon Masalin (Aston Villa)? With all due respect to those mentioned, is British football now incapable of producing goalkeepers as good if not better than many of the overseas keepers now on the books of Premiership clubs?

Some countries are known for producing quality things, Switzerland its watches, Italy its cars. British football was always renowned for the general quality of its goalkeepers. So what has happened? Has the standard fallen or is it a case of overseas goalkeepers having got better? I think the answer is a bit of both.

It's a startling fact that fewer than a third of the first-choice goalkeepers in the Premiership in 2004 were eligible to play for England. The First Division also has a good proportion of overseas goalkeepers. I think the dearth of first-class English goalkeepers is in part due to managers being reluctant to give the young ones a chance these days. I made my debut for Leicester City when I was sixteen. Pat Jennings made his debut for his first club, Watford, when he was seventeen, Ray Clemence for Scunthorpe when he was eighteen. Pat and Ray were exceptional goalkeepers, it's true, but other keepers were also given their chance when in their teens. Peter Bonetti, Jim Montgomery, Peter Grummitt, Gary Sprake, Phil Parkes and David Harvey are examples.

Young goalkeepers are not thrust into the first team these days. The pressure on managers to get results is so great they are not prepared to take that chance. With four Champions League places up for grabs and UEFA Cup places, too, the pressure on managers is immense. Money is the key. With the Premiership offering payments to clubs on a sliding scale depending on their final position in the League, there is always something to play for. A Premiership manager won't risk playing a rookie goalkeeper at the end of a season because if that lad doesn't do well, it could cost his club a lot of money.

Another reason why opportunities for young players are so limited is the play-offs. There was a time when, with three of four games left and nothing to play for, a manager would give a first-team outing to two or perhaps three youngsters, just to give them some experience of first-team football and to see how they shaped up. Today, come the final few matches of the season, very few teams have nothing to play for. The play-offs allow teams as low as eleventh in the table to harbour hopes of promotion. At the other end of the table, the system of having three clubs go down can often mean eight or more teams are involved in a relegation dog-fight. With so many teams either having an outside chance of making the play-offs and promotion or battling against relegation, no one is prepared to give young goalkeepers invaluable first-team experience.

The lack of opportunities for young, home-grown goalkeepers is a real problem and is perhaps the main reason why we are not producing keepers of the quality and in the numbers we once did. A goalkeeper is arguably at his best at the age of thirty or thirty-two, but in order to reach that standard, he has to have been playing first-team football for eight to nine years.

Managers are under so much pressure these days they just can't experiment with players. They may operate a squad rotational system but invariably every player in the squad will be experienced. If you are a number-two or number-three goalkeeper in a squad, it can be very difficult to develop.

Young goalkeepers with top-flight clubs may have plenty of money and stylish cars, but what they are not getting is experience of first-team football. The high wages paid to young players by Premiership clubs are often beyond the means of Football League clubs, which prevents them taking young Premiership goalkeepers on loan, and so another opportunity for young goalkeepers has been lost.

I mentioned earlier that when international matches were played on a Saturday, a full programme of league fixtures also took place. This offered an opportunity for a young goalkeeper to step up from the reserves and show what he could do. It happened to me. Now the Premiership all but shuts down for two weeks to accommodate England's preparations and the players' rest period. I find it odd that English cricket and rugby – both Union and League – continue as normal when their players are on international duty, but not football.

Many young goalkeepers today face the dilemma of whether to accept the big Premiership wages on offer and endanger their development by playing academy or reserve-team football or to complete their apprenticeship in the lower leagues and hope to cash in later. I think it's worth noting that David Seaman, Nigel Martyn and Tim Flowers all began their careers in the lower divisions of the Football League. Although Welsh international Paul Jones began his career at Wolves, he went from there to Stockport County before eventually returning to the top flight with Southampton and subsequently with Wolves again. When Pat Jennings began his career at Watford, they were a lower-division club, as was Scunthorpe, where Ray Clemence started. Both Gordon Banks and Bob Wilson started out at Chesterfield, as did John Osborne, who in the sixties and seventies played in the old First Division with West Bromwich Albion.

Economics is a hindrance to the development of our young

goalkeepers. The time and money spent in developing a young goalkeeper over period of five or six years are considerable. Many clubs and managers think, 'Why spend six years developing a young English goalkeeper when we can buy an experienced international from Scandinavia or Eastern Europe for a relatively modest fee.' Manchester United purchased Peter Schmeichel for £500,000 from Brondby in 1991. Even for the time, half a million pounds was a relatively modest fee, as was the £300,000 Derby County paid Estonian club Flora Tallinn for Mart Poom in 1997. I am committed to the development of young goalkeepers in this country but I wonder how many of our top clubs are? When was the last time Manchester United had a first-choice English goalkeeper? In 1990, Les Sealey was a stop-gap replacement while Alex Ferguson was looking for a replacement for Jim Leighton. You have to go back to the 1980s and Gary Bailey to find a regular first-choice United goalkeeper who was English.

I believe many clubs pass judgement on young goalkeepers too early. Goalkeeper is a specialist position. It takes years to develop into a top-flight keeper and sometimes a lad of sixteen or seventeen will offer just a glimpse of his potential.

I was fortunate to be noticed early and given my chance but many top goalkeepers were late developers. For instance, having shown only a modicum of promise when young, Joe Corrigan, Jimmy Rimmer and Tony Coton later developed and matured into the role. As former Manchester City coach Malcolm Allison is on record as saying, 'If you had seen Joe Corrigan at seventeen, no way in the world would you have thought he would turn into a top-class keeper. But Joe displayed just enough for us to want to spend time with him and take a risk with him.'

Every Premiership club has a goalkeeping coach and most First Division clubs do too, but generally there is just one. One coach can't give personal attention to every single goalkeeper from twelve-year-olds up to the first team. Consequently, most young boys miss out on specialist coaching. Even at clubs where goal-keepers are receiving one-to-one coaching there is a risk that what is being taught does more harm than good. One exercise is to have young keepers run across the goal, touch the post then run back into position before making a save. That's all well and good for building fitness and stamina but it has absolutely no role to play in developing technique. There is too much of that sort of training for goalkeepers today, which results in poor technique. Some goalkeepers even lack the basics of their art. The UEFA quali-fication for coaching badges is helping to eradicate that sort of coaching but it still goes on at clubs. The English Schools FA is also providing specialist coaching for goalkeepers. Only time will tell if this will bring benefits.

In essence, football hasn't changed from when I started in the game to the present day. The purpose is still the same – to score more goals than your opponents. What has changed is the way the game is played and the culture surrounding it. It's now much faster. Matches are played at such breakneck speed there is an argument for saying the pace of the game is now beyond all but the most skilled and accomplished of players.

In the sixties, if a team from a lower division met one from the First Division in the Cup, it was possible for the lower-division team to knock their more illustrious opponents out of their stride by harassing and hustling them off the ball. That doesn't happen nowadays. The pace of Premiership games is such that a team from a lower division can't resort to that ploy any more, and tactics tend to revolve around certain aspects of the game they feel they are better at than their opponents, such as set pieces and deadball situations.

Pitches are different, too. When I joined Stoke City in pref-erence to Derby County, one reason for my decision was the quality of the pitch at the Baseball Ground. I had spent my formative years as a goalkeeper playing on a Christmas pudding of a pitch at Leicester City. The quality of the pitch effects the quality of the football and I opted for Stoke City because their Victoria Ground pitch was much better than that at Derby's Baseball Ground. Today, practically every pitch offers optimum conditions for good football.

When I began my career, the first team, the reserves and occasionally the youth team played at Filbert Street. This was true of every ground in English football. At some clubs, training took place on the pitch as well. Drainage and the care and maintenance of soil and grass were nowhere near as good as they are today. The result was that games were played on what were basically three types of pitch during the course of a season. Pitches were firm and lush to start with, not dissimilar to what they are for much of a season nowadays. When the rains came in autumn, followed by the worst of the winter weather, the condition of pitches deteriorated alarmingly. Come February, many were little more than mudheaps. The third stage occurred with the milder weather and winds of spring. The wind would dry out the pitches and a typical end-of-season surface was bone hard, bare and bumpy.

Today most pitches are always in excellent condition. All-cover stadiums are not always a help because towering stands can prevent sunlight and wind from nurturing certain areas of the pitch. Hence in recent years we have seen very poor pitches at Chelsea and Newcastle United.

The knowledge and technology applied to pitches today is far superior to that of the sixties and seventies. Quite often pitch maintenance was rudimentary, confined to re-seeding in the close season and letting nature take its course. Many were the groundsmen who had their own theories on how to produce a top-class playing surface.

In the sixties, Manchester United visited Craven Cottage. The Fulham chairman, the comedian and TV star Tommy Trinder, kept what was referred to as an 'open-house' at Craven Cottage whereby any member of staff was free to join the Fulham directors and their opposite numbers for a drink in the boardroom after the game. Following the game against United, the Fulham groundsman was in the boardroom and fell into conversation with the wife of the United chairman, Louis Edwards. Mrs Edwards was a lady in every sense of the word but one of a somewhat delicate disposition. Having chatted to the groundsman, Mrs Edwards joined her husband who was in conversation with Tommy Trinder. Tommy had noticed Mrs Edwards talking to his groundsman. He asked her if she was enjoying her visit to Craven Cottage and was taken aback when Mrs Edwards said she was but could he do something about the language of his groundsman.

'I remarked upon the excellent condition of your pitch,' said Mrs Edwards, 'and your groundsman told me his secret was to shovel piles of manure on it when he was about to re-seed. Can you tell him to use the word "fertiliser". I find the word he used very distasteful.'

'You gotta be joking!' said Tommy, his considerable jaw dropping. 'It's taken me six months to get him to call it manure!'

It is quite literally a whole new ball game now. The footballs used in the game today are far different from those used not only when I started, but in the eighties. Today's ball is much lighter. When it comes to sending over a cross, the modern ball makes life easier for players such as David Beckham, but it can make life very difficult for goalkeepers. Players can hit the ball from thirty yards and a goalkeeper has to be constantly readjusting his position and feet because the ball, which is travelling at speed, is also swerving and in some cases dipping.

As for the reason behind the introduction of this type of ball, I can only assume it is because those charged with running the game believe it will result in more goals being scored. It's a double-edged sword. Supporters like to see goals but the new lightweight balls have placed goalkeepers at a disadvantage. They have also, to some extent, reduced the skill factor in goalscoring, at least where shooting from distance is concerned. A player may aim for a certain spot when shooting at goal but the ball may deviate through the air, fox the goalkeeper and hit the net at a different point from the one intended. The modern ball can create luck for those attempting a shot at goal but some bad luck for goalkeepers. It can also lead to goalkeepers being criticised by commentators who wonder why the keeper didn't save a shot from thirty yards when, as one once remarked, 'At that distance, he would have had plenty of time to see it coming.'

I once read somewhere that mankind had advanced more in the last one hundred years than in the previous thousand. A similar theory can be applied to football. It appears to me that the game has changed more in the last decade than it did in the previous five. The true measure of a spectator sport's health is the number of people who pay to watch it. In 2003–04 attendances were the highest they had been for forty years. The Conference is also enjoying a rise in attendances. An unprecedented number, in excess of one million, watched Conference football in 2003–04. The flagship of English football, some might say the 'Holy Grail', is of course the Premiership. People seem to like what they see, a seductive cocktail of football, showbiz kitsch and high finance. Sky are shovelling money into the game as fast as they can, other networks are chipping in for the privilege of showing selected games and highlights, and sponsors, advertisers, image agents and merchandisers are jostling for position in the queue.

Just audible in the background are a few tiny voices, lamenting that the game is not what it was. But regrets about the passing of the terraces, how football's 'social glue' has become increasingly unstuck, admission prices that cost small change and a championship that could be won by Nottingham Forest or Aston Villa are not going to change anything. What, in any case, was the alternative? In the 1980s during the dark days of Hillsborough, Heysel and Bradford, the game was being talked about as if it were a disease. It wasn't a disease but certain aspects of it were diseased. Following those tragic events, English football seemed to have no future and might have continued down the slippery slope had it not been for the Taylor Report, the efforts of the clubs and authorities to rid the game of its hooligan element and the birth of the Premiership and satellite TV. In 1985–86 the total number of people attending matches was 16,488,577. In 2003–04 it was in excess of 28 million. An increase of twelve million in a period of eighteen years is testimony to the health of the game and the fact that football is once again family orientated.

The Premiership has money and the things that money can buy, but there's a case for saying the game has lost some elements that money can't buy. Football terraces have disappeared as a result of concerns about safety and improving conditions for spectators in what is now a multi-million-pound industry. Gone with the terraces is some of football's tradition and culture. In the past, most supporters had a favourite spot on a particular terrace. Around them they would see familiar faces of fellow supporters standing in their own favourite places. There was a greater sense of community at games in the past. When I was a boy on the terraces at Leicester, the men would take part in a draw for the scorer of the first goal. One supporter would write the shirt numbers of the players on pieces of paper and those around him would pay a shilling to draw a number. Whoever had the number that coincided with the shirt number of the player who scored the first goal won the pot. Those people probably only saw each other at home games and didn't even know each other's names. The demise of these small but, to my mind, important aspects of attending a match is the price paid for safety, a seat, improved conditions and more facilities for supporters.

Those things have led to a change in the composition of crowds. Football was once almost the sole preserve of working people. Far more professional people attend games these days. Many admission prices are prohibitive for people on low incomes, although some clubs do operate a system of concessionary prices, but also football has become, to use a modern buzz phrase, 'sexy'. Football has always been talked about at work but while the previous night's match is still discussed on the factory floor, these days it is also the prime subject of conversation around the office water cooler.

In 1992 when I was still a Derby County player, Oldham Athletic and Luton Town were in the Premier League, although it takes some believing now. In recent years, the Premiership has become predominantly the preserve of big clubs with big stadiums in big cities. The Premier League has become a league within a league – in fact, you could even say four leagues within a league. At the top, the title is contested by Arsenal, Chelsea and Manchester United. Then come half a dozen teams aiming to clinch, at best, the remaining place in the Champions League or, at worst, qualification for the UEFA Cup. The third stratum contains the clubs that will neither qualify for Europe nor be in danger of relegation. For them, the carrot is Premiership money and success in the FA or League Cup, either of which qualifies them for the UEFA Cup. The lower order consists of the clubs whose sole aim is to maintain Premiership status. These clubs are involved in the battle to avoid relegation and usually include at least two of the most recently promoted teams. As a result of all this, the Premiership has not only become much faster, it has also become much more intense. The stakes are high but to compensate the players for this, so too are the wages. Whereas in the past a manager might sell his club to a transfer target by saying, 'Come and join us on the journey. This club is going places, you can be a part of that,' nowadays he is more likely to tell the player's agent, 'Your client will earn X number of pounds and your percentage of that will be Y.'

In the early nineties, concerns for safety and order were the catalyst for change. When such changes were effected, money, which has always influenced the game, became the prime cause of change. In 1992 Eric Cantona's weekly wage was £4,000. Sky paid £33,300 per match. In 2004 it is not unusual for some Premiership players to earn £60,000 per week, on top of which are lucrative commercial deals. The top players can earn twice that. As for Sky, they pay close on £6 million per match.

It's not all wine and roses. The gap between clubs in the Football League, now the Coca-Cola League, and those in the Premiership has never been greater. I feel Football League clubs should receive more financial help from 'Big Brother', especially as so much transfer money, the old way of distributing wealth among the needy, has been denied to clubs in the lower divisions.

Generally speaking, English football appears to be in a healthy state. The game's renaissance from the nightmare horrors of Hillsborough, Heysel and Bradford is one of the miracles of English sport. The game now has an infrastructure of family-friendly stadiums at all levels and supporters are treated as customers rather than terrace fodder. I sometimes wonder what our health service and public transport system would be like today if both had been the subject of the pioneering zeal that football has benefited from in the past decade or so.

I have mentioned how games, particularly in the Premiership, have become more intense, and this is reflected in how supporters watch each game. Football was once a source of pure entertainment. Supporters, such as those from my boyhood days at

Leicester, wanted to see their team win, but during the course of a game there would be much humour. In one match I remember from the early sixties, Leicester played Stoke City. At one point, the Stoke goalkeeper, who was not having the best of games, extended his right arm and made a waving motion to indicate his right-back should run wide.

'He's swimming,' remarked one Leicester fan.

'He's not swimming,' came the reply from his neighbour, 'he's feeling for the posts!'

When the television camera pans across a section of the crowd at a match today, what we invariably see are not smiling faces, but faces riddled with anxiety and angst. It's as if football is not so much entertainment any more, but something that has to be endured to achieve victory, which is the only aim, irrespective of the quality of football on offer.

With so much at stake and every Premiership match being a very intense affair, I do wonder if today's players convey as much humour as their predecessors. When I was at Nottingham Forest, the players enjoyed a good joke and a laugh. John Robertson had a droll sense of humour. Larry Lloyd and Kenny Burns were always there with a witty remark, as was Brian Clough, of course. I think most clubs possessed colourful characters and ready wits. This may have been a generational thing, but in the main I think it was down to the fact that players were not subjected to the pressures, both on and off the pitch, that today's top players have to endure. There is an argument for saying that because the clubs, supporters and media view the game far more seriously now, players have to reflect this attitude. I took my football very seriously but still enjoyed a little levity, and there seemed to be more scope for wit and humour among players in the past.

Once, Leicester City travelled to an away match at Nottingham Forest. The driver of the Leicester team coach, who was new to the job, found his way into Nottingham city centre but didn't know the way to the City Ground. When he spotted a policeman, he pulled over to ask for directions. What we didn't know was that our driver had asked a special constable on his first day of duty. He didn't know the way to the City Ground either, but he said if we waited for a few minutes, the regular bobby would arrive and provide directions. Our coach had been stopped at the side of the road, engine idling, for about ten minutes when one of the directors got up and went to ask our driver the reason for the delay.

'It's this policeman,' our driver said. 'He doesn't know where Nottingham Forest is.'

Our right-back Peter Rodrigues turned to face the rest of the team and shook his head in disbelief.

'A policeman doesn't know the way to Nottingham Forest?' said Peter in mock astonishment. 'No bloody wonder they never caught Robin Hood!'

I have read a lot football autobiographies at the end of which the author says, 'I'm glad I played in the era I did.' I have been more fortunate than most, for I can say I am glad I played in the eras I did! Apart from my league career, I won 125 caps for England, a record of which I'm very proud. Occasionally, I do wonder how many that might have been had Don Revie taken a shine to me and had Ron Greenwood not been undecided between Ray Clemence and me. I kept a clean sheet on sixty-seven occasions, which, I'm reliably informed, is also a record. Other records attached to my name include eighty-eight appearances in the FA Cup and thirty-seven World Cup games in three tournaments.

On a lighter note, I also sang on three number-one hit records. The first was with the 1970 World Cup squad and the third was with the 1990 World Cup squad. The second was with the Nottingham Forest European Cup squad in 1979, which curiously reached number one in the Swedish charts!

My career provided me with a number of very special memories outside the game, one of the most surprising being when I was the subject of 'This Is Your Life'. I was playing for Southampton at the time and had no idea whatsoever what was going on. I had been asked to attend a business meeting, I think it was, in London. I'd noticed that several times when I arrived home from training, Sue would be on the phone. When I asked her whom she had been talking to she always said it was one of her friends. I never twigged the real source of or reason for these calls. With hindsight, I should have known something was up. A friend insisted on accompanying me to Southampton station and he stayed on the platform to wave me off. I remember at the time thinking this was curious behaviour on his part, but just thought he was being overly friendly. I didn't know he had been assigned to ensure I was on that particular train when it left Southampton bound for London. On arriving at Waterloo Station I was walking along the platform when a group of porters caught my eye. They were gathered around a suitcase with their backs towards me. I thought, 'Blimey, how many porters does it take to carry a suitcase?' It was only when they turned to me as I approached them that I knew something very fishy was going on. The 'porters' were Tony Woodcock, Chris Waddle, Kenny Samson, Glenn Hoddle and Viv Anderson. I was still gathering my thoughts when Eamonn Andrews appeared at my side, brandishing the famous red book, and uttered the immortal line.

I was whisked off to a theatre and spent the afternoon in a daze as my family, friends and people I hadn't seen for years paraded before me, offering personal anecdotes of my life. People have often asked if the subjects of 'This Is Your Life' really have no clue what is going on. I can't speak for anyone else, but I was completely in the dark. It was only after the recording of the programme that I thought about those calls to Sue, and my pal at the railway station being so keen to see me off, and realised how odd their behaviour had been.

I had the honour and privilege of receiving both an MBE and an OBE for my services to football. I shall never forget going to Buckingham Palace with my family for those auspicious occasions. Meeting Her Majesty the Queen was for me as great an honour as the awards themselves. I can remember thinking, 'What am I doing here? A lad from the Braunstone estate in Leicester. This is one goal I could never have envisaged setting myself.'

I have also had the privilege of meeting a number of Prime Ministers. The England team was twice invited to number ten to meet Mrs Thatcher. I don't take a great interest in politics but having met Mrs Thatcher I remember she struck me as having a certain charisma and considerable presence. I could see why many people were much taken with her.

God willing, I still have plenty of life to live – which, I can assure you, I will do from now on within my means! I have no regrets regarding my career as a footballer. How could I possibly have any regrets when the game was so good to me? My only regrets concern the financial mess I got myself into and the drink-driving charge that resulted from my car crash in Nottingham. I put those down to experience. Experience is what we call our mistakes. No one goes through life without making mistakes but the trick is to learn from them. I have tried to learn from mine.

I still receive many requests to appear at corporate functions and do a lot of promotional work for companies. I regularly speak on the after-dinner circuit and I'm always pleased when asked to appear on television and radio. I do the occasional coaching stint when asked and generally have a busy life.

The bedrock of my life is my family. I am very fortunate to have a wife like Sue. She is not only my wife, she is also my best friend and confidante. I am very proud of our sons, Michael and Sam.

Michael is in the fire brigade and Sam, of course, has pursued a career in football. My parents have been loving and very supportive of me, for which I will also be eternally grateful. All the family are close and they mean everything to me. I am very much a family man and had it not been for the support of my family when I had problems, I don't think I would ever have overcome them.

I started playing professional football at the age of sixteen, having come from a working-class background. I have had to grow up and learn about life whilst enduring the pressure of dedicating myself to my goal of trying to be the best goalkeeper in the world. I have to say that the inner strengths that drove me on in football proved my downfall in my financial and gambling dealings. Single mindedness, a will to win, not ever wanting to be beaten, never giving up. I just didn't know when to stop. Looking back I can't remember a time I got into trouble when I had not indulged in excessive drink. Now I can take or leave the stuff. I enjoyed gambling. It was my only real release from football, with the exception of the odd binge drink. I played cards, but only on football trips to pass the time. I took to roulette and dog racing but only in a minor way. I loved the culture and atmosphere of horse racing, of watching the horses on the gallops. Owning horses was fun and successful to start with, but I went too far. I suppose that was instinctive of me. Gambling on horses was just the same. At first it was a hobby, but in time it became obsessive and a way of life to me. That's when my losses got out of control. My idea of owning property as an investment, together with my plan for breeding race horses would, I am sure, be successful today. Similarly, my idea for manufacturing sportswear. I embarked upon all those things simply at the wrong time. I believe you are born a gambler. I also believe to a certain degree that life is a gamble. I tried things and lost, which caused my family great pain. The one thing that I have learned from my past troubles is that some people are judged by the amount of money they possess, and not necessarily on their talent and ability. I think this is particularly true of the media. For me to get myself into such dire financial circumstances after all the money I had earned was a joke and a pretty sick one at that. I am not proud of that fact, but have done everything I could to put the matter right. Experiencing what I did, I learned much. I aim to put that experience to good use in the future. I miss football and to my mind the only thing that prevented me from becoming a Premiership manager was my inability to handle my finances; not my lack of ability as a manager.

I wanted to commit my story to book form as there have been many incorrect comments and statements made about me. Quite simply, I wanted you to know the true story, in all its glory, with all its warts.

I now own a lovely home and my business interests, football pension and corporate work have put me on the up again. I am very proud of my thirty years in football and some of the records I created may never be beaten. I gave it all I had and have resolved to do similar in everything I do in the rest of my life (golf clubs watch out!). I have been married for over thirty years. I have a wonderful family who have stuck by me through thick and thin, for which I am very appreciative. I am looking forward to living my life to the full from now on, but in so doing, to live within my limits. Who knows what lies around the corner? I aim to take a walk down the street and have a look.

CAREER RECORD

Peter Shilton played in 1,005 League matches between 1965–66 and 1996–97

CLUB RECORD

Leicester City	League Appearances	
1965–66	1	
1966–67	4	
1967–68	35	One Goal
1968–69	42	
1969–70	39	
1970–71	40	
1971–72	37	
1972–73	41	
1973–74	42	
1974–75	5	*Total 286*

Stoke City		
1974–75	25	
1975–76	42	
1976–77	40	
1977–78	3	*Total 110*

Nottingham Forest		
1977–78	37	
1978–79	42	
1979–80	42	
1980–81	40	
1981–82	41	*Total 202*

Southampton		
1982–83	39	

Southampton—*cont* League Appearances

1983–84	42	
1984–85	41	
1985–86	37	
1986–87	29	*Total 188*

Derby County

1987–88	40	
1988–89	38	
1989–90	35	
1990–91	31	
1991–92	31	*Total 175*

Plymouth Argyle

1991–92	7	
1992–93	23	
1993–94	4	
1994–95	0	*Total 34*

Wimbledon

1994–95	0	(named substitute but did not play)

Bolton Wanderers

1994–95	1	*Total 1*

Coventry City

1995–96	0	(named substitute but did not play)

West Ham United

1995–96	0	(named substitute but did not play)

Leyton Orient

1996–97	9	*Total 9*

TOTAL NUMBER OF LEAGUE APPEARANCES – 1,005

He made 13 appearances for England Under 23's
1969 v Wales; Holland (2), Portugal (2); 1970 v Wales; Bulgaria, Scotland.
1971 v West Germany; 1972 v Sweden, East Germany, Poland, USSR

FULL ENGLAND RECORD

1970–71   (with Leicester City)

v East Germany	Wembley	3–1	
v Wales	Wembley	0–0	

1971–72

v Switzerland	Wembley	1–1	(ECQ)
v Northern Ireland	Wembley	0–1	

1972–73

v Yugoslavia	Wembley	1–1	
v Scotland	Glasgow	5–0	(SFAC)
v Northern Ireland	Everton	2–1	
v Wales	Wembley	3–0	
v Scotland	Wembley	1–0	
v Czechoslovakia	Prague	1–1	
v Poland	Chorzow	0–2	(WCQ)
v USSR	Moscow	2–1	
v Italy	Turin	0–2	

1973–74

v Austria	Wembley	7–0	
v Poland	Wembley	1–1	(WCQ)
v Italy	Wembley	0–1	
v Wales	Cardiff	2–0	
v Northern Ireland	Wembley	1–0	
v Scotland	Glasgow	0–2	
v Argentina	Wembley	2–2	

1974–75   (with Stoke City)

v Cyprus	Wembley	5–0

1976–77

v Northern Ireland	Belfast	2–1
v Wales	Wembley	0–1

1977–78   (with Nottingham Forest)

v Wales	Cardiff	3–1
v Hungary	Wembley	4–1

1978–79

v Czechoslovakia	Wembley	1–0	
v Sweden	Stockholm	0–0	
v Austria	Vienna	3–4	

1979–80

v Northern Ireland	Belfast	5–1	(ECQ)
v Spain	Barcelona	2–0	
v Italy	Turin	0–1	(EC)

1980–81

v Norway	Wembley	4–0	(WCQ)
v Switzerland	Wembley	2–1	(WCQ)
v Romania	Wembley	0–0	(WCQ)

1981–82

v Hungary	Wembley	1–0	(WCQ)
v Holland	Wembley	2–0	(cpt)
v Scotland	Glasgow	1–0	
v France	Bilbao	3–1	(WC)
v Czechoslovakia	Bilbao	2–0	(WC)
v Kuwait	Bilbao	1–0	(WC)
v West Germany	Madrid	0–0	(WC)
v Spain	Madrid	0–0	(WC)

1982–83   (with Southampton)

v Denmark	Copenhagen	2–2	(ECQ)
v West Germany	Wembley	1–2	
v Greece	Salonika	3–0	(ECQ)
v Wales	Cardiff	2–1	(capt)
v Greece	Wembley	0–0	(capt. ECQ)
v Hungary	Wembley	2–0	(capt. ECQ)
v Northern Ireland	Belfast	0–0	(capt)
v Scotland	Wembley	2–0	
v Australia	Sydney	0–0	(capt)
v Australia	Brisbane	1–0	(capt)
v Australia	Melbourne	1–1	(capt)

1983–84

v Denmark	Wembley	0–1	(ECQ)
v Hungary	Budapest	3–0	(ECQ)
v France	Paris	0–2	
v Northern Ireland	Wembley	1–0	
v Wales	Wrexham	0–1	

v Scotland	Glasgow	1–1	
v USSR	Wembley	0–2	
v Brazil	Rio de Janeiro	2–0	
v Uruguay	Montevideo	0–2	
v Chile	Santiago	0–0	

1984–85
v East Germany	Wembley	1–0	
v Finland	Wembley	5–0	(WCQ)
v Turkey	Istanbul	8–0	(WCQ)
v Northern Ireland	Belfast	1–0	(WCQ)
v Romania	Bucharest	0–0	(WCQ)
v Finland	Helsinki	1–1	(WCQ)
v Scotland	Glasgow	0–1	(RS)
v Italy	Mexico City	1–2	
v West Germany	Mexico City	3–0	

1985–86
v Romania	Wembley	1–1	(WCQ)
v Turkey	Wembley	5–0	(WCQ)
v Northern Ireland	Wembley	0–0	(WCQ)
v Egypt	Cairo	4–0	
v Israel	Tel Aviv	2–1	
v USSR	Tbilisi	1–0	
v Scotland	Wembley	2–1	(RS)
v Mexico	Los Angeles	3–0	
v Canada	Vancouver	1–0	
v Portugal	Monterrey	0–1	(WC)
v Morocco	Monterrey	0–0	(WC)
v Poland	Monterrey	3–0	(capt. WC)
v Paraguay	Mexico City	3–0	(capt. WC)
v Argentina	Mexico City	1–2	(capt. WC)

1986–87
v Sweden	Stockholm	0–1	(capt)
v Northern Ireland	Wembley	3–0	(ECQ)
v Spain	Madrid	4–2	
v Northern Ireland	Belfast	2–0	(ECQ)
v Brazil	Wembley	1–1	(RC)

1987–88   (with Derby County)
v West Germany	Dusseldorf	1–3	(capt)
v Turkey	Wembley	8–0	(ECQ)
v Yugoslavia	Belgrade	4–1	(ECQ)

v Holland	Wembley	2–2	
v Scotland	Wembley	1–0	(RC)
v Colombia	Wembley	1–1	(RC)
v Switzerland	Lausanne	1–0	
v Republic of Ireland	Stuttgart	0–1	(EC)
v Holland	Dusseldorf	1–3	(EC)

1988–89

v Denmark	Wembley	1–0	
v Sweden	Wembley	0–0	(WCQ)
v Greece	Athens	2–1	
v Albania	Tirana	2–0	(WCQ)
v Albania	Wembley	5–0	(WCQ)
v Chile	Wembley	0–0	(RC)
v Scotland	Glasgow	2–0	(RC)
v Poland	Wembley	3–0	(WCQ)
v Denmark	Copenhagen	1–1	

1989–90

v Sweden	Stockholm	0–0	(WCQ)
v Poland	Kattowice	0–0	(WCQ)
v Italy	Wembley	0–0	
v Yugoslavia	Wembley	2–1	
v Brazil	Wembley	1–0	
v Czechoslovakia	Wembley	4–2	
v Denmark	Wembley	1–0	
v Uruguay	Wembley	1–2	
v Tunisia	Tunis	1–1	
v Republic of Ireland	Cagliari	1–1	(WC)
v Holland	Cagliari	0–0	(WC)
v Egypt	Cagliari	1–0	(capt. WC)
v Belgium	Bologna	1–0	(WC. Aet)
v Cameroon	Naples	3–2	(WC. Aet)
v West Germany	Turin	1–1	(WC. Aet. England lost on pens)
v Italy	Bari	1–2	(capt. WC)

Key: WC – World Cup. WCQ – World Cup Qualifier. EC – European Championship. ECQ – European Championship Qualifier. RC – Rous Cup; capt – Captain. Aet – After Extra-Time.

TOTAL NUMBER OF FULL ENGLAND APPEARANCES: 125

MISCELLANEOUS STATISTICS

He kept 66 clean sheets in 125 appearances for England

He captained England on 14 occasions

In 1982–83 he kept six consecutive clean sheets for England (a record)

In 12 International games from September 1988 to November 1989
he kept 10 clean sheets, conceding only two goals.

From his International debut in November 1970 to November 1978 he only
played for England outside the United Kingdom on four occasions.

In 1989–90 season he played 16 games for England which included twelve
International matches in five months.

He played in a record 37 World Cup matches. 20 World Cup Qualifying
games and made 17 appearances in World Cup Tournament Final Stages.
(a record)

He appeared in the final stages of 3 World Cups (1982, 1986 and 1990) and
was a member of the pre-World Cup squad for the 1970 World Cup in
Mexico.

He made his debut for Leicester City against Everton in 1965–66 at the age
of sixteen. He played his final League game 31 years later for Leyton Orient
at Wigan Athletic in January 1997.

He played a total of 1,391 official senior games.

Along with Ian Callaghan (Liverpool) he jointly holds the record for
appearances in FA Cup matches – 88.

When with Leicester City he kept a record 23 clean sheets in the 1970–71
season.

With Nottingham Forest he won a League Championship medal in 1978, a
Football League Cup Winners medal in 1979; European Cup Winners medals
in 1979 and 1980 and European Super Cup winners medal in 1980.

He represented England at Schoolboy, Youth, Under 23 and Full
International level.

His 1,005 appearances in the Football League is a record.

His 125 caps for England is a record.

INDEX